Library of
Davidson College

SOVIET MILITARY POWER AND PERFORMANCE

Soviet Military Power and Performance

Edited by

JOHN ERICKSON
and
E. J. FEUCHTWANGER

ARCHON BOOKS

Selection and editorial matter
© John Erickson and E.J. Feuchtwanger 1979
Chapter 1© Norman Stone 1979 Chapter 2© John Erickson 1979
Chapter 3© John Hemsley 1979 Chapter 4© John E. Moore 1979
Chapter 5© Alexander Boyd 1979
Chapter 6© Chris Donnelly 1979
Chapter 7© Teresa Rakowska-Harmstone 1979
Chapter 8© Richard Burt 1979 Chapter 9© Peter Vigor 1979

All rights reserved. No part of this publication may be reproduced or transmitted, in any form or by any means, without permission

First published 1979 by
THE MACMILLAN PRESS LTD
London and Basingstoke
and in the United States of America by
THE SHOE STRING PRESS, INC.,
Hamden, Connecticut
as an ARCHON BOOK

Printed in Great Britain

Library of Congress Cataloging in Publication Data

Main entry under title:

Soviet military power and performance.

Bibliography: p.
Includes index.
1. Russia--Armed Forces--Addresses, essays, lectures.
2. Russia--Military policy--Addresses, essays, lectures.
I. Erickson, John.   II. Feuchtwanger, E. J.
UA770.S666   1979   355'.00947   78-26158
ISBN 0-208-01779-8

Contents

List of Figures and Tables	vii
Notes on the Contributors	viii
Introduction	xi

PART I THE SYSTEM   1

1 The Historical Background of the Red Army
  Norman Stone   3
2 The Soviet Military System: Doctrine, Technology and 'Style'
  John Erickson   18

PART II THE ARMS   45

3 The Soviet Ground Forces
  John Hemsley   47
4 The Soviet Navy
  John E. Moore   74
5 The Soviet Air Force
  Alexander Boyd   88

PART III THE MEN   99

6 The Soviet Soldier: Behaviour, Performance, Effectiveness
  Chris Donnelly   101
7 The Soviet Army as the Instrument of National Integration
  Teresa Rakowska-Harmstone   129

PART IV STRATEGIC PERSPECTIVES   155

8 Arms Control and Soviet Strategic Forces: The Risks of asking SALT to do too much
  Richard Burt   157

9 The 'Forward Reach' of the Soviet Armed Forces: Seaborne
  and Airborne Landings
  Peter Vigor   183

Conclusion   212

Index   217

List of Figures and Tables

Figures

3.1	Deployment of GSFG	50
3.2	Organisation of a Tactical Air Army	51
3.3	Outline Organisation of a Motor-Rifle Division	52
3.4	Motor-Rifle Division Deployed for an Attack	59
3.5	Echelons and Objectives	61
3.6	Example of a MR Battalion Defensive Position	64
3.7	Forward Distribution System	67
6.1	Training Day Timetable	121
9.1	Russia as she existed, late 13th Century	185
9.2	The Kerch-Feodosiisk *Desant*	190
9.3	The Novorossiisk *Desant*	192
9.4	Sakhalin and the Kuriles	194

Tables

7.1	USSR. Major Ethnic Groups	130
7.2	USSR. Soviet Army Officers, Ethnic Breakdown, 1943	133
7.3	USSR. Fluency in Russian and Urbanisation of Major Ethnic Groups	138
8.1	The New Generation of Soviet Strategic Missiles	167

Notes on the Contributors

ALEXANDER BOYD was born in Sheffield and learnt Russian as a schoolboy. His interest in Russian aviation has been pursued ever since. He is now Vice-Principal of Maryland College for Adult Education in Bedfordshire where he lectures in Russian Language and Literature. He is the author of *The Soviet Air Force* and *Aspects of the Russian Novel*.

RICHARD BURT was educated at the Fletcher School of Law and Diplomacy, has held research appointments at the US Naval War College, Newport, R.I., and at the International Institute for Strategic Studies in London. He is now Defence Correspondent of the *New York Times*. He is the author of numerous articles on security and strategic matters and takes a special interest in the strategic arms limitation talks.

CHRIS DONNELLY read Russian Studies at Manchester University, has travelled widely in Eastern Europe and the USSR and studied for a time at the Moscow Energy Institute. He now holds a post in the Soviet Studies Centre at the Royal Military Academy, Sandhurst. He is the author of several articles on Soviet military affairs.

JOHN ERICKSON studied at Cambridge, became a Research Fellow at St Antony's College, Oxford, and has held university appointments at St Andrews, Manchester and Edinburgh. He is now Professor of Politics at Edinburgh, with a special interest in Soviet military affairs. Amongst his many books and articles are *The Soviet High Command 1918–1941* and *The Road to Stalingrad*.

EDGAR FEUCHTWANGER was born in Munich, went to Winchester and Cambridge and is now Reader in History at the University of Southampton. As Deputy Director of Adult Education he also has an interest in international relations and strategic studies. He is the author of *Disraeli, Democracy and the Tory Party; Prussia: Myth and Reality*, and *Gladstone: A Political Biography*.

JOHN HEMSLEY was commissioned into the Somerset Light Infantry from the Royal Military Academy, Sandhurst, where he has also worked as an instructor. When he was on the Directing Staff of the Staff College, Camberley, he visited Russia in October 1976 with a group from the college. He is now a Lieutenant-Colonel commanding an infantry battalion. He did research on the Soviet Army at the University of Edinburgh.

JOHN MOORE was a submarine commander in the Second World War and among the many naval appointments he has held since 1945 was the command of submarine squadrons and staff posts, including Chief of Staff C-in-C Naval Home Command. He retired in 1972 as a Captain, at his own request. He is the author of several books and articles on sea power, including *Jane's Fighting Ships* and *The Soviet Navy Today*.

TERESA RAKOWSKA-HARMSTONE is Professor of Political Science at Carleton University, Canada and the author of a study on *Soviet Nationality Problems*.

NORMAN STONE was born in Glasgow and took a first in History at Cambridge. He spent several years doing research in Central Europe and learnt Hungarian. He returned to Cambridge lecturing on Russian history and, latterly, on the Weimar Republic. He is the author of *The Eastern Front 1914–17*, which won the Wolfson Prize in 1976, and is now a Fellow of Jesus College and Director of Studies in History.

PETER VIGOR helped to get Poles out of Russia during the war and trained them for what subsequently became General Anders' corps. He read Russian, French and Polish at Cambridge after the war. He joined the staff of the Royal Military Academy, Sandhurst, and is now in charge of the Soviet Studies Centre there. He is the author of numerous articles and books on Soviet affairs, including *The Soviet View of War; Peace and Neutrality* and *A Guide to Marxism*.

Introduction

Churchill called the Soviet Union 'an enigma wrapped inside a riddle'. The end of the cold war, detente, and the growth of East-West contacts have not significantly diminished the hazards facing the analyst of the Soviet scene. Nowhere is this more true than in the military sphere. There is a great debate in the West about the degree of danger to be feared from a Russia newly arrived at undisputed superpower status. The profound misapprehensions about Russian strengths and weaknesses that misled friend and foe alike in two world wars serve as a warning against facile judgements.

The papers here presented seek to make a contribution to our knowledge of Soviet doctrine, style, procedure, and problems in matters military. It is a subject with such wide ramifications that no claims to comprehensive treatment can be made. Nevertheless, the various contributors to this volume, from their different standpoints, arrive at a remarkably consistent view of Soviet behaviour as a military power. They all agree that the Russian past and memories reaching back deeply into the Tsarist era still leave their mark upon Soviet military ideas today, even when it comes to the concepts governing the use of nuclear weapons and the methods of electronic warfare. The weaponry which is now available to the Soviet Union as well as to the West may have changed the nature of warfare in a way that is literally unfathomable but the human mind that has to grapple with these well-nigh insoluble problems is still shaped by past experience. The military aspect of Soviet affairs, which permeates so much of life in the USSR today, mirrors the developments in the rest of Russian society since the Bolshevik Revolution. As the year 1917 recedes further into history it often looks as if the perennial tides of Russian life will increasingly wash away the marks, apparently so deep and ineradicable, that were made by the Revolution.

Such a general perception may be said to be shared by all the contributors to this volume, as it is by many other informed observers of the Soviet Union. It still leaves wide open to debate and controversy the more detailed conclusions to be drawn about Soviet realities today and in the foreseeble future, not least in the military sphere. The common views that pervade this survey of Soviet military power and performance do not preclude, even within the same contribution, the dichotomy of view to be found in many assessments of the Soviet role in the international system. On the one hand there is a very real sense of the danger which the Soviet Union's great military potential presents. It is based on a wide spectrum of advanced technology and great economic resources; it commands a population systematically trained in the military virtues; it is governed by an ideology which combines traditional nationalism with the remnants of a universal messianic philosophy and which thereby legitimises it on a world-wide scale; it is guided by a military doctrine and style that can be expected to maximise the strengths of the Soviet system and minimise its weaknesses. On the other hand, the contributions in this volume equally strongly reflect an awareness of these weaknesses. Some sectors of advanced technology continue to be backward compared with the West and the concentration of economic resources on military production has so far failed to overcome this backwardness and may even perpetuate it. Constant indoctrination cannot overcome the lack of individual initiative which the Soviet system inculcates or the problems arising from ethnic frictions, nor can it cure the vast differences in educational standards that continue to exist. Patriotism and militarism thinly veiled by socialist rhetoric cannot disguise the ideological fatigue which has overtaken the Soviet Union. Everyone concerned with Soviet affairs must make their own judgement on the balances of strengths and weaknesses and arrive at their own estimate of danger.

The papers in this volume were written for publication and first read at a conference jointly organised by the University of Southampton and the Royal Naval College Greenwich and held at Greenwich in April 1977. The Editors would like to thank Dr Trevor Cliffe, of the Ministry of Defence, for the academic and financial support his department gave in arranging the conference. They also wish to express their thanks to Bryan Ranft, then Professor of History at Greenwich, for his advice and help. The papers express the personal opinions of their authors and do not necessarily represent the views of the organisations to which they belong. They contain no classified information and are based on open sources. The discussions which followed the presentation of each paper at the conference have been briefly summarised by Dr John Simpson, Department of Politics, University of Southampton, and by the Editors. The paper on the 'Soviet Army as the Instrument of National Integration' was not presented at the conference. The conclusion to this volume summarises the major points emerging from the lengthy general discussions with which the conference ended. Last but not least, the Editors wish to thank their secretaries, Miss Kathie Brown of Edinburgh and Mrs Mary Crowden of Southampton.

Part I
The System

1 The Historical Background of the Red Army

Norman Stone

In the months before war broke out in 1914, observers in all of the great powers of Europe had become convinced that the Russian Empire was on its way to becoming the dominant military power of the continent. Nicolson, at the Foreign Office in London, noted that it would soon become 'very considerable'; Bethmann Hollweg, in Berlin, had nightmare visions of a future in which Russian armies occupied the line from Stettin to Trieste. This vision had much to do with the Germans' decision, in July 1914, to risk, or even provoke, a European war; for the German military had become convinced that Russia had to be challenged before her army was so strong as to be quite unbeatable. The 'great programme' of Russian armament, which passed into law in 1914, provided for an increase in artillery, infantry divisions, and officer-numbers that would, by 1917, have secured the Russian army a comfortable superiority in most aspects of warfare by 1917.

The Germans' calculation proved to be correct. It was still possible, despite the great improvements made in Russia's military preparedness, for the German army to defeat Russia in the field. Beginning with Tannenberg, in the last days of August 1914, the Germans managed to throw back Russian attempts to invade the Central Powers, and by 1916 the Germans and their allies had advanced a long way into western Russia. By 1917, the western powers had lost faith in their Russian ally, whose army was generally held to be incapable of offensive action. Reports from their representatives at the front were full of gloom – as for instance when a British officer, engaged in training Russian marines in maintenance of motor vehicles, told his superiors that 'Our work has resembled swimming in glue'. The last years of Tsarism exemplified a very characteristic trait of Russian history: the gap between Russia's economic and military potential, as revealed in statistics and government reports, and her performance in the field. It is a gap which makes prediction of Russia's development very difficult. One generation later, Hitler's greatest blunder, which became all too soon apparent, was to attack the Soviet Union in June 1941. Yet this blunder, at the time, seemed to most competent observers the correct thing for Hitler to do. The German generals were so confident of overthrowing Russia that they hardly even bothered to work out a coherent plan of attack: they would kick the door in, 'and the house will fall down'. They thought they would win within six weeks. On the whole, western statesmen thought this was right – British Intelligence gave Russia about three weeks, American Intelligence a little more; Stalin himself seems to have supposed he would last about two or three weeks. This time, statesmen and soldiers were reading events in the light of experience in the First World War: they refused to accept that Russia's growth-rates in the 1930s could mean very much against the German army. Certainly, the Stalinist method of running Russia seemed to offer only starvation, inefficiency, tyranny. Few foreigners could square the various known facts about Russia with her potential, and it is not surprising that, in the two great wars of this century, western statesmen's expectations have been, on the whole, at considerable variance with the realities.

The great Russian problem – one for the 'sovietologist' as much as for the historian – has always been the contrast between backwardness and modernity in the same country. Obviously, regional differences made up part of this contrast. Some regions, such as Yaroslavl, north of Moscow, had a combination of climatic harshness, natural infertility, and religious dissent that did much to promote occupations other than farming, and hence brought about almost total literacy quite early on; others, such as the central agricultural regions, were distinguished by total illiteracy. But the contrast was essentially a reflection of the gap between the people of Russia and their élite, a greater gap than existed anywhere else in Europe. The 'established' Russia was capable of first-class military or economic performances, but these went together with – and indeed almost required – an extraordinary degree of backwardness in the lives of ordinary people. It was characteristic that classical St Petersburg, with its astonishing public buildings, should have had the worst slums in Europe: until the end of the nineteenth century, its death-rate was greater than its birth-rate. Poverty engulfed everything in the countryside, engulfed everything with the vitality of a weed, and the serfs developed, under the oppression of the gentry, ways that defied understanding by urban bureaucrats and politicians. It was not surprising that the country could only be governed by autocratic methods.

The army was, of course, the most important element in this autocratic system. Yet it, too, exemplified the contrasts at work in the country as a whole. It was, technically, often quite accomplished, and that from a relatively early date. Old Muscovy had developed her armed forces for defence against Tatars, Teutonic Knights, Poles, and by the seventeenth century the Tsarist state had developed armed forces that were large, quite well-equipped, and self-conscious. Even in Ivan the Terrible's time, the country had developed so far that Moscow was a greater city than London, and by the seventeenth century the Russian armed forces were well-enough organised to expand and defend the Empire's borders considerably before Peter the Great began his reforms. The army acted as a focus for Russian patriotism, and the ordinary people were prepared for considerable sacrifices to help the army. In 1812, for instance, there was a widespread movement of patriotism: Odessa presented the State with 280,546 roubles, Kremenchug with 7,500; the State peasants of Tiraspol gave quantities of grain, the priests of Novogorod-Volynsk, Ostrog, and Obruch found 667 roubles; even the invalided soldiers of Yekaterinoslav managed to provide 1,120 roubles ('almost all the liquid cash that they have'). The State and the people regarded the army as a vital part of the country's constitution, and although it suffered from the backwardness of Russia it was always an essential part of the country's national existence. It was an army with a mission.

The reforming Tsars of the past concentrated their attention on the army, and they did what they could to improve its technical level. Very often, this meant bringing in foreigners. Ivan the Terrible had introduced Flemish workers to improve his artillery, and a colony of Dutchmen was active at Tula, south of Moscow, in iron-casting; there were also many Germans, with their own special quarter in Moscow – indeed, the widespread use of foreigners in developing war-economic sides of the Russian economy was an important factor in the country's economic growth. Under Peter the Great and his successors, Germans and other foreigners were very widely used in the army – so much so that, in the first half of the eighteenth century, army literature was printed in German as well as in Russian, while, to this day, the ranks of officers in the army are denoted with German names. As the Russian Empire expanded into the Baltic littoral, the local nobles, mainly Germanic in origin (their Russian name is *ostzeyskiye barony*), were used to supply the army with general officers. In the middle nineteenth century, nearly two-third of Russia's generals were Protestant, i.e. of German origin. In time, their descendants would become Russified, sometimes even Orthodox in religion, but even in 1914, out of eleven army commanders, five had German names, three had Russian names, while the rest were, respectively, Flemish, Bulgarian, and Polish in origin. It was characteristic that these men were never conscious of their foreign origin; all considered themselves servants of the Russian Empire, and, throughout, the army displayed considerable talent at integrating foreigners into its ranks, at whatever level.

Although the country as a whole remained below western European levels in civilian economic affairs, the armed forces were well-supplied with matériel, and there was always a basic infrastructure capable of maintaining them in the field. There was always a solid corps of inventive professionals, capable either of adapting western discoveries or even of anticipating them. In the later sixteenth century, Russian artillery was as powerful as that of any other European army, and it was to it that Ivan the Terrible owed his victories, as for instance with the fall of Kazan in 1552. It is customary for western historians to pull wry faces on learning that Russians invented this or that piece of military equipment. The question is indeed complex, for it appears that in virtually all countries in Europe, at more or less the same time, technicians would work on similar lines and come up with similar discoveries. Russia, at least, was not behindhand in this process. Fedorov and Tokarev produced a reliable quick-firing rifle in the 1890s, and an automatic rifle in 1907; Baranovsky produced a rapid-fire cannon at the same time, capable of discharging ten rounds per minute at a range of eight kilometres; the engineer Mendeleyev invented a tank in 1911, and a Russian-made one was produced at Riga in May 1915 (with the name *Vezdekhod*); similarly a Russian engineer, Mozhavsky, managed to invent a flying-machine in which he flew for a minute or so in 1882, and Russian aircraft-technology was quite advanced by 1914 (indeed, by 1916 the field army possessed more machines than did the French army, although the types were very varied and the maintenance of them proved problematical).

Much of the effort in such inventive processes was Russian, but there was also a strong element of imitation by Russians of foreigners. In the Russian General Staff before the First World War, officers were concerned to absorb as much foreign military science as possible, as had been the case from the early days of the Tsarist Empire. Moscow University taught military science from the beginning, officers in the General Staff Academy had to know at least two foreign languages, and there was a considerable amount of translation of foreign military manuals – thus, in the eighteenth century, Russian artillery owed most to the work of two Germans, Braun and Büchner, while Russian tactics were usually worked out from foreign models, sometimes even adapted by Germans in Russian service.

The chief difficulty for the Russian army, was the backwardness of much of its man-power. This was not so much of a problem in the eighteenth century, and to some extent the seventeenth either, since the army was quite small (that of Peter the Great numbered 112,000), so that the ordinary soldiers could receive a concentrated training, and could usually be selected from the most suitable men of a particular district. But later on, the army expanded to meet the various needs of the state, with its frontiers moving forward in Asia simultaneously with large-scale war in Europe. Russia could fill out the ranks only by extending the system of conscription and by using as officer-material men who, in the eighteenth century, would not have been considered suitable. The army, in other words, represented the condition of Russian society more accurately than before. Since most of the Tsar's subjects were peasants, living at a very primitive level, this was reflected in the armed forces. By 1900, two-thirds of the soldiers (and even, reputedly, some of their officers) were illiterate. The army failed, on the whole, to produce a reliable corps of non-commissioned officers – long-serving soldiers did exist, but there were only about half as many of them per company as in Germany; and in any case they tended to 'side' instinctively with the men, not the officers. There was no sergeants' mess in the Russian army, and, except for certain cavalry regiments, the whole concept of the NCO was woefully weak – as the officers discovered when they had to face mutiny in 1917. In these circumstances, Russian soldiers' behaviour could often be astoundingly primitive. Fighting the Germans, they often did not appreciate where they were; they seldom made any attempt to escape from German captivity (and were also captured in great numbers in the First

World War); and there were episodes of a singularly revealing character, as for instance in 1915, when the telegraph to Warsaw broke down because some soldiers had cut down the telegraph poles for fuel to boil their tea.

Rightly or wrongly, the Russian military authorities never felt able to conscript on a serious scale before the First World War. It is a complete myth to suppose that the army in these years was a huge force of semi-illiterate peasants, armed with sticks, as legend has it. The military authorities never felt they could spend money on the scale required to feed and clothe their liable young conscripts (of whom, in 1910, there were nearly one million p.a.) and therefore decided to reduce the numbers of those physically liable for service by generously granting exemptions. They exempted all who failed to meet very high physical standards, all who belonged to certain privileged minorities, national or religious, all only sons or only grandsons, and all married men. In 1914–15, one million young peasants appear to have married, suddenly, and to the bewilderment of agricultural experts. The Russian army in 1914 was therefore no larger than the French army in the field – some two million men, since the French had conscripted ruthlessly, and exempted as few men as possible, despite the French population's being less than one quarter of the Russian one. It was therefore with an army quite limited in size and low in quality that Russia took the field in 1914.

It was this, and not weakness in the output of war-goods as such, that made the Russian army less effective in the First World War than it could have been. Of course, the scandals surrounding the Russian army's shell-shortage in the First World War are notorious, and one of the best-known factors of the period – the more so as there was a strange collusion on the subject between Soviet historians and émigré writers or memoirists. It was certainly true that the army lacked war-goods in 1914–15, and there were certain points in the summer of 1915 (when the Russian army had to evacuate most of Poland) when batteries were reduced to a few rounds, and soldiers had to go into action with instructions to pick up the rifle of a casualty in no-man's-land. The scandals that such episodes caused did much to weaken the hold of the Tsarist government on the people's loyalties; by the summer of 1915, there was an opposition majority in the Duma, and it had links with the great industrialists and bankers of Russia, as well as with the General Staff and the High Command.

But what was significant about the shell-shortage was not the economic weakness it supposedly revealed as much as the military disorganisation that led to the shortage and the scandal itself. Russia lacked shell in these years for the quite simple reason that she relied too far on the West – both in military doctrine and in matters of arms-production. She had neglected to lay in, before the war, either enough shell for a long war, or capacity in the factories to produce the shell. Russian writers, among them the celebrated Bloch, had indeed perceived that the war would be an immense, bloody affair of stalemate, in which cavalry would be unable to operate to much effect and armies could not advance at any speed because of their supply-problems. Men appreciated that since the armies could not rely on motor-transport, they would have to rely on railways; once beyond their railheads, they would therefore encounter impossibly difficult problems of supply. Bloch, and other writers in Russia, well understood that, in circumstances of this kind, victory would have to be achieved by raining artillery shell on the enemy until he collapsed.

Where they went wrong was to suppose that the war would be short. Most people assumed it would be 'over in six weeks'; some Russians imagined a six-month war. The reasons for these assumptions were not strictly military. They were, rather, economic, even fiscal. Everyone accepted the prevailing orthodoxies. Economies in western Europe were held to be so dependent on exports that they would collapse if the exports came to a stop (indeed, the initial motive in the British blockade of Germany was not so much the arresting of imports to Germany as of exports from her: British exports were expected to take the place of these, a calculation that proved wholly correct). Consequently no trading country could afford a long war without mass unemployment, even economic collapse. Besides, and here the Russians adopted the western-European view with a literalness that western Europeans themselves found excessive, the cost of a long war would be impossible to meet. The government could not pay for it out of income, and would therefore have to run a large deficit. No one supposed that the public would grant credit on such an enormous scale to the government, which in any case would, after the war, be unable to pay interest on this scale. Moreover, almost no one imagined that the war could be paid for by taxation – an income tax or an excess-profits-due would be too expensive to collect, and would harm business by removing incentives (a story unfolded by the Opposition in Great Britain when income tax was raised, in 1915, to two shillings in the pound). In fact there were serious reasons against imposition of direct taxes in Russia, and to the end of the war such taxes were not more than a gesture. The Russian excess-profits-due raised about enough to pay for twenty hours of the war, and the income tax paid for the rest of the week-end. Other countries were not much better – German direct taxes paid for six days' war-time expenditure, Austro-Hungarian for four. It was only in Great Britain that a serious percentage of war-expenditure was covered by direct taxes. In the event, the governments paid for their war-effort mainly by having the National Bank produce paper-credits, to be redeemed at the end of the war by reparations of some sort or another. The inflation that resulted from this bore out all the fears of the experts before 1914; but, to their surprise, economies did not collapse, except in Russia, where orthodoxies were applied, as usual, more rigorously than elsewhere.

The consequence of such orthodoxies was that the Russian army concentrated its armament on stocks of shell for a six-month war. From experience in the Far East a decade before, about two thousand rounds of shell per gun were thought desirable, and the army thus had some seven million laid in. Resources were concentrated on the stock-piling, and not on capacity to make shell: armament, in other words, in 'width' but not 'depth'. When money became free, it would be used to buy shell, not machinery to make it. In the conditions of 1914, a great part of the stockpiled shell was fired off by the end of the year, and thereafter the country had to rely on factories and arsenals producing about half a million rounds per month, at a time when monthly needs reached two or even three million. Even so, reactions were sluggish. Not many officers in the War Ministry had faith in the capacity of Russian businessmen to convert their plant to war-time use, and consequently, when shell seemed to be needed, recourse was had to foreigners. Yet the foreigners – in the main, American – turned out to be not much better than Russian suppliers in their record of efficiency or delivery dates. It was partly their inexperience; it was partly the difficult matter of inter-Allied finance (who would pay for Russian orders in the United States?); and it was partly a matter of transport. At all events, foreign deliveries of finished war-goods were not impressive, and by March 1917, not even ten per cent of the orders passed since 1914 had actually reached Russia.

The whole matter was bedevilled by a very characteristically

Russian feature – the mistrust that prevailed between the infantrymen and the artillerymen. In brief, the artillerymen did not suppose that the infantry really did need the quantities of shell demanded. They thought that the infantry generals were exaggerating their requirements, because of the low quality of the troops. Shell was expected to do work that infantry ought to have been doing – for instance, the disruption of an enemy patrol. Besides, the peculiarities of the Russian army before 1914 had left infantry officers with too much say in the direction of artillery. In many of the army corps, the senior artillery officer was left merely with inspecting duties, because the infantry commanders felt that, if left to themselves, the artillerists would let the infantry down (as had frequently happened in the Russo-Japanese war). They would refuse to engage in preliminary bombardment, or to give proper support to attacking infantry. This was partly a matter of money – the military budget not being large enough to supply shell in great quantities, so that, in peace-time, each gun was forbidden to use more than forty shells p.a. in practice. It was particularly a matter of the gap between the educated, highly-trained artillerists and the infantrymen, who were regarded, both by cavalrymen and artillerists, as 'cattle', simple peasants with no notion of real warfare. The artillery chiefs were so adamant on these points that no suitable tactical manual for co-operation between them and the infantry could be produced until just before the war, and even then it was an extremely vague document. This had several harmful consequences. At ground level, corps commanders allowed infantry officers to give orders to artillery batteries; so the artillery chiefs reacted, in 1914-15, by supposing that the shell-crisis merely reflected the wasteful ways of infantrymen in the field, and would go away as soon as the artillery officers were allotted their proper responsibilities. To tales of shell-shortage, they therefore reacted with considerable sluggishness, and did little to plan increases in output from the various arsenals, let alone from converted civilian factories. Foreigners, such as the Frenchman Pyot, who suggested ways of stream-lining the war economy, were informed that they should mind their own business, and great industrialists or bankers, anxious to keep their industries going in war-time conditions, were also cold-shouldered.

There was a further harmful consequence of such attitudes, in so far as the artillery chiefs concentrated on the sectors of their affairs that had little to do with straightforward infantry action. They concentrated to an overwhelming extent on fortresses, and expected these to do the work of defence. From the 1880s onwards, an extraordinarily high proportion of non-supply allocations in the Russian military budget went to fortresses and fortress-artillery. Novogeorgievsk, protecting Warsaw, was built up; so were Kovno, Ivangorod, and the barrier-fortresses on the Narev, as well as Grodno. In the later nineteenth century, when the Franco-Russian alliance was far from secure, it perhaps made sense to concentrate resources in this way. But the development of quick-firing artillery, and especially the development of heavy artillery, made these fortresses dangerous traps. In the early part of the twentieth century, heavy shell could knock virtually any material apart, and fortresses, however strong, offered a very obvious target. Moreover, it was in the nature of fortresses that they could not be flexibly defended: once the place had been surrounded, there was no way in which reserves, the key to defence in the First World War, could be brought up. Consequently, sensible generals in that war would abandon their fortresses without a fight, as the French did at Verdun and elsewhere, and concentrate their defence on a trench-system which offered far less obvious targets and which could be easily reached by reserve-forces. It was much to the discredit of the artillery chiefs in Tsarist Russia that they failed to espouse the creative alternative. They reacted to the increasingly obvious weakness of fortresses, not by abandoning them, but by investing yet more in them. They demanded quantities of heavy shell and heavy fortress artillery, in the expectation that the fortresses could be defended by an artillery-duel. At every increase in the budgetary allocation for artillery, they would demand (and frequently obtain) more money for their heavy fortress guns than for the field artillery, of whatever type. Two consequences of this were disastrous: in the first place, the field army, with just over six thousand mobile guns, had barely more guns than the fortresses, with five thousand (half of them very modern); moreover, the failure to concentrate on infantry-support artillery meant that not enough money could be found for high-trajectory light artillery, which turned out to be the most important field-piece in the circumstances of immobile trench-warfare in the First World War. Russian divisions had three or four light howitzers, where German regular ones had twelve, as well as some heavy howitzers. Yet the Russian fortresses collapsed, in the summer of 1915, with great rapidity. Novogeorgievsk fell after a fortnight's siege; Ivangorod, Grodno, Brest-Litovsk were simply abandoned; Kovno fell after a few days, in circumstances so lamentable that its commander was given a hard-labour sentence. The real harm was shown when the Germans were able to announce that they had captured, not only a hundred thousand prisoners, but also some four thousand guns and three million shells in these various places. The only one that offered serious defence was, paradoxically, the weakest of the fortresses, Ostroleka, where the commander, unable to rely on his walls, was forced to develop a trench-system outside them and use the fortress, as sensible commanders did, merely as a larger version of a dug-out.

The same factor of immense mistrust between artillerymen and infantrymen also produced a serious division in the field, between heavy and light artillery. The infantry generals managed to assert control, at least of the light artillery, attached to the divisions in the trenches. The artillery chiefs insisted on controlling the heavy, long-range, artillery in the same way as before, and the consequence was that little liaison existed between the two. This, rather than shortage of material, led to such disasters as the Lake Narotch offensive of March 1916. In an effort to help the French, who were facing German attacks at Verdun, the Russian High Command launched an attack on the German part of the eastern front. An enormous superiority of number was built up: twenty-three divisions to seven-and-a-half. There were a thousand guns to three hundred, and shell-supplies in abundance. Yet the offensive came to an end, after four days' action, and casualties of over 100,000, with almost no gains. The light artillery was commanded at infantry corps level, and concentrated on infantry tasks, while the heavy artillery was managed by a separate command altogether, with not much liaison. It fired inoffensively into woods, in a bombardment known as 'General Smirnov's *son-et-lumière*'; the infantry, attacking through the slush, even found themselves being bombarded by their own side, from lack of liaison. It was an engagement that convinced most of the Russian generals of the front facing Germany that they had better abandon all offensive action until there were such quantities of heavy shell available that nothing could possibly survive on the other side. As the result, two-thirds of the Russian front saw no action of any seriousness until virtually the end of the war, with consequences in terms of morale that 1917 was amply to show.

In reality, production both of artillery and of shell showed that the country could produce the goods once difficulties of an organisational kind had been cleared away, even if the army establishment was too disunited to make proper use of the artillery. The government, after much hesitation, finally took the plunge into lavish spending that the war-industrial effort required. It enlisted the co-operation of big business and the banks; a Special Council for Defence was instituted in the spring of 1915, and by the end of the year it functioned well enough, in allocating orders and credits to civilian factories for war-production. The result was that Russia, which even in 1914 had developed the sinews of industrial strength, began to produce war-material in great quantity. The rifle-crisis, the shell-crisis, became things of the past; by January 1918, the Red army was able to rely on a Tsarist stock of eighteen million shells when it started to fight the Civil War, and by the early 1920s the Bolsheviks were able to produce even tanks from factories that had been organised for such purposes in Tsarist days. The war did come to an end through revolution, prompted by the collapse, from disorganisation, mainly of food supplies to the towns; and yet by 1917 the signs were certainly present that Russia would soon be a super-power, capable of dominating the field in a European war if ever the matter were decided in narrowly military-economic terms.

The traditional difficulty was, then, not so much on the material side, but more on the organisational one. The ordinary soldiers were frequently too backward for any very sophisticated system of tactics, and hence also of strategy, to be followed. It was characteristic that the Tsarist army, and to a large extent also the Red army, neglected a principle such as fire-and-movement, which required independent action from small parties of men operating under a non-commissioned officer, and instead concentrated on 'wave' tactics, lining up a mass of men with officers to front and rear, making sure that they behaved in an almost automaton-like way. Such formations were of course very vulnerable to machine-gun-fire, but no-one seems to have suggested a different system. Similarly, the discipline of the Russian army was also much stricter than in other European armies, even the German one. Although officer and man were expected to be on good terms, there was always a high degree of formalism in the military structure. Saluting was a complicated ritual, that had civilians rubbing their eyes in disbelief; until 1917, the ordinary form of address for an officer was a complex formula of German (eighteenth-century) origin which meant calling an infantry captain 'High-Born'.

Overall, circumstances in the Tsarist army were such that administration tended to dominate every other consideration. The country was so immense, the tasks of the army so variegated, the gap between the educated section of it and the uneducated one so great, that the simple effort of keeping the army going at all was generally enough to absorb all energies. It was for this reason that, over most of the Tsarist past, the army was dominated not by its High Command in the field, but by the organisers in the rear. A General Staff of a serious kind did not emerge until 1906. Before then, the War Minister, in charge of administration, was the real chief of the army; it was he who controlled the Main Staff, one of the sections of which was called *Generalny Shtab*, in which a few officers desultorily planned whatever might come their way. There was no central planning authority, and hardly even a serious war-plan, until 1906; and even when a General Staff was set up, independent of the administrative machine, it could not dictate its will to the various sections of the army – cavalry, infantry, artillery, engineers (for fortresses and railways) – without running into serious obstruction. The General Staff remained independent of the War Ministry only for two years, until 1908; and thereafter the War Ministry, which controlled officers' appointments, deliberately used the promotions-machinery to assert central control through a system of clientage, with all the divisions and hatreds within the officer-corps that such tactics were likely to bring about. The generals of 1914–18 really divided between friends and enemies of the War Minister, Sukhomlinov; and the two sides made certain that, when one of the other side's number was appointed to a particular command, one of their own would be appointed to be his chief of staff. In consequence, the army and corps head-quarters in the Russian army in the First World War were usually marked by immense dislike between commander and chief of staff, who, in the case of I Army in August 1914, communicated only in writing. The frequent cases in the First World War of armies and corps failing to co-operate, of light and heavy artillery going their separate ways, may frequently be ascribed to factors of this kind, which did much to discredit the whole general officer-class in the eyes of subalterns.

The prevailing atmosphere in the army, the fear that the men would be unable to match up to European standards, the dominance of administrators and the weakness of planners, produced two results that mark the Russian army to this day. On the one hand, there was a considerable defensiveness: when in doubt, planners and administrators would alike concentrate heavily on defence, with fortresses and fortress-artillery well to the fore. It was this ultimate defensiveness of attitude that made the plan of attack in 1914 such a feeble affair. On the other hand, the army authorities greatly over-rated the effects of matériel alone: they would build up artillery in particular, even at the expense of sophisticated tactical systems, and they neglected the force that sheer will-power may have in war. The army was always a focus of Russian patriotism, and, against a weak, Asiatic enemy of imperialism, always with some sense of mission; but against a strong, western power, considerations of defence proved to be overwhelmingly strong.

SUMMARY OF DISCUSSION

In presenting his paper Dr Stone emphasised how greatly traditional Russian military attitudes and assumptions had been shaped by the contrast between backwardness and modernity, by the gulf between the mass of the peasant population and the educated élite, and between administrative confusion and technological competence. In particular he stressed again the effect of this on the nature of the officer corps: a part of the élite, and as such isolated from their men, yet recruited from a diversity of elements because of the general shortage of educated people, and thus very divided amongst themselves. Such an officer corps was fundamentally defensive-minded: it distrusted its human material and put its faith in the accumulation of matériel; it could not conceive of taking the offensive against an enemy always regarded as superior.

Much of the discussion focused on the problem of Russian defensive-mindedness and how far it still prevailed at the present time. In particular the question was asked to what extent the expectation that the Soviet Union might launch a *Blitzkrieg* type of attack in Europe could be supported from traditional Russian military attitudes. Some speakers pointed out that under French influence offensive tactics had been adopted in the Tsarist armies and there had been occasions in history when Russian armies had successfully taken the strategic offensive. On the whole there was agreement that even today the Soviet Union was unlikely to initiate military action except in circumstances in which it believed that it could win relatively swiftly and comprehensively. On the other hand it was pointed out that there existed in the Soviet Union a mixture of ideology, militarism, and belief in the armed forces as 'the school of the nation' that was potentially explosive. While the continued validity of Russian traditions through 1917 and 1945 was emphasised there was no belief that historical analogies constituted an exact guide for the future.

REFERENCES

L. Andolenko, *Histoire de l'Armée Russe* (Paris, 1967)
I. I. Rostunov, *Russki front pervoi mirovoi voynoi* (Moscow, 1976)
V. I. Shunkov (ed.), *Voprosy voennoi istorii Rossii, 18 i pervaya polovina 19 vekov* (Moscow, 1967)
H. P. Stein, 'Der Offizier des russischen Heeres im Zeitabschnitt zwischen Reform und Revolution 1861–1905', in *Forschungen zur osteuropaeischen Geschichte* (Berlin, 1967, vol. XIII, pp. 346–507)
N. Stone, *The Eastern Front 1914–1917* (London, 1975)
P. A. Zayonchkovski, *Voyennye reformi 1860–1870gg.* (Moscow, 1952)
—— *Samoderzhavie i russkaya armiya na rubezhe 19–20 stoletiy 1881–1903* (Moscow, 1974)

2 The Soviet Military System: Doctrine, Technology and 'Style'

John Erickson

Present excitements over the 'Soviet military build-up' are considerable, to say the least, though the recognition of this phenomenon has been astonishingly tardy. The historian of Soviet military policy would insist quite properly that Soviet society had long ago embarked on a permanent military build-up, signalled by the introduction in 1928 of the first Five Year Plan: nor do Soviet accounts shy away from affirming this rationale. As for mass, the same historian would point to that traditional Russian predilection for quantitative solutions to military problems, not to mention the proclivity towards over-insurance – though the irony is that both the Imperial Russian and the Soviet military systems have over-insured against the wrong things. Nor is the business of elucidation helped by those caprices of selectivity which abound in the western press and which are designed to serve a variety of causes, be they budgetary, political or emotive: a persuasive example is the reaction of the Western press to Soviet naval programmes, whereby much of Admiral Gorshkov's work has been done for him by our own journalistic hyperbole. Governments and military agencies (NATO in particular) cannot escape censure, for they would have the public believe implicitly in a 'threat' whose dimensions, location and deployments they refuse to disclose in any commonsense and credible manner. Bringing up the rear are the academics, who have generally failed to produce any reputable work on the *Soviet military system*: not the least discreditable aspect of this performance (or the lack of it) has been the failure to present any assessment of the Soviet General Staff, that massive and unique organisation which functions as the 'brain' of the formidable Soviet military machine – *mozg armii*.

While there may be arguments over the details of particular Soviet military programmes (ICBMs, warship building, modernised aircraft, and so on), those same arguments are impeded – at least in public circles – by a lack of understanding of how the Soviet military system at large operates. This involves indentifying Soviet military processes – choices and preferences – without superimposing upon the analysis non-Soviet perceptions and requirements. Let us approach this by way of negative proof: a simple linear exposition of Soviet military programmes (the quantitative buildup) explains little or nothing and, on the contrary, may complicate the picture by failing to illuminate particular 'fits', namely, that between general and theatre war, or modernisation cycles and the demands of technological improvement as opposed to tactical innovation or yet again the interrelationship of the several arms and services. One example must suffice here to prove those several points: the new infantry combat vehicle, the much vaunted *BMP* (infantry combat vehicle, 11–12 tons, 73-mm gun, AT-3 ATGW launchers, 7.62 mm MG, 8 troops), is a case in point, for here was a vehicle quite specifically outlined as a battlefield requirement in *Voennaya Mysl'* (*Military Thought*: the General Staff journal) in 1960, a vehicle produced for the nuclear battlefield (where it might encounter only light opposition) and yet now being wrenched into a different environment, the conventional mode where the *BMP* could well face heavy opposition, even a breakthrough operation. Thus we have a situation in which the Soviet command is attempting to derive a revised role for a combat vehicle with this unique origin, all suggesting a military version of Pirandello's play, *Six Characters in Search of an Author*. The same argument, or one very similar, can be applied to the recent improvements in the Soviet ground forces, resulting in a formidable 'build-up' – Soviet compensation for perceived shortcomings in their own performance: the lack of protection for march columns (compensated now by the introduction of the SA-8), the shortage of artillery in the fire preparation phase (amended by the massive infusion of artillery over the last five years), and the shortage of infantry on the axes of tank thrusts (corrected by the use of BMPs in the attack, though the tank forces are concerned that the infantry might dismount and thus slow the armoured attack). This is indubitably a Soviet response to their *own* perception of shortcomings in tactical performance.

How, then, does the Soviet system operate? It cannot be by the mere quantitative accretion of weapons: nor can it be by abstract adhesion to doctrine, nor yet again without some reference to the performance of the troops in the field and on the ground. Fortunately we have a very extensive model, one supplied by harsh Soviet experience and confirmed by subsequent Soviet analysis – the devastating, near annihilating German surprise attack of 1941, a disaster on an unexampled scale which now serves as a paradigm for the Soviet leadership, civilian and military alike. How did 'the system' respond and what, if anything, was fundamentally wrong? The debate was both anguished and protracted, as might be expected: it could even be said that it has never finished, for only recently Marshal Kulikov (at the time Chief of the Soviet General Staff) pointed to the dangers of inflexibility in the 'Soviet system' and to its possible lack of responsiveness in the face of global threats, threats which could be sudden and unexpected – the Gaullist strategy of *tous azimuths* in reverse, as it were.

Unravelling (or decoding) this Soviet commentary, we can determine three elements which are of overriding importance – *doctrine* (military doctrine, the '*accepted system of scientifically founded views on the nature of modern wars and the use of armed forces in them*'), *technology* (military technology in its own right as well as 'levels of armament', that is, both quantity and quality) and, finally, '*style*', the performance of the soldier and battlefield efficiency at large. This is the triad upon which Soviet experience rests and which works its way into the Soviet system in its entirety: by way of proof, we have the extensive commentaries of Colonel Anfilov (himself a General Staff officer) on the 1941 paradigm, three overlapping and interleaved commentaries – *Nachalo Velikoi Otechestvennoi Voiny* (1962), *Bessmertnyi podvig* (1971), and latterly *Proval 'Blitskriga'*, (1974). Closer examination of these volumes and the exegesis involved in these three 'explanations' – together with a variety of military-political commentaries by Party leaders and military commanders alike – confirms that this is a basic model of Soviet experience.

Let us first put this into Soviet terminology: doctrine is *voennaya doktrina*, technology is *vooruzhenie* (best translated not merely as 'armament' but also as 'armament norms') and 'style' – *effektivnost'*, a term comprehending efficiency, effectiveness, and battlefield performance in terms of the individual soldier and troop control, 'command and control' in Western usage. The next problem is to put these concepts into the total Soviet context. The argument runs as follows: doctrine, military doctrine, embracing 'operations in depth' was fundamentally sound, even as it was developed in the 1930s, but the lack of available technology (both in quantity and quality) made the doctrine 'unworkable' – for example, not until tank armies were organised, equipped, and assembled in 1943 could the concept of mobile operations and deep penetration work effectively. Equally, in terms of 'style' or performance, the old Civil War theory of morale, which substituted élan and revolutionary morale for technological competence – 'revolutionary will' acting as compensation for gross shortcomings in armament – had to give way to a new concept of battlefield performance, with physiological as well as psychological implications, including the 'management' of the modern battlefield. In this latter area, 'style', traditionalism, and innovation are most intimately combined, for here are the time-honoured qualities of the Russian soldier linked with his adaptation to modern equipment and tactical innovations.

The debate on the disasters of 1941 – which still continues in highly selective fashion – swung through its various phases, all of them as anguished as they were intense: once the Stalinist deceptions (or rather self-deceptions) were stripped away in the mid-1950s, the Soviet command embarked on a searching analysis of the *débâcle* and sought for means to avoid any repetition of near catastrophe. The first and fundamental question to decide concerned the viability of Soviet military doctrine (including war planning processes): in brief, if the Soviet command could not make provision for modern war, including the appropriate operational forms, then 'the system' was indeed endangered. To put it another way, in the fashion of the Soviet analysts, why did 'doctrine' not produce the required results? Closer inspection revealed that it was not the imperfections of doctrine but the shortcomings in 'armament norms' – *vooruzhenie* – which had to be held to account: for example, mobile operations were impossible in the absence of lorries or the proper exploitation of railway links, not to mention air lift. In 1943, when the tanks, lorries, and SP guns rolled out of the factories in the proper quantities, then 'doctrine' worked and was amply vindicated: 'operations in depth' – *gluboki boi*, first adumbrated in the 1930s by Tukhachevskii, Isserson, and officers of the General Staff, embodied in *PU-36* – was the Soviet answer to the *blitzkrieg*. At first, it seemed to have failed, but given the requisite 'armament norms', then it worked admirably. Of course, fitted into a modern context, it required an extension into 'military economics', the relationship between 'strategy and economics' (to subsume the substance of an important study by Major-General Lagovskii) and the development of a whole theory of *oboronosposobnost'*, 'defensive capacity' in the widest sense of the word. Mobilising ideological orthodoxy, in order to establish the primacy of the defensive imperative, it is not surprising to see Major-General Lagovskii producing a study on Lenin's view of defensive capability – *V. I. Lenin ob ekonomicheskom obespechenii oborony strany* (Moscow, Voenizdat, 1976). Here is a managerial input, or a claim to it, by the Soviet military command.

Thus the vindication of doctrine. What, however, is meant by 'armament norms'? This is not merely a simple quantitative approach, though *mass* is an important principle. The process of settling 'armament norms' is related to a huge, systematic investigation of wartime operations at large, setting numbers against 'performance' – for example, the evolution of the 'armament norms' of the rifle division, or the maintenance of 'sustained combat capability' (*zhivuchest'*) in tank formations. This has resulted in the elaboration of battlefield 'norms', part typology and part preplanned concept. The breakthrough operation is a case in point, examined in typological detail by officers of the Frunze Academy in a major work, *Proryv podgotovlennoi oborny strelkovymi soedineniyami* (Moscow, Voenizdat, 1957): the 'norms' for breakthrough operations are studied here in exacting detail. The same approach can be discerned in a very recent study, that of General Radzievskii, which adopts the same typological *point de départ* in examining Soviet tank operations – gross losses, the recycling rate (battlefield repair), duration of operations, casualty rates in personnel, and the methods needed to maintain 'sustained combat capability', all expounded in *Tankovyi udar* (Moscow, Voenizdat, 1977).

So far we have examined the connection between the viability of doctrine and the implementation of 'armament norms'. Doctrine can only 'work', that is, accomplish battlefield missions successfully, if the requisite 'armament norms' are met: close typological analysis can establish those norms and a 'norm' can be duly identified as that combination of 'armament levels' with procedures in order to equal battlefield success (in other words, those successive 'buys' of equipment required *to win*). There remains, however, the significance of procedures, perhaps best subsumed under the general heading of 'style', ranging from the morale and performance of the individual soldier to the intricacies of modern automated command and control, 'troop control' – *upravlenie voiskami*. Clearly the Soviet theory of morale is closely involved here. If doctrine and armament norms had to be brought into closer alignment in the early years of the war, then so had there to be changes in the approach to individual performance – a move away from substituting 'revolutionary will' for technological progress and the amelioration of 'discipline of the revolver'. A new model of battlefield performance had to be developed, which has now advanced into the fields of 'military-engineering psychology', the man-machine match and the management of 'large military systems' (LMS), as well as looking more closely at the performance of Soviet sub-units and thence the individual soldier. That approach has resulted in a bifurcation in Soviet training practices, to 'morale-political preparation' and 'morale-psychological' training (the latter much more overtly military), while the common bond between both is the implementation of discipline in all its accepted orthodoxy.

It is clear that a simple linear approach to Soviet military policy will not suffice: that would not explain the past, clarify present developments, or elucidate the future. Even more, it does great violence to Soviet perceptions, many of them derived from their wartime experience, a dwindling but still important residue of operational knowledge. The past and present Soviet preoccupation has been with the properties of 'the system' – its viability, flexibility, and survivability, wherein 'the system' is perhaps best understood as the amalgam of doctrine-technology (armament norms) – 'style'. Such a formulation looks both backwards and forwards, back to the whole tradition of Russian war-making and on to the requirements of the modern, automated battlefield: inevitably, the original model has been extended to include Soviet experience of the large-scale post-war military exercises (such as *DNIEPER* in 1967 and *DVINA* in 1970), together with the evaluation of the several local wars, the Middle East and Vietnam being the most prominent. Soviet military analysts closely monitored American experience in the air war in Vietnam, succinctly summed up by the late Marshal Grechko, who confirmed that 'scientific-technical intellect is intensely working on the problem of increasing the survivability of aircraft and helicopters and giving them a greater striking power when they break through modern air defence systems.' Similarly, operations in the Middle East 'have put a new slant on the problem of the relationship between offensive and defensive actions of ground forces . . . . '

Of the three components of this system, 'style' – performance, or effectiveness at large – is perhaps the most important, though frequently elusive in its operation: it is, for example, difficult to find a suitable translation for that much used Soviet term *effektivnost'*, which may signify efficiency much as it conveys the context of effectiveness, referring both to operations at the strategic level to the performance of the sub-unit and the effectiveness of the individual Soviet soldier. Elucidation of these problems is not helped by the inexactitudes of Soviet terminology and the obfuscations of actual discussion, though this is readily understandable in view of the sensitive nature of theme. The questions which spring to mind are legion: how adaptable is the system, how responsive is it to present and projected threats – what 'scientific foresight' (*nauchnoe predvidenie*) can it muster and apply – what is the degree of true combat readiness, how effectively is it absorbing the artefacts of the 'revolution in military affairs' (*revolyutsiya v voennom dele*)? There are many brave words uttered on these variegated themes, but it was Trotskii who built up the Red Army in the days of the Civil War and who had the first – possibly the last – word on the subject, when he referred to *brodyachaya Rossiya*, 'vagabond Russia' as his worst foe: how much of this still prevails?

It is logical to begin with doctrine, which comprehends a number of military technicalities and forms part of a wider relationship – military doctrine as official state policy on military questions, military art (*voennoe iskusstvo*) concerned with 'the theory and practice of engaging in combat', and military science (*voennaya nauka*) which is 'a system of knowledge concerning the nature, essence, and content of armed conflict' – though we can legitimately understand 'doctrine' as the full range and sweep of Soviet strategic thinking. Until recently it was fashionable to deride Soviet strategic ideas as crude and unsophisticated, the product of military ignoramuses unable to comprehend the metaphysical niceties of American civilian theoreticians: latterly, this view has been revised to recognise the consistency, cogency, and contemporary relevance of Soviet military ideas. While western concepts centred increasingly on a 'cost-effective' approach to strategic forces and a 'managerial' concept of strategy – using many euphemisms to hide that grim word 'war' from the outset, and in the wake of the Great

Patriotic War with its gruesome toll of 20 million dead, Soviet military planners set out to face the central problem of war, now rendered more devastating with the advent of nuclear weapons. What was regarded as 'unthinkable' in the West had to be rendered 'thinkable' in the Soviet Union, for the survival of the system and its society was at stake. It was natural, therefore, that there should be a strong defensive input into this strategic evaluation and understandable also (though incomprehensible in some western circles) that any Soviet concept of 'deterrence' could not be isolated from a defensive commitment: while western commentators argued that 'deterrence' and 'defence' were incompatible, the Soviet argument insisted that 'deterrence' without 'defence' was as irresponsible as it was inane.

This outlook was reflected consistently in Soviet terminology, where *oborona* – defence – is generally used to signify this 'defence/deterrence' concept, as opposed to the rather esoteric language of 'deterrence' as such, *ustrahsenie* or *sderzhivanie*. If there is a cornerstone to this whole strategic outlook, then it is survival, based on a war-waging capability and the recent development of that margin of strength which will enable the Soviet Union to emerge, if not as 'victor', then with visible and viable advantage. In brief, this is a 'battlefield philosophy', with its emphasis on damage-limitation and counterforce (to use western terms): the Soviet command put its trust in fire-power and sought from the earliest days of the strategic weapons programme to maximise this. Nor, as we shall see, did they lose sight of numerical solutions. (It is worth noting in passing that the early stages of the Soviet missile build-up were in the charge of senior Soviet artillery officers.)

It is in this context that we can observe the origins of *the* Soviet build-up, engaged irreversibly in the mid-1950s: with the years of Stalinist immobilism ended (though much stirred discreetly under the surface under the aegis of the Military-Scientific Directorate of the General Staff, set up in 1953), Marshal Zhukov set about implementing a re-organisation designed to fit the Soviet armed forces and Soviet society at large for war under nuclear conditions. For their own reasons, the political and military leadership had rejected the notion of 'mutual deterrence' – espousing that cause cost Malenkov his political head, for his opponents suspected that 'mutuality' of this process much as they despised a concept of deterrence in which the Soviet Union was deterred, as opposed to 'deterring' in its own right. Defence in its active and passive modes was pushed through vigorously, with massive investment in an air defence programme (*PVO strany*) and the re-activation of civil defence preparations (*grazhdanskaya oborona*), not to mention the start upon the dispersal and hardening of potential targets. Nor is it impossible to ignore that singular work, *Voennaya strategiya* (*Military strategy*) produced under the auspices of Marshal Sokolovskii and essentially the first Soviet manual or primer dealing with the conduct of nuclear war, an imperfect work in many respects but one to be set against the background of the 'special collections' at General Staff level revealed by Colonel Penkovskii – this was not, as some American commentators tried to adduce, a delicate, metaphysical disquisition on 'flexible response' but a brute, compelling study instructing the Soviet command to think about the 'unthinkable' – nuclear war.

Nor was the economic aspect of strategic war planning neglected in this phase. In 1955 Soviet allocations to defence (and space operations, culminating in *Sputnik*) amounted to some 11 per cent of GNP, falling somewhat to 8 per cent in 1958 but rising thereafter with the promulgation of the Seven Year Plan (1959–65), fixing Soviet defence expenditures at about 13.1 per cent of GNP by 1961 and increasing throughout that decade. In rough and rather indeterminate form Soviet 'total strategy' was emerging for all the world to see: Khrushchev's eccentricities, including his Cuban missile 'quick-fix' and his own minimax solution to afford the greatest fire-power at minimum cost, were short-lived. The Soviet military command could scarcely be satisfied with verbal manipulations of a non-existent 'superiority', nor did mighty terror multi-megaton warheads, whatever their city-annihilating properties, satisfy their requirements for battlefield counter-force capability, committed to knocking out enemy 'nuclear batteries'. So much depended on Khrushchev's notion that a future nuclear war would be no more than a spasm exchange, a matter of hours, and thus eliminating the need for general purpose forces or extensive home front preparations from active participation. Khrushchev's missile mania led to some alarming results: that mania did not extend to furnishing a numerically superior bombardment force, it rested on assumptions of minimum strength, it allowed the political admission of 'mutuality' in deterrence, it led to the drastic reduction of general purpose forces (hollowing out the Ground Forces to a mere 75 divisions) and – *horribile dictu* – to the prospect of permanent strategic inferiority for the Soviet Union, as the price of a strategic compact with the United States. The gap, which now yawned before the Soviet command, had to be closed at all costs.

The debate on strategic options, launched in the immediate post-Khrushchev phase, was of crucial importance: closing the nuclear firepower gap in terms of US-Soviet ICBM strengths, refashioning the relationship between strategic strike and general purposes forces (the ground forces had lost their status as an independent command in 1964 and it was to be three years before this was restored), matching Soviet objectives more closely with Soviet capabilities and abandoning Khrushchev's one-sided, 'one-variant' military policy. The result was to superimpose 'a military build-up' on *the* build-up, a phase extending over a decade and more and including expansion, modernisation and diversification.

Certain significant conclusions can be drawn from this protracted and substantial debate – clearly, Soviet strategy recognised (and still does recognise) the sensible need to avoid nuclear war as a possible contingency (if waged by the United States and her allies, for here is power enough to destroy the Soviet Union), but by the same token the Soviet Union was unwilling (as it is now) to entertain any concept of deterrence which would *increase* Soviet vulnerability, either through being fastened into the 'balance of terror' at a time when that 'balance' was grossly distorted in American favour or else by being committed to 'mutual assured destruction' – since there was no mutuality involved and 'assured destruction' invalidated any concept of effective defence. In other words, the Soviet command was not inclined to trade vulnerabilities as the guarantee of security: it was military weight, not measured weaknesses which pointed the way to safety in an unstable world.

In addition, the Soviet command has never accepted the nuclear weapon as an 'absolute' in war: nor could it conceive properly of concepts such as 'limited nuclear war' where military technology provided the limiting mechanisms, since Soviet doctrine affirmed that wars are defined by their political objectives, not by the level or type of weaponry engaged. As for 'deterrence', Soviet opinion quite properly recognises that this cannot lead to 'victory', meaning the survival of the Soviet system and the elimination of any threat to it. Equally, there is no sense in 'absorbing' an enemy strike merely to enjoy the luxury of retaliation. The Soviet Union 'absorbed' enough for many lifetimes in 1941 and henceforth 'active offensive actions' are mandatory and seizing the initiative is the decisive factor. Such complexity imposes its own complications in clarifying Soviet strategic posture: the Soviet stance is not one of unequivocal 'first-strike' (to use our terminology), the Soviet command does not subscribe to a 'second-strike strategy' but that is not to say that it is not interested in residual strategic capabilities (the development of a mobile ICBM version of the SS-20 could attest to this, or the withholding of SLBMs). If anything, the Soviet view concentrates on a 'damage-limitation/time-winning' strike – which propaganda might invest with successful properties, but which military realism considers more cautiously, as we shall shortly see. In sum, the Soviet position – quite unlike that in the West – is not that of repeating that if war comes, 'deterrence' has somehow 'failed': the advent of war means simply a shift to damage-limitation, the utilisation of strategic forces to eliminate military threats to the USSR, and the struggle to gain measurable advantage. It follows, therefore, that 'deterrence' has never been and never could be a measure of 'sufficiency' for Soviet strategic force levels: to argue that Soviet force levels exceed the needs of 'deterrence' is an absurdity when they never were designed primarily for deterrence – though the Soviet leadership, with its military and political segments, clearly understands the *political* strategy of war-avoidance.

The heart of the matter is the strategic 'disruptive strike' (not unlike the wartime artillery technique of *kontropodgotovka*, a delicately timed fire blow designed to unhinge an enemy blow . . .); however, this 'disruptive attack' might not cripple capitalist society, enemy launchers might remain unscathed, command and control and military installations remain intact to some degree, and transportation still operative – hence the consideration of a more prolonged struggle and the resort to an *'all arms' solution*. This argument makes any concept of 'sufficiency' relative and places a premium on *forces in being*, including the rapid deployment of available military technology, while the Soviet command ponders on the 'fit' of the several theatre operations to main strategic blows – including new prescriptions for extensive war at sea.

'Winning' has been the subject of much Soviet polemical exchange (and alarmed western commentary): stripped to its essentials, the Soviet argument seems to centre on 'useful advantage' – that is, the capacity to ensure the survival of the Soviet system as a recognisable military power, as a viable political entity and as a working military-economic system, a doctrine predicated as SANE (survival and national existence) in contrast to MAD (mutual assured destruction) concepts. 'Retaliation' offers little to the Soviet Union, for having suffered a devastating blow, the results may be so catastrophic that surrender may be the only option: as for 'mutual deterrence', this offers only passivity, nullifying any seizure of the initiative.

Translated into missions, battlefield/bombardment assignments, the ICBMs of the Strategic Missile Forces (supplemented by long-range aviation and SLBMs) will ensure 'destruction of the enemy's nuclear means of attack', the elimination of military bases, the dislocation of command and control, the paralysis of the economy and transportation (a mixture of counter-force with selective counter-value targets). The Soviet Navy must 'contain aggression from the sea', inhibit seaborne nuclear strikes against the USSR, with a massive anti-submarine warfare effort conducted by combined air-surface-submarine task forces and Soviet submarines also operating in the combined task force mode. The Air Defence Command (*PVO Strany*) relies on a massive manned interceptor/SAM/radar network to fend off air attack, is presently adapting this system to deal with the cruise missile, and shows no diminution of interest in an improved ABM system; 'active defence' is backed by an expanding passive civil defence system, which may not be able to protect the Soviet population at large, but which can secure some greater survival for vital command and production centres. Theatre forces, with the Ground Forces as their main arm, will also strike out to eliminate enemy nuclear means, enemy formations, and enemy command and control – with surprise and deception vastly assisted by EW (electronic warfare), associated with the rapid concentration of superior forces, the uninterrupted high-speed offensive into the whole depth of enemy defences, whether this offensive is conducted in a nuclear or conventional mode, with a possible influsion of chemical weapons.

Here, then, are doctrinal prescriptions: the next question to ask is the manner in which 'armament norms' and technology are fitted (or not fitted, as the case may be) to make doctrine 'work'.

The 'numbers game' is crucial to Soviet military policy, though this is not to be construed as the blind pursuit of mass for its own sake – a solution discredited by the experience of 1941–2. The true relationship is that between doctrine – operational requirements – and 'armament norms', for strategic and general purpose forces alike. The build-up of Soviet strategic forces has certainly followed this pattern, with the emphasis on fire-power and yield. While matching the US ICBM forces in numbers, first attaining 'rough parity' and then exceeding it, the SALT-1 agreement in 1972 provided some unexpected bonuses: alarmed at what appeared in the late 1960s to be an American move to a 'deterrence/defence' mix, by which a major American defensive (ABM) effort would have disjointed Soviet plans, the numerical ceilings of SALT-1 smoothed Soviet strategic planning, invested the Soviet Union with what it perceived to be a permanent numerical superiority, and blunted any US defensive effort through the ABM treaty, while in no way inhibiting Soviet passive defence programmes, which contribute in their own way to diminishing an opponent's strategic strike capability and thus to enhancing Soviet survivability.

Obviously the Soviet command has done its sums in orthodox military fashion, as in the study 'Effectiveness of large target destruction', setting out the mathematical expectation of targets to be destroyed, the development costs of the missile systems involved, the cost of a single missile launch installation and the probability of the destruction of a typical target with a single missile, and so on. In equally obvious fashion the implementation of the Soviet counterforce/countervalue targeting doctrine requires specific numbers and types of ICBMs: not only must launchers be included but also reload capability (and refire capability), which could bring numbers up to *four times* the nominal ICBM deployment and must attain a minimum of 1×1. 'Cold-launch' techniques clearly facilitate reload/refire.

The heart of the Soviet strategic system is the 'heavy bombardment' ICBMs, initially the SS-9s now followed by the SS-18 (with a payload in the region of 16,000 lb.): the follow-on profile of the Soviet ICBM force may well consist of that essential 'core' (300 or so large, or heavy ICBMs), supplemented by 500 SS-19s, SS-17s, or whatever models of MIRV-ed modernised ICBMs are finally deployed. To the numbers of ICBMs must also be added the number of warheads (due to multiple warheads). Assuming that the SS-18s could carry 10 MIRVs, the SS-19s six and the SS-17s four, then the Soviet warhead total could rise in the early part of the next decade to 5,000 – and all with heavier yield than anything in the US arsenal. Accuracy is of great importance here and allowing for the time-lag as Soviet engineers improve accuracy, then Soviet bombardment options – aimed at knocking out US silos – can be calculated in terms of a 'two-on-one' strike (two warheads to each

US silo) and then a 'one-on-one' attack. The critical force level for MIRV-ed ICBM launchers is in the region of 800–850, for this affects the US-Soviet 'exchange ratio' in marked fashion and all in Soviet favour. (This is to assume that the US 'MX' mobile ICBM is not developed and not deployed: anything over 100 MXs would once more throw the Soviet 'numbers game' into disarray.) A Soviet build-up in the immediate future to maximum force levels (all within the provisions of any SALT-2 agreement), at the same time improving warhead accuracy to 0.15 of a mile at least, must lead inexorably to the capability to initiate nuclear war with an expected outcome of 'measurable advantage'.

Strategic defence, a vital element of the 'survival/advantage' equation, consumes huge resources of men, aircraft and missiles – 2,650 manned interceptors, over 10,000 SAMs, and many thousands of radars, not to mention the early-warning/ABM complex in the Moscow region. Modernised manned interceptors—MiG-23, MiG-25, and the formidable Su-15 (in several variants)—have updated Soviet air intercept capability, but low-flying targets and the advent of the cruise missile must seriously complicate the defensive problem, which must wait on a 'look-down/shoot-down capability' as well as improved fire-control radars and missile seeker heads. Available ground-based jammers to impede hostile bombers cannot provide full coverage of Soviet territory: low-altitude coverage would be appreciably improved by bringing a more advanced Soviet airborne warning and control aircraft (AWACs) into service, though none has yet made its appearance (save for the limited numbers and limited performance of the Tu-126). Low-altitude radars are being developed, together with the hypersonic SA-10 missile operating with CW (continuous wave) radar, but gaps in the defences remain to be plugged. A temporary Soviet solution could be a resort to sheer numbers, deploying more radars and more missiles – while every negotiating tactic is utilised to inhibit US development and optimised deployment of the cruise missile. (The scale of the problem is at least suggested by one American estimate which argues that at least 1,000 interceptors in the same class as the US F-14 and improved missiles deployed at 600–1,000 sites will be needed to enhance Soviet air defence.)

However, 'doctrine' or the whole strategic spectrum and the potentialities of advanced, not to say exotic military technology may be brought into startling alignment depending on Soviet progress with directed-energy beam weapons and high-energy lasers used as 'satellite killers'. The logic stretches back somewhat in time, to that ABM Treaty of 1972 which stripped the US ICBM force of any defensive system, while the Soviet Union not only improved its limited ABM system and intensified its damage-limiting civil defence programme, but also looked forward to the directed-beam energy weapon as the true neutralising instrument against the ICBM and its warheads. Fanciful this may be, but eight successive Soviet tests of a prototype beam weapon suggest intentions both grim and intensive.

'Armament norms' and the adoption of a more advanced military technology also dominate the Soviet approach to the battlefield, seen in this context in its much more familiar outline of armour, artillery, motorised infantry, and tactical air. Studies of 'battlefield performance' have continued without respite since the 1950s, though it should not be forgotten that in 1942 the Soviet command ordered OR teams to evaluate operations in the wake of combat units. Detailed studies under the rubric *'Po opytu Velikoi Otechestvennoi voiny 1941–1945 gg.'*, poured out in the 1950s: the archives of the Soviet Ministry of Defence were systematically combed, producing profiles of tank army, 'combined arms' army, and air army operations and so down to division. The result was a whole series of operational typologies, embracing weapons hold-ings, structures, expected effectiveness, anticipated losses, and measurement against operational reality. This has also given rise to one of the richest tactical-technical military literatures in the world, such as Colonel V.P. Istomin's *Smolenskaya nastupatel'naya operatsiya (1943 g.)*, or General Kurochkin's volume *Obshchevoiskovaya armiya v nastuplenii* – to cite but two examples, a distillation of failure and success respectively.

The evolution of the Soviet ground forces is remarkable in a number of respects: for all the talk of 'mass', the ground forces concentrated on building up comparatively small mobile units, adapting tactics to type of structure and designing armour with a nuclear battlefield in mind. The high ratio of combat strength to support – a noticeable Soviet feature – was achieved by centralising logistics support, by fitting a great deal of training into the operational framework, by keeping down the size of formations and units and, finally, by maintaining a 'mixed' force of cadre/active divisions. In terms of weapons, the ground forces have passed through three main stages – with the armoured fighting vehicle as the core, supplemented by increasingly sophisticated infantry combat vehicles (the BMP being the latest version) and, latterly, self-propelled guns (122-mm and 152-mm).

The real revolution occurred in the mid-1950s, when the ground forces were committed to and equipped for high-speed, offensive operations and doctrine affirmed the primacy of the offensive, as well as confirming the prescription of 'operations in depth' – where the first lesson to learn was the integration of nuclear weapons into a war-fighting system. Soviet attention was concentrated on the breakthrough phase, involving high-intensity operations only on selected sectors – hence the selective distribution of logistic resources and the availability of fire support, largely indirect fire. Much of this was based on an analysis of the breakthrough operations of 1944–45 (with adjustments for the properties of modern weapons). A distinctive feature was the relationship between tactical performance and logistical requirement (much misunderstood in western circles, which persisted in its parrot-talk of a Soviet 'weakness' in logistics – when an armoured breakthrough against an opponent lacking depth in his defences would require little sustained logistical support).

Over the past two decades the ground forces have gradually evolved a genuine dual capability – nuclear and/or conventional; indeed, the 'build-up' of the past ten years has been explicitly in the direction of augmenting conventional weaponry, though this does not imply an outright preference for a conventional campaign. 'Battlefield norms' have been adjusted correspondingly – rates of advance, fire, and combat engineer support, logistical back-up and (not least in importance) improvements in command and control. The 'combined-arms' concept now reigns supreme, though like Orwell's equality, some arms are more combined than others. The improvements in and diversification of weapons have produced further twisting complications in implementing this battlefield combination, in particular, the misgivings of the armoured forces in having to wait for full fire suppression (or a dismounted infantry attack), thus slowing down the high-speed attack, the introduction of *direct fire* resources (self-propelled artillery) but the difficulties of handling decentralised artillery, the growing complexity of co-ordinating air strikes with artillery, the pressing requirement to improve the speed and accuracy of *target acquisition*; the burden of protecting the soft targets presented by combat engineers deployed well forward, the necessity to maintain flexibility in fluid battle situations, the lack of provision of air cover/air support in the regimental area and, as ever, the inflexibility of communications. (See chapter 3.)

Here is a classic example of the doctrine-technology-performance triad, though with one interesting variation. 'Armament norms' have now been almost met in full (with Soviet tank and motor-rifle formations densely 'packed' with weapons), so that either doctrine (tactical utilisation and handling) must be adjusted or 'performance', particularly at the sub-unit level, substantially improved. The Soviet command can either increase the size of its formations or else swell reserve stocks in order to support 'sustained combat capability' (*zhivuchest*'): on present evidence, they are choosing the latter course. 'Operational norms' are involved here, as are 'loss co-efficients', all subject to the closest statistical scrutiny by the Soviet military command. For example, present 'loss co-efficients' (20 per cent of manpower per 24 hours of operations) will only keep a motor-rifle division in the line for five days, yet the commander must retain sufficient manpower/fire resources for any final decisive assault, hence the interest in 'sustained combat capability'.

In terms of overall capability, there is an interesting development in terms of a Soviet concept of an 'independent theatre war option', namely, de-coupling general war from a high-speed theatre campaign in Europe, and 'limited war' in the Soviet sense of being limited by *political* objective rather than by level of weapons; selective targeting and damage limitation would go hand-in-hand, assisted by developments in high accuracy conventional, chemical, and radio-electronic weapons, all geared to the overriding Soviet concept of decisive battlefield victory, the destruction of the enemy's war-making potential, a short war, and rapid post-attack recovery. The principle remains *the maximum effective application of military force*. Soviet air power would have a critical role to play in this situation (and in other battlefield contexts). Advances in Soviet combat aircraft, improvements in range/payload, can now give operational effect to an offensive air doctrine, a capability embracing the whole Eurasian land mass. Meanwhile, the Soviet conventional build-up serves a double purpose, both to win a conventional campaign and to exploit a nuclear strike or strikes, conducted with *low-yield systems* as well as the larger weapons. A protracted conventional campaign in the European theatre does not appear to be part of Soviet planning, but the relationship between 'a more extended campaign' and 'sustained combat capability' is obviously under close scrutiny, an intriguing correlation of doctrine and technology in its own right.

Thanks to developments in armament and technology, we are seeing for the first time an adjustment in the previous Soviet view that rapid escalation to the use of nuclear weapons was inevitable. Forces built in the early 1960s for a short nuclear conflict have been extensively modernised and invested with the capability of conducting conventional war, all with the intention of depriving NATO of exercising its own nuclear option. Here doctrine is lagging behind technology, though we must distinguish between doctrine formally enunciated and informally received, an important qualification and one demonstrated in the early 1970s when the conventional mode in the *initial phase* of operations received much greater attention, all without any 'official' airing.

Nowhere is the transformation of doctrine and the modification of tactics by technology and brute 'armament norms' more striking than in the recent development of the Soviet Navy. Unable to benefit to any extent from its own experience during the Second World War, the Soviet naval command turned to the German navy for light on the handling of the submarine arm and learned from these post-war analyses that independent employment of submarine had failed. The submarine had to be fitted into task or strike forces with surface vessel and air components, each acquiring targets for the others as well as for itself. The missile, even in its 'strapped on' form, also revolutionised the Soviet approach to naval tactics and with this growing sense of tactical competence came the affirmation of the 'naval mission' in the grand sense. Once again, the Soviet Navy has built up to heavy 'armament norms', maximising firepower though not without some provision for survivability. That latter factor, the survivability of the medium- or large-size surface combat vessel, has been the subject of some acrimonious dispute within Soviet naval circles, with Admiral Gorshkov insisting that without surface strike forces the concept of 'balance' would be hopelessly disrupted. For the neutralisation of western power to project power ashore from naval forces, to ensure Soviet utilisation of sea spaces for military-political purposes, and to ensure the domination of waters conjoint to the Soviet Union (including the approaches to western Europe), a 'balance' of naval capability is clearly necessary. (See chapter 4.)

Will 'the system' work, or more precisely, will it work under conditions of maximum stress? This may seem a bizarre question in view of the Soviet military build-up and an increasingly diversified military programme extending over 25 years and more, during which time 'doctrine' and 'armament norms' have been brought into much closer alignment; yet it is this very progress which has given rise to the problem of 'style', or 'performance' or 'effectiveness' – the Soviet terminology is as extensive as it is opaque – at all levels of the system. 'Style' itself might appear to be a questionable term, at once intangible and almost too ethereal for the grimy business of waging war, but consider one Soviet formulation in this context – *shtabnaya kultura* (literally 'staff culture'). In practice the Soviet command means to convey by this the requirement for a good professional style of work, deftness, order, precision, an expression of the all-round competence of the staff officer born of his general education or 'cultural' background. The same formula also hides a dilemma, for here is a social system which demands conformity and obedience, even as the military demands flexibility and a show of initiative, above all, in modern, high-speed operations.

Here we must return for a moment to the war the Soviet Union waged, the 'Great Patriotic War' and look briefly at the lessons of 'style', for all its generality perhaps the most sensitive issue of all. There were explicit reasons why a particular mode of war-waging was adopted between 1941–5 – the impact of technological inferiority in the early years of the war, the failure to exploit resources, the anachronism of a purely 'revolutionary' theory of morale, the inefficiency of the Party as an administrative instrument, the early mismanagement of economic mobilisation, and the problems of 'super-centralisation' worked by Stalin in person. One of the most extraordinary aspects of Soviet wartime experience is that disconcerting but ultimately effective relationship between centralisation, even 'super-centralisation', and improvisation. That latter style was extended in the early period of the war to the organisation of the *high command* and here 'style' has more than a touch of the traditional Russian imprint, including the revival of the *Stavka* (General Headquarters): there must be command-in-being and, of course, a commander-in-chief duly designated. Why is it, then, that only in October 1977 was Brezhnev (painfully hoisted through senior military ranks to the elevation of Marshal of the Soviet Union) almost coyly revealed as *Verkhovnyi Glavnokomanduyushchii*, Supreme Commander? (This most significant disclosure, made almost casually, is to be found in Colonel-General G. Sredin, First Deputy Chief/Main Political Administration, *Voennyi Vestnik*, 1977, No. 10, p. 10: under 'Istochnik sily i mogushchestva'.) Was there no operational C-in-C before this? That seems to be inconceivable. Did the military command, possibly the General Staff, wish to break irreversibly with a past 'style', or, assuming that Brezhnev had held this post for some time, why was it so carefully concealed?

Operational command and control does reside in a 'command-in-being' organ, namely, the General Staff of the Soviet Armed Forces which is responsible for the centralised control of all branches of the Soviet armed forces. Their peacetime organisation is more an administrative arrangement, whereas in war (or in any immediate pre-war situation) General Staff battle staffs, already much practised in their operational duties, would exercise command and would co-ordinate. For example, *operational* command of the four 'Groups of Forces' in eastern Europe and the combat-ready forces (including tactical air) in the sixteen military districts is vested in the General Staff. Brezhnev's rival for the post of Supreme Commander may well be not some military *arriviste* but a computer, or banks of computers: the problem of 'style' in high command arrangements might well have to be resolved in the struggle between what could be called the 'political' dimension of command and military-engineering requirements. With reference to the General Staff, if we are talking of style as a matter of tradition, then we are witnessing a return to (or, at least a rejuvenation of) the élitism of the Imperial *Genshtabistyi*, the General Staff officers who came to dominate the Imperial Army and the Imperial military system.

In not dissimilar fashion, the problem of command and control – *upravlenie voiskami* ('troop control') – exhibits the same admixture of traditional 'style' with advancing technology. *Shtabnaya kultura* at all levels, from army to battalion, has a specific role to play here. Many of the contemporary arguments are subsumed by Colonel-General D. Grinkevich (Chief of Staff, Group of Soviet Forces/Germany) in his article 'Upravlenie voiskami na uroven sovremennykh trebovanii' ('Command and control in response to contemporary requirements'), emphasising that effective command and control 'has become just as important a condition for victory as the quality and quantity of weapons. . . .' Colonel-General Grinkevich makes the point quite neatly: the opposite of 'style' is clumsiness and he inveighs quite heavily against this, as well as using 'the same old way' to make decisions and to organise the sequence of work. An equally important function of command and control is to maintain a high state of combat readiness, to prepare action data, and to maintain co-ordination, plus the organisation of ECM (electronic counter-measures). The staff is the 'basic organ of control'; staff officers must avoid stereotyped thinking, formality for formality's sake, and the easy way out, often the way of over-simplification.

Sections of the command place increasing faith in the automation of troop control, reflected in the recruitment to the General Staff of officers with engineering qualifications and the emphasis on *ASUV* (automated control systems), not to mention 'military engineering psychology' (sometimes translated as 'human factors engineering') and the 'man-machine match'; hence Grinkevich's castigation of those who rely on 'old methods'. However, the emphasis on the machine raises fresh problems: what is 'command' and what are the effects of officer training and education when the 'pilot-engineer' or the 'navigator-engineer' or the 'infantry-engineer qualified' officer knows more about technology than about handling a tactical situation? It is little wonder that Marshal Kulikov called for urgent reconsideration of the officer training programme.

All these issues must be viewed against a diminishing stock of Soviet operational experience and a military establishment which has not been committed to large-scale action for more than thirty years. Massive manoeuvres and frequent exercises are prominent, but subject also to the criticism that the atmosphere is that of a 'hot-house' (*teplichnyi*) with much contrivance, artificiality, and *uproshchenie* (simplification). While the 'large military system' (LMS) may be put through its paces, difficulties arise at lower levels, particularly with the sub-unit, where the dichotomy between centralised direction and a show of personal initiative is at its sharpest. Two examples must suffice – that of a battalion commander who followed 'the book' but took 40 minutes to 'consider' his decisions and issue the requisite orders, thus leaving only 50 minutes to complete the approach march, deploy, and attack (all manifestly impossible); and that of a motor-rifle battalion commander who failed to bring in helicopters for fire support because 'the plan did not call for this'.

Ineptitude such as this is not confined to the Soviet Army, but 'the system' contributes to its own difficulties, relying at one and the same time on drills and 'habit' (*navyk*) to implement tactical performance, yet demanding 'initiative' and what is called *tvorchestvo* (literally, 'creativity' but better rendered as tactical deftness), all the subject of a recent military study *Initsiativa i tvorchestvo v voennom dele*, (Moscow, Voenizdat, 1976). At the same time, the Soviet command has been obliged to ask itself not only 'what is a soldier?' (in view of his changed role) but also 'what keeps the soldier in his front-line position under conditions of maximum physical stress and psychological strain?' Clearly, ideology, faith in the Communist Party, is not the cement which holds soldiers together. The answer, which would have gladdened the heart of many an Imperial Russian officer, is *discipline*, though not quite 'the discipline of the revolver' which was the hallmark of the Civil War style and not a disciplinary pattern which is meant to be a substitute for technological/weapons inferiority. Discipline throughout the system and realism in training is at the heart of the present Soviet method, a 'style' which is redolent of the great 'military-pedagogic debates' of the 1880s and 1890s; and in view of that expansive background there ought to be some caution in speaking too glibly of Soviet 'rigidity' – the answer has to be in the ambiguities and the tensions of 'will', the durability of 'habit', the resilience of 'drills', and a dash of heroism. The Soviet command is not averse to appealing to true soldierly qualities, speaking at once of hardship but also extolling skill, self-sacrifice, and courage. Here is a theme which is simultaneously melancholy and rewarding, a hint of the traditional reluctance on 'donning the grey coat' (joining the army) but recourse to a tradition of unsurpassed fighting qualities. Little wonder that Soviet conscripts are paraded before the battle honours of their regiments and divisions. . . . (See chapter 6.)'

With the implementation of a pre-call up military training scheme for Soviet youth in schools, in factories, and on collective farms, the expansion of the DOSAAF programme (more specialised youth training for military service), a conscription system, and prolonged reserve service, much has been made of the 'militarisation' of Soviet society. For those too readily impressed by this phenomenon, it can be a salutary exercise to read Professor Curtiss's major work *The Russian Army under Nicholas I, 1825–1855*, for here was all-pervasive, massive militarisation (all ending in the *débâcle* of Russian arms in the Crimean War, it should be said). What we have been seeing in Soviet society for some decades, as Colonel Odom has pointed out so succinctly, is a traditional policy decked out in Marxist-Leninist guise and buttressed latterly by what I have elsewhere called the 'pseudo-ideology' of defence-mindedness and primacy for defence requirements, *oboronosposobnost'*, doggedly argued and persistently paraded – replete with an ironic twist, for it is scarcely Leninism and recalls more strongly Trotskii's thesis urging the development of Soviet society as the bonding of three major activities—sport, productive labour, and military training—into one *kolossal'nyi kollektiv*, a giant military-political and military-economic syndicate. There is every reason for the Soviet Union to pursue its present 'militarisation', though we should be cautious in any interpretation of this process, burdened as it is with social and political paradoxes: a neutralised military establishment in a militarised state, the problem of the political control of a technology-intensive establishment, the military implications of demographic change and the justification of external commitment to colonial-expansionist undertakings.

In evaluating the Soviet system and its 'style' it would be a mistake to emphasise the imprint of tradition at the expense of the impact of innovation (and vice versa), but amidst all the intangibles and imponderables of 'style' there are some curious parallels, if not actual continuities. It has been observed that while the Americans are bellicose but not martial, the Russians are martial but not bellicose. However, latterly the Soviet Union has adopted a posture which is at once bellicose and martial. For those who would recall it, this is almost the self-same 'style' which contributed substantially to the undoing of Imperial Russia, when numbers alone could provide no salvation, gigantism tripped ever more clumsily over its own clay feet, and the requisite 'performance' – *effektivnost'* – was simply not forthcoming.

What is needed? The answer was formulated many years ago: it was and is still ' . . . criticism, checking of facts, independence of thought, the personal elaboration of the present and the future, independence of character, the feeling of responsibility, truth towards oneself and towards one's work.' Thus spake none other than the organiser of the Red Army, Leon Trotskii, as far back as 1923.

SUMMARY OF DISCUSSION

In presenting his paper Professor Erickson stressed again the importance of looking at the Soviet military system through Russian rather than western eyes. Survival was at the centre of Soviet military doctrine; many things stemmed from this, for example, their different view of deterrence from the

West and the rejection of mutual assured destruction. In the discussion the speaker pointed out that there was no discrepancy between the unity and coherence of Soviet doctrine, which he had postulated, and the bureaucratic frictions from which the Russian military system had suffered in the past and which continued to be a feature of it in the present. He pointed out, however, that the General Staff now had the ultimate say in weapon procurement and adjudicated in inter-service rivalries. Normally, its requirements would be accepted by the political leaders. Difficulties might arise if, after a change of political leadership, the General Staff added demands arising from the needs of military management to their resource demands. Professor Erickson also did not see any discrepancy between the current offensive Soviet strategy and the reluctance of the Russians in the past to take offensive initiatives because of their sense of inferiority. The current need for offensive operations in Soviet doctrine would be underpined by improvements in morale. A choice had been made in favour of morale based on traditional disciplines rather than ideology. The stress on the offensive was tactical; because of historical fears, the lessons of 1941, and despite detente the Russians still saw NATO as a potential aggressor.

SELECT BIBLIOGRAPHY

English Titles

H. J. Berman and M. Kerner, *Soviet Military Law and Administration*, (Cambridge, Mass., Harvard University Press, 1955)

John Shelton Curtiss, *The Russian Army under Nicholas I 1825–1855* (Durham, N.C., Duke University Press, 1965)

H. S. Dinerstein, *War and the Soviet Union* (revised edn.) (New York/London, Praeger, 1962)

John Erickson, *The Road to Stalingrad* (London, Weidenfeld & Nicholson/New York, Harper Row, 1975)

Matthew P. Gallagher, *The Soviet History of World War II. Myths, Memories and Realities* (New York/London, Praeger, 1963)

Raymond L. Garthoff, *The Soviet Image of a Future War* (Washington, Public Affairs Press, 1959)

—— *Soviet Military Policy, A Historical Analysis* (New York/Washington, Praeger/London, Faber and Faber, 1966)

Leon Gouré et al., *The Role of Nuclear Forces in Current Soviet Strategy* (University of Miami Centre for Advanced International Studies, Washington, 1975 edn.)

Eike Middeldorf, *Taktik im Russlandfeldzug. Erfahrungen und Folgerungen* (Darmstadt, E. S. Mittler, 1956)

William E. Odom, 'The "Militarization" of Soviet Society', *Problems of Communism*, Vol. xxv, No. 5, (September–October, 1976), pp. 34–51.

Norman Stone, *The Eastern Front 1914–1917* (London, Hodder & Stoughton, 1975)

Russian Titles

V. A. Anfilov, *Nachalo Velikoi Otechestvennoi voiny* (Moscow, Voenizdat, 1962)
——*Bessmertnyi podvig* (Moscow, Nauka, 1971)
——*Proval 'Blitskriga'* (Moscow, Nauka, 1974)
V. V. Druzhinin and D. S. Kontorov, *Voprosy voennoi sistemotekhniki* (Moscow, Voenizdat, 1976)
N. M. Fendrikov and V. I. Yakovlev, *Metody raschetov effektivnosti vooruzheniya* (Moscow, Voenizdat, 1971)
B. G. Grigor'ev, *Ekonomicheskii i moral'nyi potentsialyi v sovremennoi voine* (Moscow, Voenizdat, 1970)
L. N. Gor'kov, *Podgotovka i vvod informatsii v ASU* (Moscow, Voenizdat, 1976)
A. A. Grechko (Marshal SU), *Vooruzhennye sily Sovetskogo gosudarstva* (2nd edn.) (Moscow, Voenizdat, 1975)
F. I. Ivanov, *Reaktivnye psikhozy v voennoe vremya* (Leningrad, 'Meditsina', 1970)
S. P. Ivanov (Army General), *Nachal'nyi period voiny* (Moscow, Voenizdat, 1974)
A. I. Kitov et al., *Sovremennaya armiya i distsiplina* (Moscow, Voenizdat, 1976)
V. K. Konoplev, *Nauchnoe predvidenie v voennom dele* (Moscow, Voenizdat, 1974)
M. P. Korobeinikov, *Sovremennyi boi i problemy psikhologii* (Moscow, Voenizdat, 1972)
S. N. Kozlov et al., *O sovetskoi voennoi nauke* (2nd edn.) (Moscow, Voenizdat, 1964)
V. G. Kulikov (Marshal SU: Ed.), *Akademiya General'nogo Shtaba* (Moscow, Voenizdat, 1976)
——'Sovetskaya voennaya nauka segodnya', *Kommunist*, 1976, No. 7, pp. 38-47.
A. Lagovskii, *Strategiya i ekonomika* (Moscow, Voenizdat, 1957)
I. N. Loshchilov, *Perspektivy primeneniya vychislitel'noi tekhniki v voennom dele* (Moscow, Voenizdat, 1976)
A. M. Nekrich, *1941 22 iyunya* (Moscow, Nauka, 1965)
N. N. Popel 'et al., *Upravlenie voiskami v gody Velikoi Otechestvennoi voiny* (Moscow, Voenizdat, 1974)
P. N. Pospelov (Ed.), *Sovetskii tyl v Velikoi Otechestvennoi voine*, Moscow, 'Mysl', Vols. 1-2, 1974.
A. B. Pupko, *Sistema: chelovek i voennaya tekhnika* (Moscow, Voenizdat, 1976)
I. N. Shkadov (Army General: Ed.), *Voprosy obucheniya i vospitaniya v voenno-uchebnykh zavedeniyakh* (Moscow, Voenizdat, 1976)
A. F. Shramchenko, *Voprosy psikhologii v upravlenii voiskami* (Moscow, Voenizdat, 1973)
——*Takticheskie ucheniya* (Moscow, Voenizdat, 1975)
S. M. Shtemenko, *Novyi zakon i voinskaya sluzhba* (Moscow, Voenizdat, 1968)
P. V. Sokolov (Ed.), *Voenno-ekonomicheskie voprosy v kurse politekonomii* (Moscow, Voenizdat, 1968)
V. D. Sokolovskii (Marshal SU: Ed.), *Voennaya strategiya* (Moscow, Voenizdat, 1962, 1963, and 1968)
Taktika v boevykh primerakh, (5 vols: Division, regiment, battalion, company, section) (Moscow, Voenizdat, 1974-76)
P. N. Tkachenko (Ed.), *Matematickeskie modeli boevykh deistvii* (Moscow, 'Sov. Radio', 1969)
M. V. Zakharov (Marshal SU), *O nauchnom podkhode k rukovodstvu voiskami* (Moscow, Voenizdat, 1967)

A. S. Zheltov (Ed.), *Soldat i voina* (Moscow, Voenizdat, 1971)
(Collective authorship) *Voennaya inzhenernaya psikhologiya* (Moscow, Voenizdat, 1970)

Select Technical References

M. P. Atrazhev et al., *Bor'ba s radioelektronnymi sredstvami* (Moscow, Voenizdat, 1972)
E. S. Fridenson, *Osnovy raketnoi takhniki* (Moscow, Voenizdat, 1973)
V. S. Frolov, *Inertsial'noe ipravelnie raketami* (Moscow, Voenizdat, 1975)
L. G. Golovkov, *Gibridnye radetnye dvigateli* (Moscow, Voenizdat, 1976)
V. P. Glushko (Ed.), *Razvitie otechestvennogo raketnogo dvigatelestroeniya* (Moscow, 'Mashinostroenie', 1973)
N. I. Morozov, *Ballisticheskie rakety strategicheskogo naznacheniya* (Moscow, 1974)
V. I. Petrovskii and O. A. Pozhidaev, *Lokatory na lazerakh* (Moscow, Voenizdat, 1969)
A. M. Sinyukov, *Ballisticheskaya raketa na tverdom toplive*, (Moscow, Voenizdat, 1972)
S. A. Vakin and L. N. Shustov, *Osnovy radioprotivodeistviya i radiotekhnicheskoi razvedki* (Moscow, 'Sov. Radio', 1968)
V. I. Varfolomeyev and M. I. Kopytov (Eds.), *Proektirovanie i ispytaniya ballisticheskikh raket* (Moscow, Voenizdat, 1970)

Part II
The Arms

3 The Soviet Ground Forces

John Hemsley

The Soviet Army is the second largest army in the world. The six non-Soviet members of the Warsaw Pact take their organisations, tactics, and the great majority of their equipments from Russia. Some twenty-seven other countries throughout the world equip their armies with varying amounts of Soviet equipments, and some thirteen armies are trained by Soviet training teams and missions.

Over the past eight years there has been a significant increase in the capabilities of the Soviet ground forces which has resulted from an increase in the manning strengths of organisations, and the introduction of many new and technically advanced equipments. This is all in line with the emergence of a Russian concept of theatre war as distinguished from a strategic (global) war with its inevitable use of ICBM.

Soviet military doctrine is based on the development of a dual capability – i.e. for both nuclear and conventional warfare. It seems most probable at the moment that they would be prepared to commence with conventional operations in the event of a war in Europe; however their tactics and equipments are such that they retain the option of going nuclear at any stage. The Russians regard the use of chemical weapons in the same way as they regard nuclear weapons, that is as weapons of mass destruction; and the initial use of either will be subject to political decision at the highest level. They might hesitate to use CW against an enemy with a good defensive or retaliatory capability unless they felt tactically obliged to do so. However, chemical release might possibly be given well in advance of nuclear release, in which case chemical weapons would be used freely as a normal complement to conventional munitions. Once the decision to go chemical had been taken, authority for their use would probably be delegated down to divisional commander level.

TACTICAL DOCTRINE AND CONCEPTS OF OPERATIONS

Soviet tactical doctrine is based on the philosophy of offensive operations taking place within the context of a short campaign. This doctrine is characterised by the employment of two main principles, namely firepower and manoeuvrability. The principles of war for the Soviet ground forces might be listed as follows: advance and consolidation, morale, offensive action, adequate reserves, surprise and deception, concentration, economy of force, manoeuvre and initiative, combined arms and annihilation.

These principles lead to a concept of operations in which the stress is laid upon concentrating vastly superior forces on to a particular sector in order to make a decisive armoured breakthrough. The accent is on deep armoured thrusts through to strategic objectives rather than seizing and holding ground at a tactical level; difficult country and large urban areas will be bypassed by first echelon armies and cleared subsequently by second echelon armies or even second echelon fronts. As first echelon formations become exhausted or are brought to a halt second echelon formations are passed through to keep up the pressure and maintain the momentum of the offensive. Airborne forces may be used in depth, particularly at strategic targets such as areas where reinforcements and supplies will be disembarked, air heads, rail heads, and so forth; helicopter-borne forces are more likely to be used against tactically critical targets not more than 4–6 hours ahead of the leading troops, for example, to draw off reserves or secure an important piece of terrain. The logistic system is efficient and designed to meet the needs of a rapid advance over long distances; it works on the principle of delivering combat supplies from the rear to forward sub-units.

Formations at all levels of command adopt an *echelon system*, dividing their forces into first and second echelons. (Only in rare cases will a force operate in one echelon, in which case a sizeable reserve will always be earmarked.) Echelons are used for all phases of war and should not be confused with reserves. In general, the second echelon is one-third the strength of the first echelon and the reserve is one-ninth the strength of the first echelon; however, second echelons are normally termed reserves until they are given a mission or objective. In offensive operations it will be seen that there is direct relationship between the various levels of command, their echelons and objectives.

The Soviet Ground Forces

The Soviets place great emphasis on all arms co-operation particularly at higher levels, and it is important to appreciate the priority which they give to electronic warfare, particularly the degree of integration which exists with artillery at formation level and below, and chemical defence.

Particular effort is given over to detailed reconnaissance, both ground and air, before and during every operation. It will be seen that all levels of organisation contain reconnaissance elements; these forces being used in the role of flank protection and rear security as well as forward reconnaissance.

ORGANISATION OF THE SOVIET GROUND FORCES

In wartime, the Soviet Army will be grouped into Fronts which are formed from the peacetime Military Districts and Groups of Forces; each Front being roughly equivalent to a NATO Army Group. In major theatres, Fronts would be grouped under a Theatre HQ (or TVD).

A Front has no fixed organisation and its scale of armies and supporting elements will depend upon its task. It would, however, invariably command a Tactical Air Army and is likely to be allocated an airborne division complete with its airlift. The 'Group of Soviet Forces Germany' (GSFG) which is deployed in the GDR provides a good example (see the deployment map, Figure 3.1).

A *Tactical Air Army* has no standard organisation but would include fighters, light bombers, reconnaissance and transport aircraft, and helicopters. A typical organisation is presented in the diagram of an air army organisation (Figure 3.2).

Armies are formed from either predominantly tank formations, in which case they are termed Tank Armies, or from motor rifle formations, whereupon they are known as Combined Arms Armies (CAA). Airborne formations are allocated to Front organisation, and airborne regiments may be allocated to under command of an Army for a specific operation.

Armour

A *Tank Division* has three tank regiments and a motor rifle regiment integral to its organisation, a total of 325 tanks. Each tank regiment has three battalions each of three tank companies. The standard

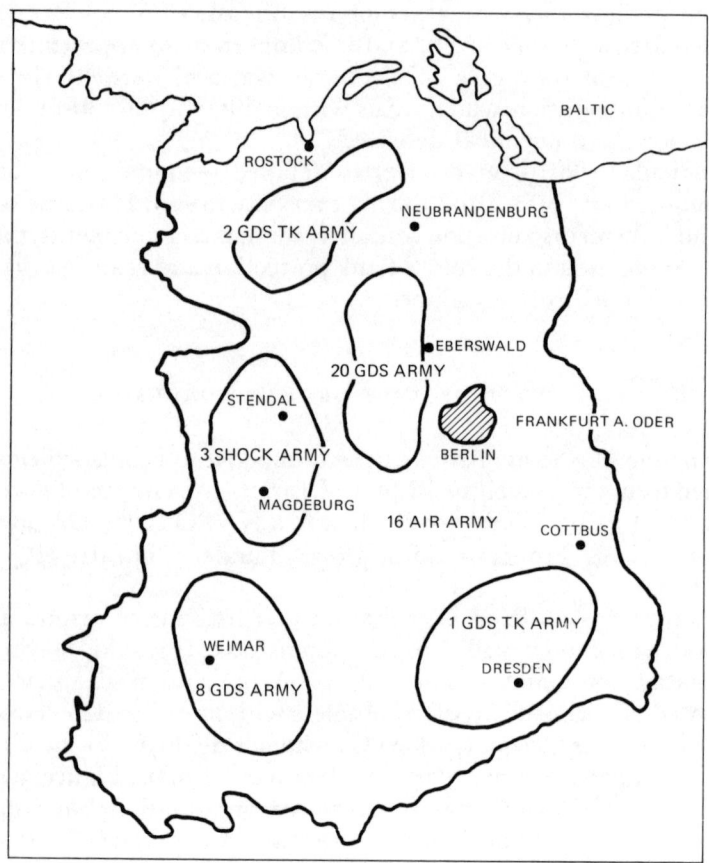

FIGURE 3.1 *Deployment of GSFG*

equipment in all the tank formations is the T-62 medium tank. However, with forces as large as those possessed by the Warsaw Pact, the time frame for a replacement of any new equipment on a large scale of issue, such as a main battle tank, could take place over as much as a ten-year period or more. Therefore, some units may still possess the older T-55 tank, or may now be currently re-equipping with the new T-72. There is no integral infantry at present in the tank regimental organisation, although in GSFG the inclusion of a motor rifle company has now been identified. At present its role is thought to be purely one of local defence for regimental headquarters.

The Soviet Ground Forces

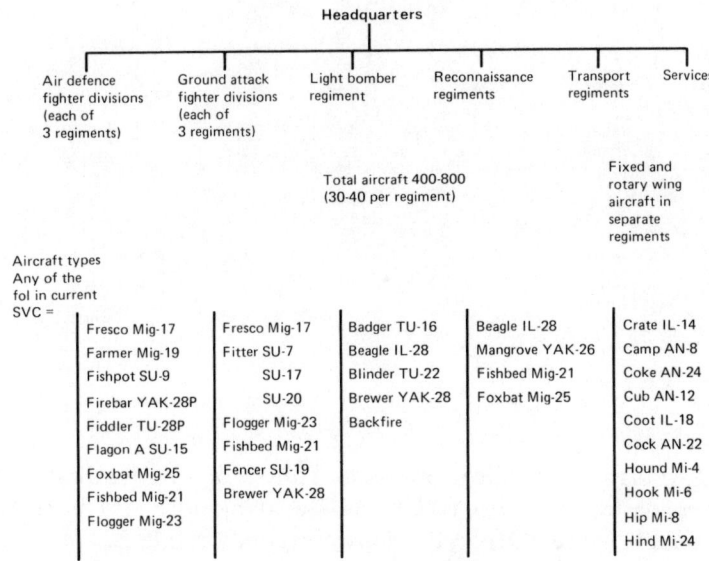

FIGURE 3.2 *Organisation of a Tactical Air Army*

Motor Rifle Troops

A *Motor Rifle Division* has three motor rifle regiments and a generous allocation of tanks to support the infantry. As well as the 40 tanks in a motor rifle regiment tank battalion (as opposed to 31 in the normal tank battalion) there is a tank regiment of 95 tanks and an independent tank battalion consisting of a further 51 tanks. Altogether a grand total within the division of 266 tanks – only 59 less than in a tank division. This makes the motor rifle division a most formidable formation in the field, and, unless the ground is really open and suitable for purely armoured movement, one might expect to find motor rifle formations operating in the first echelons with a tank formation in the second echelon poised to exploit a breakthrough. Again, motor rifle troops would invariably be used to force the crossing of an obstacle or to seize a bridgehead in a deliberate attack.

A *Motor Rifle Regiment* has three battalions as well as integral tank support in the form of a tank battalion of 40 tanks. The motor rifle battalion has three companies each with 10 APCs. There is still a

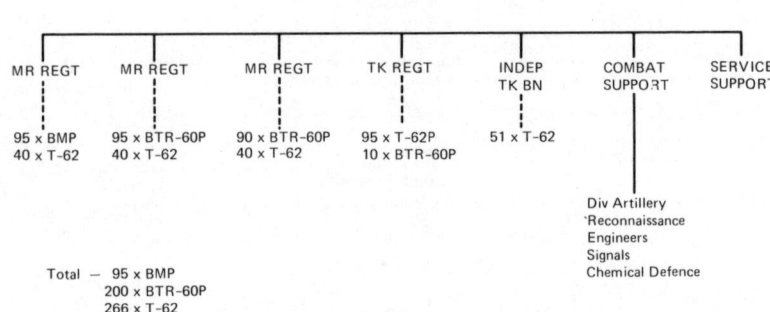

FIGURE 3.3 *Outline Organisation of a Motor-Rifle Division*

mix of APC in motor rifle formations. Motor rifle divisions have one regiment equipped with BMP and the remainder still have the BTR-60 PB (see Figure 3.3). However, motor rifle regiments in tank divisions all have BMP or, where a re-equipment is not yet complete, the older BTR-50 PK. The combination of BMP and BTR-60 PB equipped motor rifle regiments within motor rifle divisions makes the motor rifle division better able to exploit changes in terrain and enemy resistance: it can respond flexibly to the different types of opposition it encounters, as well as making best speed across country when not able to use roads. Also, the greatly enhanced firepower (particularly in anti-tank capability) of the BMP equipped motor rifle regiment, coupled with the increase in tanks in the tank strength of motor rifle regiments, will allow the motor rifle division to engage all but the most tank heavy formations it may encounter.

Airborne Troops

Airborne formations are organised on different scales to motor rifle formations, their grouping tending to reflect their tactical employment at the time. Tactical employment is discussed later on.

Artillery

Nuclear and chemical delivery means are organic to formations down to divisions. The main nuclear delivery means are the SCUD B and FROG-7 systems. (It is possible that the 152 mm (M – 1973) SP gun has a nuclear capability.) Most other Soviet artillery pieces have a chemical capability. The BM-21 is particularly suitable for delivering the highly toxic blood agents in sufficient concentrations to be tactically effective.

Air Defence

The Soviet Command has developed an extremely comprehensive family of equipments to cover the whole spectrum of low-level air defence. These are based on surface-to-air missiles (SAM-6, -7, -8, -9) complemented by mobile, multi-barrelled air defence machine guns, the most recent of which is the SP quadruple-barrelled ZDU-23-4 with its integral radar. With this multiplicity of equipment, it must be assumed that low level air defence fire control gives rise to some problems. In addition many vehicles are fitted with a 12.7 mm heavy machine gun on an air defence mounting.

Anti-Tank

The Soviet Command is most conscious of the requirement for an effective anti-tank capability, and anti-tank units exist in combined arms armies and in all motor rifle and airborne formations down to battalion level. The anti-tank capability of Warsaw Pact forces has been greatly enhanced by the introduction of BMP with its ability to launch SAGGER.

Field Artillery

The Soviet Army regards artillery, together with tanks, as the most important arm. All operations are carefully planned around detailed and massive artillery fire support, which is closely integrated with electronic warfare measures both ESM and ECM. It is worth noting the introduction of the 122 mm and 152 mm SP guns which will supplement their large holding of wheeled artillery, but it would appear at present that there is no question of the Soviets carrying out a total replacement of wheeled artillery by SP. This is in accordance with their principles of maintaining a balanced mix in equipments and organisations.

Engineers

Engineer units are included in all formations to regimental level. Particular attention is paid in attack to route clearance, crossing of water and other obstacles, and minefield clearance, while in defence, to rapid digging-in of men and equipments, and assisting with the provision of communication trenches.

Electronic Warfare (EW)

The Soviet Army places very great importance on all aspects of offensive and defensive electronic warfare and the significance of this upon the conduct of battle should be fully appreciated. EW units are integral to Front, army, and divisional organisations, and at the lower levels their tactical employment is very much tied in with the artillery. It is important to understand the definitions and relationship of the two main aspects of Soviet EW. These are Electronic Support Measures (ESM) and Electronic Counter Measures (ECM). It can be seen that ESM provide two different forms of information from the same source – SIGINT/ELINT for the formation commander, and Steerage for the jammers. The radio intercept/DF company has an ESM capability (including non-communications EW) but holds no jammers on establishment. A DF platoon must have a minimum of three stations whilst a radio intercept unit would probably have five intercept positions operating on VHF. The divisional reconnaissance battalion also possesses a DF and intercept capability. A similar organisation exists at Army level but would still have no jamming capability. Jammers will probably be placed under command at army level for specific operations. These jammers will be capable of successfully jamming any enemy radio link in a corps area. It is likely that jammers would be used in conjunction with artillery in an attempt to disrupt specific parts of the enemy command system at critical moments in the battle. There will therefore be close co-ordination between the reconnaissance troops (which contain intercept), artillery, and EW troops. Consequently the artillery and EW plan is synonymous, with ESM acting as a target acquisition system. Modern tactical command and control systems depend upon electronic systems, all of which are vulnerable to EW. The Soviet Forces are particularly conscious of both their own vulnerability and the advantages to be gained by possessing a well-co-ordinated, offensive EW capability.

TACTICS

We have traced elements of Soviet tactical doctrine and stressed the importance that is attached to the 'primacy of the offensive'. Three basic factors have evolved from the resulting military philosophy, namely reconnaissance, the use of massed firepower, and manoeuvre and mobility.

Principles of Offensive Operations

The aim of a Front offensive is to destroy opposing forces by penetrating deep into enemy territory; an example in north-western Europe could be the River Rhine. This is achieved by launching deep thrusts aimed at smashing through the enemy's main defensive positions, probably bypassing areas of difficult going in order to maintain momentum, and then destroying the remaining enemy reserves in the rear areas. The Theatre Second Strategic Echelon would be available to clear major bypassed areas as necessary. A Front would normally operate in two echelons against a properly deployed opposition. One would expect to see perhaps three armies deployed in the Front first echelon with two armies held in the second echelon. Again, depending on organisation and terrain, an army would normally deploy two or three divisions in its first echelon and one or two in its second echelon. Motor rifle divisions would normally be seen in the first echelon, tank divisions being held in the second echelon ready to exploit a breakthrough unless the ground is particularly open and suitable for purely armoured movement.

Sector widths and depths of operations will vary considerably according to the terrain, objectives, and the strength of the forces used. It should be noted that the deployment widths for an actual attack will always be narrower than the allocated sector widths for a general advance. It is not axiomatic that a formation has to fill its sector during an advance, although at divisional level and below, those parts of the sector not covered specifically by a formation would certainly be covered by reconnaissance elements of some sort. The policy on bypassing opposition or difficult terrain is laid down at a level not below that of army commander. A Front would expect to maintain an average advance over a short campaign of some 50–60 kilometres per 24 hours in nuclear operations, and 30 kilometres per 24 hours in conventional operations.

The Advance

Soviet offensive philosophy depends heavily on the accuracy and speed of their *reconnaissance and target acquisition*. Great importance is placed upon reconnaissance at all levels and this is integrated, co-ordinated, and controlled by intelligence staffs at the headquarters at each level. The main means of target acquisition are air reconnaissance, electronic intercept and DF, deep penetration reconnaissance and sabotage teams, motorised reconnaissance (this is based on specialist all arms reconnaissance units but may be supplemented or reinforced by normal tank or motor rifle troops), and artillery observation (including field radar). The long range reconnaissance company of the divisional reconnaissance battalion will operate up to 24 hours or more ahead of the divisional forward elements. The remainder of the divisional reconnaissance will operate on the division's intended main routes up to 12 hours or more ahead of the main body. Regimental reconnaissance will operate less covertly across the regimental front and may be accompanied by special reconnaissance elements of engineer, artillery, and chemical troops.

Reconnaissance troops are equipped with the PT-76 light amphibious tank which is now being replaced by the reconnaissance version of BMP (BMP-R?), BRDM, and motor-cycle combinations mounting machine guns. These are specialist vehicles providing a distinctive signature which will, however, tend to disappear when PT-76 is replaced by BMP-R. Battalions operating in the advance-guard role will also provide their own reconnaissance. Unprotected flanks will be covered either by specialist reconnaissance units or by patrols drawn from normal motor rifle or tank units. The Russians are particularly conscious of the need for security of their rear areas and will employ patrols as a cover where necessary. In the advance, a division may employ a forward detachment (*peredovoi otryad*) of regimental or battalion group size. Its aim will be to seize an important tactical objective such as a defile or crossing over an obstacle. It moves as fast as possible in front of the main body, bypassing all opposition in order to achieve its objective. A forward detachment may also be used to link up with and support a helicopter-borne landing.

Air reconnaissance will normally be conducted by pairs of reconnaissance aircraft flying low and fast using visual, photographic, and electronic methods. Reconnaissance aircraft are capable of opportunity attacks on ground targets, particularly air defence weapons. The initial scale of effort produced by a Front would be in the order of 120 sorties per day of fighter reconnaissance and 100 sorties per day of light bomber reconnaissance. Drones and other airborne reconnaissance devices are under development.

Tactical formations for the advance will normally move forward in columns for the sake of speed and control and will then deploy into battle formations before making actual contact with the enemy.

The Attack

There are two main types of attack, namely the *hasty attack*, which can take the form of an encounter battle at low level, i.e. company, battalion, or possibly regimental level, or a quick attack when enemy prepared positions are first encountered. In both cases attacks are made by leading units in order to confirm or probe for further intelligence on enemy dispositions, or by taking the opportunity of trying to make quick tactical gains. This type of attack could quickly escalate from a company or battalion probing attack into a regimental quick attack by the leading regiment in a divisional advance. The other main type of attack is the *deliberate attack* which is mounted against a well-prepared defence, normally as a result either of the availability of really good combat intelligence or after a hasty attack has failed. The main difference which characterises the hasty attack from the deliberate attack is the importance of speed in order to maintain the momentum of the advance. This is exemplified by a rapid deployment from the line of march and by a less concentrated fire plan directed at predicted rather than adjusted targets. Otherwise the principles remain basically the same for both types of attack.

Deliberate Attack

The divisional commander and his staff will base their plan for the attack on the information available from all forms of reconnaissance which have been mentioned earlier as well as the additional combat intelligence obtained through troops in contact. The deliberate attack would normally be mounted by the formation whose troops are already in contact. The division would move into an assembly area while detailed orders are given out by commanders. A divisional assembly area would occupy some 400 square kilometres between 20–40 kilometres back from the FEBA (Forward Edge of the Battle Area). Regiments normally occupy a tactically sited assembly area of about 100 square kilometres. Orders at all levels are extremely detailed and junior commanders are required to see the ground wherever possible.

Soviet troops are trained and have the capability of fighting at night. However, current doctrine tends to the view that the problems of control make it undesirable to launch night attacks for formations above regimental level. If a night attack has to be planned, then it would probably be timed for the second half of the night so that the divisional second echelon would not be committed until after first light.

The accent is on armoured breakthrough wherever possible. Motor rifle troops will be allocated in support of tanks where necessary and for a deliberate attack would normally dismount out of effective anti-tank range and assault the enemy positions on foot, supported in the case of BMP by its 73 mm gun and coaxial machine guns. At regimental level, depending on the circumstances, the commander may allocate tanks from his tank battalion to the motor rifle battalions or he may employ his tank battalion as an independent sub-unit, either within its own boundaries or across the whole of the regimental front leading with first echelon into the attack. (See Figure 3.4 for an example of a motor rifle division deployed for attack.) Any one of several combinations is open to the commander and a similar option exists for the motor rifle divisional commander in the way in which he employs his independent tank battalion.

Front and Army artillery is normally allocated to first echelon divisions, which in turn will allocate some of their organic and/or allotted artillery to leading regiments – particularly on the main axis. Similarly a regiment may place some of its artillery in direct support of leading battalions. Artillery is grouped into divisional groups (DAG) and regimental artillery groups (RAG), which enables control to be retained at the highest practicable level. Artillery groups normally tend to follow the main thrust line of their respective formations. A detailed and comprehensive fire plan covering both adjusted and predicted targets and lasting some 20–30 minutes will precede a deliberate attack. An ammunition dumping programme involving comprehensive logistic support would be carried out prior to the commencement of this fire plan.

Anti-tank reserves are formed and the anti-tank fire plan is co-ordinated at the highest level. All Soviet field artillery possesses an

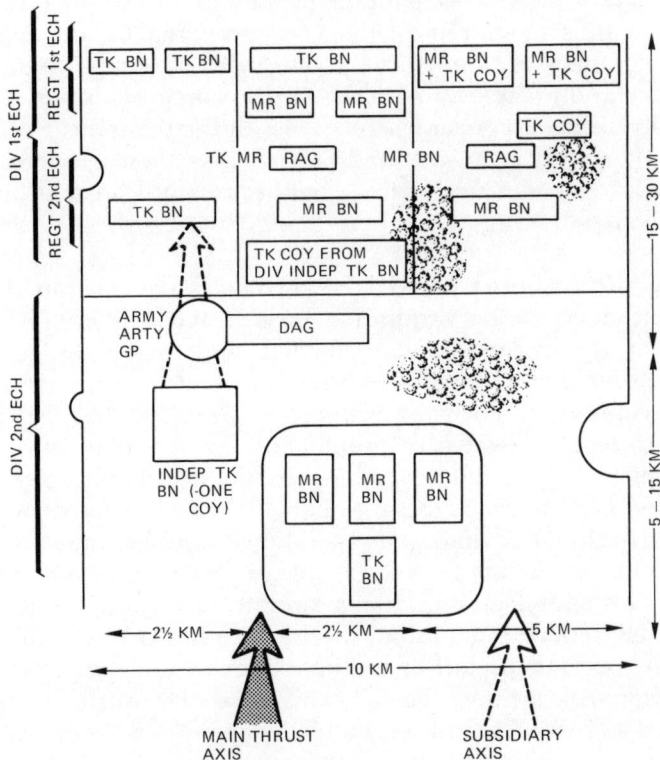

FIGURE 3.4 *Motor-Rifle Division Deployed for an Attack (One Possible Formation)*

anti-tank capability (ammunition holdings contain five per cent anti-tank) and is trained and prepared to meet enemy armoured counter-attacks by direct engagement. Anti-tank reserves contain an engineer element for minefield and obstacle laying, and their role requires them to be able to deploy rapidly to meet armoured counter attack threats.

Indirect tank fire can be used to augment the conventional artillery fire plan, in which case tank units from the divisional second echelon would normally be deployed forward close to the first echelon regimental artillery groups. It should be remembered that tank regiments have no organic artillery in their organisation.

Engineer equipment for rapid obstacle crossing is held well forward. Tanks with mine ploughs or rollers are likely to be allocated on a basis of one per tank platoon to the leading echelons. The accent is upon rapid minefield breaching by the leading elements; follow-up units carry out more thorough minefield clearance and make existing lanes safe. Leading battalions would normally aim to create at least six lanes through a minefield using mine plough attachments and/or explosive hose devices. On encountering a minefield tanks would normally lead with motor rifle troops following through the lanes created by the forward tanks.

It has already been pointed out that EW is closely integrated with reconnaissance, target acquisition means, and artillery. REC is aimed at the disruption of sequential control systems, and its resources include both reconnaissance elements and firepower for the disruption of enemy electronic control systems. Selective jamming would also figure prominently in any plan of attack, although control would never be exercised at a lower level than divisional headquarters; more probably it would be fixed at army level. In the initial period of any operation it would seem reasonable to expect a tactical air army to be able to provide up to 600 sorties per day for fighter ground attack aircraft. Control of air support would be retained at Front headquarters. FGA aircraft will normally operate in pairs or multiple of pairs, and are capable of delivering strikes using the following weapons – nuclear bombs, conventional bombs, cluster bombs, napalm, cannon, rockets, chemical and machine guns.

Relationship between Objectives and Echelons

The interrelationship between the immediate and subsequent objectives and echelons at the various formation levels has already been discussed. The initial objective of the higher formation is always the subsequent objective of the next lower formation (see Figure 3.5). Objectives will always be clearly laid down for subordinate formations by the senior commander.

Soviet commanders lay great stress on the *intelligence process* and the gathering of adequate information about the enemy prior to conducting any operations. The formation chief intelligence staff officer tasks and controls all intelligence gathering elements under command, in particular reconnaissance troops. The main intelligence requirements at any stage are location of nuclear delivery means, location and identification of enemy reserves, location of

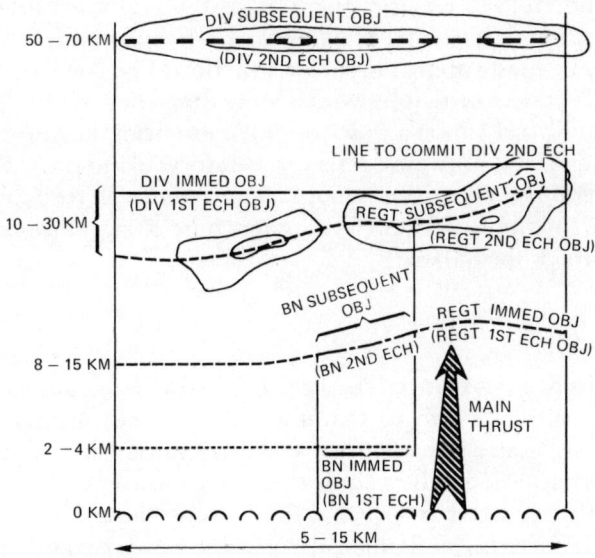

Distances between first and second attacking ech may be:

Div	Regt	Bn
fwd and rear bns	fwd and rear coys	fwd and rear regts
15 – 30 km	5 – 15 km	1 – 3 km

FIGURE 3.5 *Echelons and Objectives*

headquarters and command and control centres, location of gun areas, and detailed identification of forward battle positions.

The constraints imposed upon the use of chemical warfare have been mentioned already. The Soviet Command regards the use of CW in the advance and attack as a useful method of sealing flanks or blocking the movement of enemy reserves (persistent agents), or as an adjunct to normal conventional firepower (non-persistent agents).

Meeting Engagement (Encounter Battle)

This is essentially a clash between two mobile forces such as might be encountered by a Soviet formation in the advance to contact or pursuit meeting a counter-attack force. Despite the doctrinal importance that is given to this concept, there is some evidence of

Soviet concern as to whether the standard of junior leadership will prove good enough to cope effectively with the demands that would inevitably be made upon it in such a situation. The concept depends very much on the principles which were described in the advance, and the tactics rely upon a quick deployment from the line of march with artillery and anti-tank reserves well forward to provide a firm fire base for the assaulting troops. The essence is to deploy and defeat the enemy quickly before he has time to organise his forces into an attack formation.

The Assault River Crossing

If the speed of advance envisaged by the Russians during a European offensive is to be maintained, then they are well aware that they are going to have to cross one or more water obstacles in each 24-hour period. Their equipment, organisations, and training are clearly designed to ensure that the crossing of water obstacles is a normal part of a day's advance, designed to be carried out from the line of march wherever possible. Closing up to a river line or consolidating a bridgehead is not regarded as a separate phase of the battle. All aspects of river crossing reflect the following key Soviet principles – reconnaissance, early planning and thorough organisation, destruction of the enemy in the area of the obstacle by massive firepower, speed and surprise, crossing on a broad front, rapid development of the bridgehead and subsequent breakout, skilful and rapid engineer techniques, and comprehensive air defence.

There are three types of assault river crossing: *Opportunity Crossing*, in effect, a bounce crossing that would normally be carried out by a forward detachment or a helicopter-borne force in order to secure a crossing before the enemy could carry out effective demolitions; *Immediate Crossing*, on a normal advance the groups in contact would usually attempt an immediate crossing from the line of march on a broad front; *Deliberate Crossing*, carried out as a set piece of operation if an immediate crossing has failed and the water obstacle has been developed as a well-prepared defensive position. This equates with the deliberate attack.

After a heavy preliminary artillery bombardment, a deliberate river crossing would almost certainly be spearheaded by motor rifle troops. These may well cross the obstacle in their APCs using them as assault craft should the exit bank prove too difficult thus forcing them to dismount. These troops would then quickly establish a bridgehead between $1\frac{1}{2}$–4 kilometres deep, sufficient to clear the area of all direct-fire weapons. Tanks would then be crossed as soon as possible using either deep wading techniques, or bridging and/or ferries. Once units have crossed they do not halt to consolidate but immediately press forward into the enemy positions or to continue the advance. Bridging sites would be opened as soon as possible and a division would aim to cross on a broad front with at least four crossing sites per regiment.

Pursuit

The Soviets move over to the pursuit phase once the enemy main defensive positions have been defeated or if they are attempting to break contact in a general withdrawal. The Soviet doctrine stresses that decisive defeat of an enemy force can only be achieved by vigorous and continuous exploitation of tactical advantage; therefore they will attempt to follow up closely, maintaining contact with the enemy, with the aim of eventually encircling and destroying him. The pursuit may be carried out on the same axis as the withdrawing enemy or on a parallel axis or both. Maximum use would be made of armoured heavy formations, and forward detachments of reinforced battalion or regimental strength would operate boldly up to 50 kilometres ahead of the main body against specific targets in depth – such as bridges, defiles, airfields, and so forth. Assuming that air superiority would now largely lie with the attacker, use would be made of helicopter-borne forces or even airborne forces in depth. Chemical strikes could also be used at this stage to seal off flanks and deny areas of ground to a withdrawing enemy. Formations in the pursuit will normally only employ one echelon and retain a reserve for contingency planning.

Defence

Although defence is regarded as a temporary expedient only, it is recognised that tactical defence will occasionally be necessary. It can be adopted in order to consolidate captured objectives, cover withdrawal, gain time to regroup or concentrate forces, and hold ground while an offensive is mounted in another sector. The principles of defence are based on holding areas of tactical importance with well dug in motor rifle troops; retaining mobile anti-tank reserves in the second echelon to block penetration;

retaining a strong armoured counter-attack force, and the use of an integrated fire plan to create fire pockets flanked by artillery barrage lines. (See Figure 3.6 for an example of a motor-rifle battalion defensive layout.)

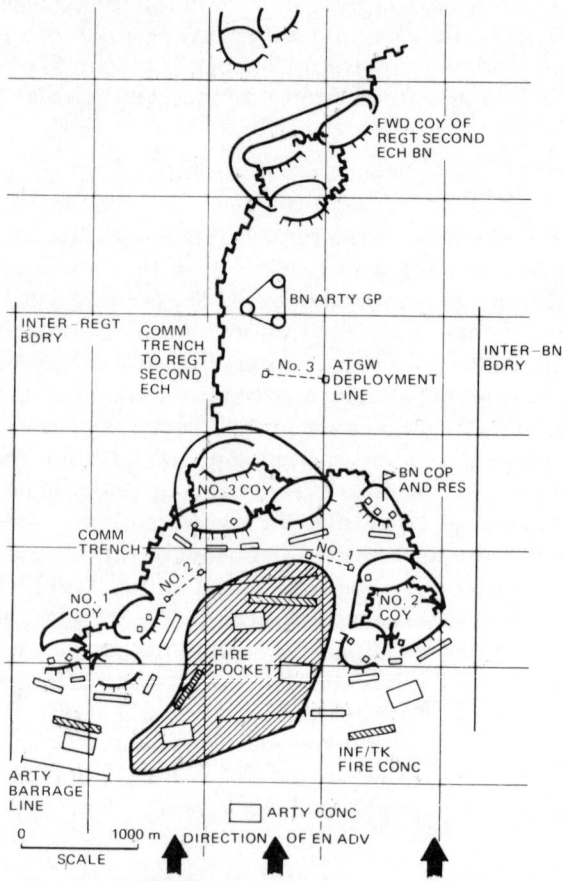

FIGURE 3.6 *Example of a MR Battalion Defensive Position*

Airborne Operations

Airborne operations are basically of two types – *parachute operations* carried out by specialist airborne troops, which may be followed by the air-landing of further troops once suitable landing grounds have been secured, and *helicopter-borne assaults* which are normally made by motor rifle troops. Soviet usage emphasises the bold use of airborne troops, in order to exploit the depth of the initial mass nuclear strike, since ground forces advancing at 60 km a day will take some three to four days to reach the rear of the area it covers; maintain the momentum of the armoured attack by securing communication centres, river crossings, and defiles ahead of major thrusts; draw off or contain enemy reserves; seize airfields, either to destroy them or to open them for subsequent airlanding or air operations; destroy enemy nuclear delivery means and disrupt control, movement and supply in the rear areas, and disrupt control (headquarters), movement and supply.

Parachute Operations

Parachute forces may be used from company up to regimental strength to support a ground formation commander's tactical manoeuvre, or may be employed in a divisional drop operating against a strategic target in great depth. They may be required to operate for up to seven days before being relieved by the main ground forces (if at all). It is unlikely that parachute operations would be initiated until a large measure of air superiority and air defence neutralisation had been established over the whole area of the flight path during the fly-in. Each Front is likely to be allocated on airborne division.

BMD, GAZ-69, and the 57 mm SP assault guns can all be heavy-dropped. It is thought that the 85 mm self-propelled assault guns can only be air landed. About 110 CUB aircraft are required to lift one regiment.

The Soviet Army believes that the success of a parachute operation depends on: secrecy and surprise; effective air defence of the fly-in and the suppression of anti-aircraft weapons along the flight path; neutralising the enemy, and particularly his tanks, in the area of the dropping zone; and providing fire support by air strikes and by missiles and artillery of the advancing ground forces.

The Airborne Landing

A *nuclear/chemical attack* could be made on the area of the dropping zone (DZ) about 20–30 minutes before the drop. The *fly-in* is protected by fighter cover and by a massive effort, using all available delivery means, to neutralise enemy air defence weapons along the flight path. *Landing.* Drops will frequently be made by night. Whenever possible, the assaulting force is dropped in one wave on or astride its objective. A regiment is allocated one or two DZs, each about 3 by 4 kms in size. Subsequent drops are normally made on the initial DZs, although alternative DZs are designated. Protection is quickly organised with anti-aircraft and anti-tank weapons in the first wave.

NUCLEAR WARFARE

It is quite clear that tactical nuclear weapons will only be used as a result of a top level political decision. The doctrine applying to the release of nuclear weapons obviously supported the concept of an initial massed strike, where up to one-third of all available warheads would be used. However, recent writing would indicate that the massed strike concept may have received some modification and it is possible that the Russians are now thinking in terms of some sort of selective release or graduated response.

Nuclear targets in likely order of priority are enemy nuclear delivery means, headquarters, reserves, known defensive positions, logistic installations and communication centres; and the following nuclear delivery means might be used:

SCUD – held at army level, but could be deployed in support but not under command of divisions;
FROG-7 – four held in the divisional FFR battalion;
152 mm SP gun – guns over 150 mm are assessed as having a nuclear capability.

There is no great change in the *tactics* as a result of the transition to nuclear warfare. The main points to note are (*a*) the accent will be on even greater mobility, a greater degree of dispersion and, when necessary, concentration in a particular sector for a shorter period of time; (*b*) frontages may well be wider, sector widths would certainly be increased and objectives could be in greater depth; and (*c*) alternate headquarters would certainly be used and would play a more significant role in the command and control system.

LOGISTICS

The Soviet logistic system is designed to fit the requirements of a short offensive lasting only 10–12 days, although base area stocks of combat supplies are sufficient for a much longer period. The general concept is based on divisions holding five days' stock on wheels as a reserve whilst normal replenishment is carried on for as long as possible. Armies would hold one or two days' stocks on wheels. The logistic system differs mainly from western armies in that supply is carried out by forward distribution (see Figure 3.7). Units and sub-units hold limited reserve stocks and do not possess a logistic A or B echelon on the British style. It is based on centralised planning; holding reserve stocks well forward, achieving maximum self-sufficiency within field formations, strict resupply priorities of missiles (warheads and fuel), ammunition, POL (petrol, oil, lubricants), stores and rations, efficient use of available transport, captured stocks and forward distribution.

The rear services are represented at all headquarters down to regimental level and are responsible for co-ordinating and controlling all aspects of logistic support.

Ammunition is accounted for in units of fire (UF) for each weapon. It is demanded and allocated for an operation in multiples of UF.

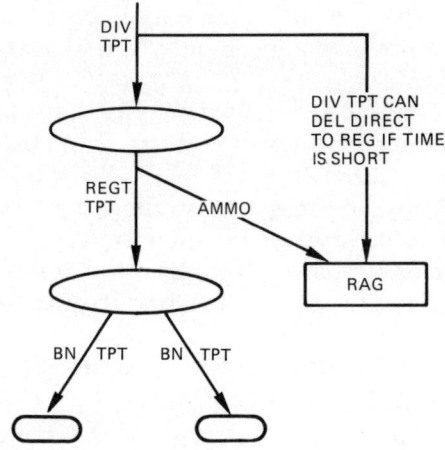

The philosophy of resupply 'rear to front' applies particularly in main thrust areas, where it will be a priority if there is a shortage of transport. Units in areas of secondary thrust may have to provide their own transport rearwards to collect C supplies on occasions.

FIGURE 3.7 *Forward Distribution System*

Ammunition distribution is based on the normal supply chain but transport can deliver direct to gun positions in order to speed up the system. Wherever possible dumping is carried out so that normal scales of artillery holdings can be retained on unit transport in the event of a sudden move forward.

The Soviet concept of operations makes *POL* supply particularly important. It will be noted that most Soviet vehicles have a good fuel range often supplemented by the addition of auxiliary fuel tanks. Forward delivery can be made by tactical pipeline which could be laid for specific operations direct to forward units.

Fresh and dry rations are available. Water supply in the field is the responsibility of the engineers and medical services; water trailers are held in all units. Although higher formations are responsible for the evacuation of casualities, returning empty transport of all kinds would be used for casualty evacuation.

The general principle of recovery and repair is based upon high standards of maintenance, rapid route clearing, and repair only if this can be effected speedily. The mechanical repair effort in forward units is relatively small and complete replacement by units is normally made. The Soviets classify repairs into *light* – small repairs which can be undertaken by unit or regimental repair teams; *medium* – repairs requring main assembly replacements; and *heavy* – major overhauls which can only be undertaken in army or Front workshops.

Since only a short war is visualised, *reinforcement* is likely to be by a complete regiment or division rather than by sub-units or individuals.

The Soviet Army now has a streamlined and efficient logistic system, tailored to its strategic offensive concept. The future will probably see the development of a high-mobility load carrier and the increasing use of helicopters for logistic purposes. The philosophy is based on a fallback to formation stocks if necessary. However, this would create problems in terms of artillery ammunition under the current doctrine should resupply be held up for a long period.

THE SOVIET SOLDIER

The problems of recruitment, training and effectiveness of the Soviet soldier are more fully discussed in Chapter 6 below, and it is not proposed to deal with them here. The author agrees substantially with Mr Donnelly's findings and conclusions.

Despite, or perhaps because of, the close attention which is paid to Soviet military training and the great demands which are made on the officers and NCOs, there are certain discernible problems which constantly recur. The first is posed by the character of the soldier himself. The Russian, and by association many of the other inhabitants of the USSR, is not only hardy and capable of great self-sacrifice, but also can be lazy with little sense of urgency and easily depressed by failure. Much of the effort put into organising 'Socialist Competition' between units as well as political education is done in an attempt to generate enthusiasm during a fairly unpleasant two years' national service. The demands that political activity makes on both spare time and training time are irksome to many professional officers. Despite the enormous military budget in the USSR, there are vast shortages of training and support equipment as well as items of everyday use in the army, so that the slogan 'economise' features regularly in the military press. Well instructed though the young officer may be, he often has problems in man management, and the lack of a strong NCO cadre makes his early career an arduous one.

The problems of morale amongst Soviet troops invading Czechoslovakia in 1968 underlines the brittleness of effective control. The Soviet Army has not undergone any significant trial by combat for over thirty years and there is no doubt that the Army of today is very different from the Army of 1945. The questions of whether the troops are physically capable of fighting the type of non-stop war the Soviet Army intends to try to fight, whether they will accept the massive casualties that were such a feature of the last war, whether ideological contact with the West will weaken their resolve to attack, especially in the event of military failure, cannot be answered except by trial. No amount of the 'realistic' battlefield simulation that is such a feature of Soviet exercises can compensate for the actual experience of war. Nevertheless, the military authorities do everything possible to ensure that, if it does happen, the Soviet soldier will meet it successfully.

CONCLUSION

It has not been the purpose of this paper to examine the strengths and weaknesses of the Soviet Ground Forces vis-à-vis, say, NATO forces. Nevertheless, a brief comparison of the two by way of drawing up some form of a quantitative and qualitative balance sheet gives an interesting summary of the possible effectiveness of Soviet tactical philosophies.

On the credit side, the Warsaw Pact has, first, a numerical superiority backed up by immense fire power and, in particular, close air support. Secondly, the Pact possesses the aggressor's advantage of strategic and tactical surprise, and hence will have the initiative to concentrate a superior force against a chosen sector. Thirdly, their equipment policy is based upon three principles: quantity, a paradoxical amalgam of simplicity and specialist sophistication, and the continuous updating of successful equipments. Therefore, it is good, reliable, they have plenty of it, and have achieved a degree of standardisation within the Warsaw Pact which can only be the envy of NATO. Finally, recent improvements arising out of a complete overhaul of the Soviet logistic system allow the effective and sustained support of high-speed offensive operations. These improvements include modernisation of the infrastructure and increases in the transport lift, including air transport.

However, there are some important factors on the debit side: the Soviets will be fighting on unfamiliar ground and their rather rigid battle procedure may cause them to experience uncalculated delays with subsequent dislocation to their planned operation timings. They will be compelled to take some risks in order to maintain the required rapid rate of advance. It is probable that the current planned grouping of formations and units would cause congestion on routes and this inflexibility could lead to severe disruption of plans. Finally, the Soviet soldier is a tough and efficient opponent but he is no superman. He faces many of the problems which arise in conscript armies, plus a few which are peculiar to the USSR; furthermore, there are some political strains within the Warsaw Pact. The standard of junior leadership is low. Nevertheless, it is possible that what we in the West think of as a weakness may to the Soviets be a strength. It is at least arguable that somewhat inflexible tactics and a rigid doctrinal approach may be a sensible system to adopt for an army based on conscription and with a low standard of junior leadership but possessing a vast numerical superiority in men and equipment.

In conclusion, it behoves us to remember a quotation by a

sometime SACEUR, General Lemnitzer, who said: 'Military planning must be oriented only to the capabilities of a potential enemy and not his assumed intentions. Intentions can change overnight.'

SUMMARY OF DISCUSSION

The initial discussion on Colonel Hemsley's paper centred on the contradictions between the Soviet claims that GSFG was a defensive formation, and the fact that it was clearly structured for an uncompromisingly agressive role. Colonel Hemsley pointed out that during the 1960s exercises had been based on an initial defence, followed by an offence, but by the 1970s they were concerned totally with the offence. He also argued that there was a mismatch between the Tank Army concept, which was best suited to the open spaces of Poland and Russia, and the likely combat area of western Europe, which was hilly and heavily urbanised. This was likely to lead in the future to the conversion of the Tank divisions into Motor Rifle formations, which would be better able to cope with west European terrain, though such a conversion could encounter stiff resistance at the level of the individual units. A discussion then ensued on the degree of warning time available to NATO and the amount of logistic preparation that would be necessary before the Soviets could mount an attack. The speaker pointed out that although GSFG could move with little warning, they were unlikely to do so before second echelon units in the western military districts of the USSR had been mobilised, and this would take some time. However, they could act immediately if only a limited attack were planned. In any prolonged conflict, the NATO forces were likely to run out of supplies long before the Warsaw Pact forces, and thus a prolonged encounter would not be to NATO's advantage. The question of the use of BMPs in a raiding role was then raised, and it was pointed out that this idea was largely a product of mistranslations, as in the Soviet military literature a raid was a forward penetration, and did not involve any return to a jump-off point. Finally, a speaker mentioned that the Soviets have changed their low-level infantry tactics, and instead of driving APCs at targets, they now used the APC to provide supporting fire while the infantry attacked the target on foot.

NOTES AND REFERENCE MATERIAL

Though reference is made throughout the text to the T-62 Soviet battle tank, it should be remembered that a new tank, the T-72, is now coming into front-line service: weighing an estimated 40 tonnes, the T-72 (sometimes identified as the T-64) mounts a smooth-bore main gun whose calibre is 125-mm, using ammunition with semi-combustible cartridges, with 28 rounds housed in the automatic loader and an additional 4 more ready rounds in the turret. There is a 3-man crew, thicker armour (100-mm) than the T-62, and an improved track/suspension system. Another marked feature is the incorporation of a base-length stereoscopic rangefinder. With a 920 HP engine, the T-72 has a reported speed in the region of 43 mph: the T-72 thus embodies a good power-to-weight ratio. Some 6–800 have already been reported in GSFG and over 2,000 have already been produced.

Reference material

Voennyi Vestnik (*Ground Forces Journal*) for 1975–May 1977
Taktika v boevykh primerakh (5 vols: *Divizya, Polk, Batal'on, Rota, Vzvod*) (Moscow, Voenizdat, 1974–76)
A. Kh. Babadzhanyan (Marshal of Armoured Forces, ed.), *Tanki i tankvye voiska* (Moscow, Voenizdat, 1970)
P. A. Rotmistrov (Chief Marshal of Armoured Forces), *Vremya i tanki* (Moscow, Voenizdat, 1972)
G. Biryukov and G. Melnikov, *Antitank Warfare*, Moscow, 'Progress', 1972. (Official Soviet translation)
A. F. Shramchenko (Colonel), *Takticheskie ucheniya* (2nd edn.) (Moscow, Voenizdat, 1975) (On tactical training and field exercises)
Y. Novikov and F. Sverdlov, *Manoeuvre in Modern Land Warfare*, Moscow, 'Progress', 1972. (Official Soviet translation)
P. I. Konoplya and N. A. Maikov, *Tankovyi batal'on v boyu* (2nd edn.), (Moscow, Voenizdat, 1972)
A. S. Belonovskii, *Eleketrooborudovanie bronetankovoi tekhniki* (Moscow, Voenizdat, 1976)
A. I. Kitov (Colonel, ed.), *Sovremennaya armiya i distsiplina* (Moscow, Voenizdat, 1976)
V. V. Serebryannikov and M. I. Yasyukov, *Initsiativa i tvorchestvo v voennom dele* (Moscow, Voenizdat, 1976)
A. A. Beketov *et al.*, *Maskirovka deistvii podrazdelenii sukhoputnykh voisk* (Moscow, Voenizdat, 1976)
Savkin, V. E. (Colonel), *Osnovnye printsipy operativnogo iskusstva i taktiki* (Moscow, Voenizdat, 1972). (USAF Translation: *The Basic Principles of Operational Art and Tactics*, 'Soviet Military Thought' series, Washington, D.C., n.d.)
A. A. Yepishev (Army General), *Some Aspects of Party-political Work in the Soviet Armed Forces* (Moscow, 'Progress', 1975). (Official Soviet translation)
I. Babenko, *Soviet Officers* (Moscow, 'Progress', 1976). (Official Soviet translation)
Uchebnoe posobie po nachal'noi voennoi podgotovke (6th edn.), (Moscow, Voenizdat, 1975) (Official Soviet handbook on pre-call up military training.)

Friedrich Wiener, *Die Armeen der Ostblockstaaten*, 2nd edn. (Munich, Bernard & Graefe, 1977). (In translation, Friedrich Wiener and William J. Lewis, *The Warsaw Pact Armies* (Carl Veberreuter, Vienna, 1977)
John Erickson, *Soviet Military Power* (London, RUSI, 1971)
Lawrence L. Whetton (ed.), *The Future of Soviet Military Power*, (New York, Crane-Russak, 1976)

John Erickson, 'Trends in the Soviet Combined Arms Concept', *Strategic Review* (Washington), Vol. V, No. 1
——'The Soviet NBC Programme: Defensive and Offensive Modes', lecture given at NBC Defence Centre, 9 Nov. 1976
——'Soviet Ground Forces and the Conventional Mode of Operations', *RUSI Journal* (June 1976)
C. N. Donnelly, 'Soviet Techniques for Combat in Built Up Areas', *International Defence Review* (1977) No. 2
FM30–40, Handbook on Soviet Ground Forces, (Washington, US Government Printing Office, 1976)
Arthur Volz, 'Soviet Chemical Warfare Capability' *Radio Liberty Research* (Oct. 1976).

4 The Soviet Navy

John E. Moore

In a recent lecture Professor Galbraith reviewed the arms competition between the USA and the USSR. He produced two contrasting reasons for this competition. The first, the more conventional, is that the present situation is the result of 'an irreconcilable conflict between inherently hostile systems'. His second reason is that there is 'a symbiotic relationship' between the military forces and the arms manufacturers, each relying on the other for their existence and subsequent growth. Accepting this fact, there could also be a similar relationship between the two super powers.

The second of these views, even though containing some elements of truth, suggests that there is little to be gained in a study of the aims of the great powers as evidenced by their military policies. I make no apology for these general references in a discussion of the situation of the Soviet navy in the world today. Unless the whole situation is reviewed and an overall appreciation of all aspects of military power and political objectives is taken one is very likely to become over-parochial in one's appreciation.

Certain clichés have become only too common in discussions of the Soviet fleet. One of the more misleading is that 'the Russian is a land animal.' This fails to define what is meant by 'the Russian' and also fails to take into account historical truth. Over a thousand years ago some of the tribes which were later to be absorbed into the whole mass of Russia were at sea trading, fishing, or for conquest. From this point the maritime history of the country developed in the same uncertain way as in many others, including England. By the time that the First World War broke out, the Russian sailor had made his presence felt in a number of ways – in exploration, in warfare, and in trade. In naval affairs there had been a readiness to adopt new ideas which was not always reflected in the thinking of other navies. The main problem which confronted them was the social organisation inherent in the Russian system, breeding a lack of leadership amongst the officers. Although at the turn of the twentieth century the Russian fleet was fourth in the world in numbers, its efficiency was shown up in a tragic light during the war with Japan which, from a naval point of view, came to an end with the cataclysmic battle of Tsushima. Between that date of 1904 and the involvement of the Russian states in the First World War many good ideas and plans were nullified by the overwhelming weight of bureaucracy. The performance of this fleet in the years 1914–17 was, not surprisingly, unimpressive. The period immediately following the October Revolution saw that navy allowed to moulder away at a time when the majority of the new politicians were more concerned with the situation ashore.

It was thus not until 1926 that any form of new construction programme was considered, although a certain measure of refit had taken place amongst the ships of the fleet. It is possibly significant today that early consideration was given to the construction of submarines. However, at the time of the Spanish War when Stalin found that his reinforcement of the Communist forces in that country was inhibited by the presence of both German and Italian submarines, the lesson of the need for sea control was absorbed. It was possibly this lesson which spurred on a building programme which, by September 1939, reached a total of 219 warships under construction including three battleships, two battle cruisers, 10 cruisers, 45 destroyers and 91 submarines. This programme was inevitably gravely interfered with by the German invasion and thus, in July 1945, there was little but a mixed bag of pre-war and lend-lease vessels in a fleet which had shown very little ability during the previous four years.

It was in this month that Stalin gave instructions that a fleet 'still stronger and more powerful' must be provided. As usual with such pronouncements this took little account of the current situation. The main surface ship-building yards had been destroyed and construction was confined to inland river yards and those in the Far East. As the western yards were rebuilt, construction of pre-war designs recommenced although at this time new designs must have been on the drawing-board. The Soviet navy was still suffering from a grave lack of experienced officers as a result of Stalin's purges in the 1930s but had learnt a considerable amount from the contacts made during the war with western navies and also the equipment and designers captured from the Germans.

Although the death of Stalin in 1953 brought an end to his planned big ship fleet it is quite apparent that there were already many designs available which were to start a revolution in Soviet naval construction. The first surface-to-surface missile in destroyers went to sea in 1957 in the Kildin class. These and their immediate successors were no more than conversions based on existing hull designs and one need look for no more lead-time than three or four years, although the design of the missiles themselves would have probably been initiated well before this.

It is as well here to consider the situation confronting the Soviet leadership as the Korean War came to an end in 1953. As a country the USSR had lost twenty million people and a third of its industrial capacity in the four years of the Great Patriotic War. Although geographical gains had been made as a result of that war there must inevitably have been a feeling that such a catastrophe must not occur again. Mother Russia must be protected and in 1953, at a time when the first aircraft armed with nuclear missiles was capable of flying from American aircraft carriers, the conclusion of hostilities in the Far East released great fleets with recent war experience. In all, at this time, the US Navy had 28 large carriers and 75 light carriers on its list whilst the Royal Navy had 18. Against this formidable array the Soviets began to deploy those craft best suited to nullify or, at least, give battle to this stupendous imbalance. So the craft were designed to carry the weapons which could best meet this need. Surface-to-surface missiles in cruisers and destroyers and similar conversions in their submarine force were pressed ahead with great vigour.

The submarine programme had benefited more than any other from the lessons learned from the Germans. Between 1951 and 1957 240 Whiskey class submarines and 25 of their larger sisters of the Zulu class were produced in Soviet shipyards. This astonishing performance was typical of what was to come in the future. Once a design had been accepted it was pushed ahead without recourse to prototypes and years of trials. If the first ships of the class were unsatisfactory then the programme was halted and the equipment switched to other purposes. As a result the build-up of the Soviet Navy has been unparallelled in its speed.

At the same time as these submarines were under construction, other plans were being formulated. In 1955, two years before the first US ballistic missile submarine was laid down, the Soviets launched their first submarine-oriented ballistic missile. This was not impressive by modern standards but in 1956 the first Zulu conversion carrying two of these weapons was at sea, to be followed by the Golf class which was specifically designed for the task and later by the nuclear propelled Hotel class. Even allowing for a shortened lead-time this means that the decision must have been made at least by 1950. It was not until December 1959 that any western navy possessed a similar capability.

In the air the Soviet navy had also greatly improved its situation. By the early 1950s there were four thousand aircraft manned by the SNAF. These were all shore-based but included long-range jet aircraft of the Badger type with the first air-to-surface weapons and a large number of fighters which were designed for the protection of the home bases. These last were soon to be removed from the naval inventory but it still left a considerable power for both reconnaissance and strike.

The emergence of the Soviet navy as we know it today began to accelerate from the date of the appointment of Admiral Sergei Gorshkov to the post of C-in-C in January 1956. Gorshkov had been promoted to Rear Admiral at the age of 31 and was 45 when Khruschev finally placed him in overall charge of this increasing fleet. The appointment of C-in-C is an amalgam of the posts in Great Britain of First Sea Lord and the erstwhile First Lord of the Admirality. In no way daunted by this vast task, he set to work to implement the instructions of his political bosses. The fleet of big ships envisioned by Stalin was cancelled but, at the same time, the need for Soviet naval power had been made evident to the hierarchy in the Moscow Kremlin. In October-November 1956 the Anglo-French descent on Suez and in July 1958 the intervention of the American naval forces in the Lebanon proved a point which had not been lost on Stalin twenty years before. From now on there was a steady and increasingly methodical build-up of the Soviet navy. Battleships, old cruisers, and destroyers were scrapped and attention focused on the development of missiles, both cruise and ballistic as well as anti-aircraft, and the improvement of propulsion. The much heralded arrival of the US Navy's Polaris force brought great efforts in the development of anti-submarine warfare. By 1967 the first of a new class of helicopter-carriers, unlike any other built in the world, was nearing completion. She came at a time when the problems of A/S warfare had been greatly enhanced by the deployment of the American A2 Polaris in 1962 and the even longer range A3 missile in 1964.

Even so, if one examines the ships which were available to Admiral Gorshkov at this time it must be admitted that great strides had been taken. Among the cruisers the Kresta I class was to be followed in 1968 by the Kresta II. The Kynda missile-cruiser had first commissioned in 1962 and in the same year the first of the Kashin class destroyers had entered service. This last was a particularly notable advance as she was the first all-gas turbine ship to enter naval service in any country. New designs of frigate with mixed diesel and gas turbine propulsion had arrived in the first half of the 1960s simultaneously with the development of another totally new idea, the missile-armed fast attack craft. There was no doubt of the originality and vision of the Soviet naval designers.

In the same year, 1963, that the first British nuclear submarine was commissioned the Soviet navy was completing the last of the fourteen strong November class nuclear submarines which had been in production since 1958. There was then a pause as the lessons were absorbed and in 1967, a year of great importance in this history, the first of the Victor class fleet submarines appeared. Of a new design she was shorter, quieter, and faster than her predecessors. A similar hull form was used for the Charlie class which followed in 1968. In these latter submarines a new missile system had been built in to overcome the problems which faced the captains of the previous cruise missile submarines. In the converted Whiskeys and the Echo class nuclear-propelled boats there was always the requirement to surface before firing their weapons. In the Charlie this was overcome with the creation of a new dive-launched missile and once again the Soviet designers had moved a very large step forward.

We have already mentioned the arrival of the Zulu V ballistic missile submarine in 1956 and the building of its immediate successors, both diesel- and nuclear-propelled. A proportion of these was converted to carry longer range missiles of the SS-N-5 type and it was in the fateful year of 1967 that the reason for this tardy retro fitting became evident. The first of the Yankee class, carrying sixteen ballistic missile tubes in the hull in the same manner as the American and British designs, was commissioned. Her missiles had a range of 1,300 miles and it was not very long before the first were deployed to the Eastern American seaboard. Thirty-four of this class were constructed over the next seven years and there was the expectation that improvements in her missile range would shortly

The Soviet Navy

be seen. The improvement was even more dramatic than expected. In 1972 came the first of the Delta class, monstrous submarines carrying twelve of the new SS-N-8 missile with a range of 4,200 miles. This capability meant that these submarines would be capable of covering the whole of the area of the USA and Canada as well as Europe and a large area of China without ever leaving the immediate area to the north of Norway. The Soviet Union may have had an anti-submarine problem with the extension of the range of the Polaris missile – NATO now had an almost insuperable anti-submarine problem with the arrival of the Deltas. Not content with the Delta I, the Soviets produced the Delta II in 1973, an even larger monster carrying 16 missile tubes. In 1977 the SS-N-18 missile with a range beyond 5,000 miles entered service. Four years after the first Delta was at sea the lead ship of the USN's Trident programme was laid down with the expectation of commissioning in 1979.

By July 1976 Gorshkov had produced a fleet with astonishing capability and which for the last fourteen years had been obeying his instructions to get to sea. The building programme had, admittedly, slowed down but still included two or three of the very powerful Kara class and Kresta II class cruisers. Both classes are armed with long-range SS-N-14 anti-submarine missiles which probably have an anti-ship capability and with considerable additional armament, both missile and guns. The Krivak class destroyers which first entered service in 1971 are still being produced at a steady rate of about four a year. Amongst the smaller ships new ideas had been seen in the production of the Grisha class corvettes and the very powerful Nanuchka class with its 150 mile surface-to-surface missile battery. The rest of the fleet had been similarly well provided with a new class of tank landing ships following the large numbers of its predecessors, while afloat support had not been neglected and a new class of these ships was in series production. A country which had always taken a keen interest in mining was not to be left behind in this field and new classes of mine countermeasure vessels were also coming off the slips. Ashore the Soviet Naval Air Force was being strengthened by the addition of backfire, long-range strike bombers and also possessed a very considerable and very long-range reconnaissance capability. The only major factor missing from a 'balanced fleet' on this date was organic air. In July the long-anticipated arrival of the aircraft carrier Kiev in the Mediterranean did much to remedy this defect.

She was swiftly seen to be a remarkable vessel and, in the same way as the Moskva before her, was a complete departure from normal western practice. With a heavy battery of surface-to-surface weapons, strong surface-to-air defence, a considerable gun battery, anti-submarine weapons and sensors, this was something totally new to naval observers. But the aircraft she carries are by no means capable of carrying out all the functions of those normally associated with a fixed-wing carrier. Not only is the performance of the V/STOL aircraft somewhat suspect, but so also is the drill and equipment provided on the flight deck. But this very considerable step forward, which shows that the long-standing dispute in the Soviet navy concerning the value of aircraft carriers has been resolved, must be taken very seriously. We have seen so often in the past that Soviet designers move with a rapidity unknown in the West and this ship may well be the forerunner of new classes in the fairly forseeable future.

Comparative studies of the world's navies must inevitably take into account the role of those forces. In looking at various fleets today one is impressed by the many variations which have taken place as the result of a consideration of this very fact of role. The Chinese navy is almost entirely concerned with coastal defence, its great strength lying in its submarine force and its light forces armed with missiles, guns, or torpedoes. It is the failure of various politicians and analysts to take account of this aspect of navies which frequently results in ludicrous comparisons such as those made in the US Congress in March 1977 when one member was busily comparing the tonnages of the fleets of the USA and USSR.

The role of the Soviet navy is one that deserves considerable investigation. Its Commander-in-Chief, Admiral Gorshkov, has stated a very simple overall aim. He says that, 'The Navy's mission is to protect state interests on the seas and oceans and to defend the country from possible attack from this direction.' Now this in its simplicity is all-embracing. He is suggesting that his aim in the creation of the modern Soviet fleet has been to provide an all-purpose force capable of operations world-wide. Although in his writings he has been known to allude to the dangers of building 'all-purpose' ships this is, in many ways, what he has achieved amongst the larger units. Although the majority of these are classified as anti-submarine ships they carry the capability for both anti-surface and anti-air operations in addition. When he talks of the navy as being 'a powerful instrument of defence in the oceanic areas, a formidable force for the deterrence of aggression, which is constantly ready to deliver punishing retaliatory blows and to disrupt the plans of the Imperialists', he is speaking of something far more than a force aimed only at the defence of Mother Russia. At one time the Admiral spoke of the very satisfactory situation in which the Soviet Union is placed because of its vast resources of raw materials. In this he was of course absolutely right because there are only five of the major strategic materials which have to be imported and these only in comparatively small amounts. Were he to provide an analysis of the raw material requirements of the NATO countries and to forecast the forces needed to defend those imports the results would not only be of great interest but would falsify a number of the conclusions which he reaches on the possible employment of NATO naval forces. Even the mighty USA is dependent on the importation of over fifty per cent of fourteen of the twenty major strategic materials. If this is converted into numbers of merchant ships upon the ocean which would require protection in the event of hostilities, the balance quite clearly is set against the Gorshkov argument.

The Soviet navy's first consideration is clearly defence against a sea-borne nuclear attack, with a capability of riposte should they be put in the second strike position. The latter, we have seen, has been achieved and is virtually invulnerable. But the defence task changed with the introduction of submarine-launched missiles – the emphasis altered from an anti-carrier policy to an anti-submarine policy. The detection and destruction of submarines carrying Polaris, Poseidon and, eventually, Trident missiles must be a primary consideration. The question is whether this can best be done by surface ships, submarines, aircraft, or more unconventional means such as satellites with sophisticated detection devices or a combination of these methods. The present order of battle is, therefore, interesting – on the anti-submarine ticket there is a building programme of A/S oriented carriers, two helicopter-cruisers, fourteen cruisers with four building, and fifteen missile destroyers. All building of major surface ships is now switched to anti-submarine operations. But on the submarine side the balance is very different – of the twelve boats built each year the pattern is, roughly, six ballistic missile submarines, two cruise-missile boats, two conventional diesel-electric boats, and only two nuclear attack submarines. In an underwater world where the most efficient listening platform and the most deadly weapon carrier is the nuclear attack submarine the Soviet Union today possesses only 39 of this type with a building programme far smaller than it could achieve were it determined to press the issue of defence.

Unless there is a significant advance in satellite detection and tracking, the surface forces are unlikely to home on to any western SSBN. The geographical problems of the USSR make it unlikely that any major use of a system such as the American SOSUS can be achieved and, if it were, the surface ships would be at continual risk and their comparatively small force of nuclear attack submarines insufficient to prosecute any such detections. Therefore, allowing for the decisions of the highly competent Soviet naval staff, what is the purpose of this fleet? In addition to those we have already isolated as having a primary A/S function there is still a huge force for the protection of the homeland – 68 cruise missile submarines, 250 diesel submarines, 20 cruisers, 95 destroyers, 120 frigates, 185 corvettes, as well as 350 fast attack craft, over 400 minesweepers, and over 250 amphibious craft. As the naval forces of the West diminish so these numbers remain static, even though some proportion is in reserve. One can only gaze thoughtfully at these figures and conjecture against what vast armadas they are aimed. They are certainly far greater than anything needed today when the aircraft carriers of the USA would be used in tactical, or sometimes strategic, defence against a Soviet assault on the Central Front, when the possibility of an invasion of Soviet territory is almost laughable, and when the USSR has no need for sea-lines of communication in times of crisis. A Russian friend recently remarked, 'We ate cabbages in the last war – we can eat cabbages again.' Unfortunately for the West NATO has insufficient cabbages.

So if this huge naval panoply is too large for the task of 'defending the country' what other aspects of Gorshkov's aim remain? 'To protect state interests on the seas and oceans' is the other side of the coin and so the naval planner must give thought to what evidence exists as to where 'state interests' lie. The manipulations in Angola, the secret treaty with Iraq, the affirmations of support for African insurgents recently pronounced by President Podgorny give more than a hint of policy trends. These, amongst a host of other indicators, give the planner a great deal to consider – matters which will affect not only his dispositions but his building programmes. In the last ten years the western navies have become reactive to the

Soviet fleet, a change of emphasis too often forgotten but forced on NATO staffs by reductions in defence spending.

Since 1962 the expansion of Soviet operations and interests overseas has been steady and, in some cases, dramatic. In that year, as the Cuban crisis brought increasing realisation of the part a navy can play in international affairs, the fleet was making its first tentative moves on to the high seas. Gorshkov was, and remains, insistent on this as a necessity in all naval training. Small deployments to and from the Baltic and Mediterranean were followed by exercises in the Norwegian Sea and by 1966 extended Arctic operations and a squadron deployment through the Atlantic, round Cape Horn, and thence to Vladivostok were evidence of a growing capability. In 1968 a series of visits in the Indian Ocean was followed by a permanent, if fluctuating, presence in that area. As Soviet survey and research ships prodded further and further into the oceans, the fleet was not far behind. In 1969 came the first Caribbean expedition, and the first Okean exercise in the spring of 1970 brought a flood of ships into all areas except the Eastern Pacific and Australasia. So the pattern has expanded and the situation today is strangely reminiscent of British deployments in the heyday of an earlier Imperialism.

The overall result has been the establishments of friendly havens in many places. Cuba, Conakry, Luanda, Mozambique, Mauritius, Berbera, Umm Qasr, Aden, Hodeida and, more recently, Libya are amongst ports and areas now well-known to Soviet navigators. Others will no doubt be added as the years go by and more and more political initiatives are backed by port visits. These are not bases in the accepted sense, although storage, communications, and missile facilities exist at Berbera. But they all possess that inestimable virtue of being havens where maintenance can be carried out, stores and fuel embarked, and people transferred without the expense of a massive fleet train. Their existence means that a well-sustained force can remain in an area for an indefinite period whilst political manoeuvres reach their climax.

This is surely the meaning of the second half of Gorshkov's aim. With a well-entrenched KGB throughout the world capable of engineering a crisis on command, the presence of a ship or a squadron ready to answer any calls for help or support is, as history shows, a great step towards political success. Here the new Soviet aircraft-carriers could be of immense value, either alone or as the kernel of a task-force. With both fixed-wing and helicopter capability, able to operate all forms of missiles and artillery, and with a full inventory of sensors, ECM equipment, and communications their presence would be invaluable. A couple of destroyers, a landing ship, a fleet support ship and Kiev could maintain station in an area for a very long period and, as numbers grow and the West becomes even more hard-pressed to find adequate numbers to carry out surveillance, so do the chances of success increase.

One great question-mark remains – what is the efficiency of this huge fleet? Here, as always, one enters into areas of estimation which are very difficult to back with facts. So far as the ships themselves are concerned such an estimate is easier to achieve than it is when considering the manpower and is probably a sound starting point.

The ships' hulls, despite some rather odd design features, have proved themselves capable of withstanding the weather in all parts of the world. Considering the number of ship-days spent out of area, the mechanical availability appears to compare very favourably with western standards. Sensors certainly work and the communications necessitated by the close control exercised from Moscow must be adequate and efficient judging by results. The occasions on which the various armaments are fired or launched are very rare but examination of guns and launchers on the rare occasions on which they can be seen suggest that these are well-maintained. Accommodation and air-conditioning is primitive by western standards, reminiscent of a pre-war British ship, although below-decks hygiene and cleanliness are of a significantly lower standard. The officers' accommodation is comparatively palatial though dull and unimaginative – a less individual approach is again similar to the austere conditions of 1939–45.

So the ships work; but there are areas where the technology incorporated in them lags behind that of western fleets, notably in submarine detection. Here one can imagine that a vast R and D programme is in hand and, with the anticipated new generation of nuclear submarines, the arrival of improved and enhanced sonar systems may not be far away. As the West continues to export modern technology to the Warsaw Pact countries it is only logical that some advantage will accrue from this liberal attitude.

The manning of the Soviet navy presents that most difficult of all mixtures – a professional officer corps directing a conscript Lower Deck with the assistance of senior ratings some of whom are volunteers, some conscripts. The officers themselves are proficient technicians and it is significant that a considerable proportion of the seaman officers hold technical degrees. This is a natural outcome of their training in the eleven schools which cater for this intake. These schools are so parochial that their products enter the fleet, after four years training, as specialist officers – sonar, radar and so on – a fact which clearly worries Admiral Gorshkov who is continually seeking a broad approach to naval matters. This is hardly likely to occur, however, for two reasons. The first is that an officer may spend all the time from first appointment to second-in-command in the same ship. The second is that a very compartmented approach is inevitable when dealing with conscript junior ratings.

These young men enter the service by call-up at the age of eighteen after a certain amount of basic training in the equivalent of state-controlled cadet forces. If going to sea, the new entry will do six months' shore training and then join his ship for a $2\frac{1}{2}$-year stint. On arrival he will spend a few weeks being trained on the job by his predecessor and will then continue for the rest of his time in the same job unless he is particulary bright. In this case he can be cross-trained – in fact he will be taught an additional job – and may in his last year find himself as a Petty-Officer. At the age of 21 he will enter the reserve unless he volunteers to sign on, in which case his advancement to Chief Petty Officer is very rapid. It is hardly surprising that a system such as this throws a very heavy technical burden on the officers and senior ratings and the turbulence in the drafting community may be imagined when it is remembered that the total of officers and ratings is about 425,000 whilst the annual intake of trainees is a little over 100,000.

The overall position for manning the ships is not one which would delight a western naval staff. The commanding officers range from Rear-Admirals in some of the ballistic missile submarines to 28-year-old Lieutenant-Commanders in some of the newer destroyers. Whilst the submarine service is allowed the best of the ratings in most cases, manning these vessels is becoming more and more difficult. The overall production of senior ratings has also proved a problem and considerable incentives are offered to those who re-engage. Added to all this is the degree of centralisation of command which would be unacceptable in any western navy. This may have resulted from the inexperience of commanding officers at the period of initial overseas expansion in the early 1960s, but that need should now be past. There is certainly no longer any excuse for an admiral to take charge of his flagship when entering harbour – a situation which is still reported from time to time.

The general command structure is on similar lines to the state control of the merchant marine and fishing fleets. All are subject to instructions from the USSR but are also beneficiaries of a centralised meteorological and routeing service of considerable efficiency. It is this attitude of obedience which, while having its strengths, must inevitably bring in its train lack of flexibility and initiative. The need for effective communications is therefore paramount and any failure of this organisation could possibly result in chaos.

What, then, of the future? The most senior officers of the Soviet navy are now elderly by any standard and their successors are already standing in the wings. Bearing in mind the long lead-time for any major warship, even in Russia, the pattern must be ineluctably set for the next eight years at least. But weapons can be changed, sensors made more efficient, tactics improved and, above all, intentions changed. This is a fleet with great strengths and equal weaknesses, but its very size and the lavish financial support accorded it ensure that, unless the western countries are prepared to provide adequate surveillance and counter-force, it will be in a position to dictate to those countries in the years ahead.

SUMMARY OF DISCUSSION

In the discussion following Captain Moore's paper, the author argued that the major reason for moving directly from design to series production of warships was to save time. He also emphasised that, except in the Mediterranean, the Russians rarely operate a fleet structure with an Admiral in command, all actions normally being co-ordinated from Moscow. This led to a vigorous debate about the nature of the command structure of the Soviet navy and its relationship to the General Staff and the political leadership. It was pointed out that the General Staff commands the missile submarine force, and that there was little knowledge of how the air force, navy and army co-ordinate their activities in areas such as the Baltic or the Northern Fleet areas. Captain Moore responded by pointing to the fact that such problems did not arise in peace-time as the navy operated only on a single service basis, with disagreements being referred back to Moscow for decision. SSBN boats tend to have older, more senior officers in command, perhaps because these vessels might at some time be required to take independent action.

Captain Moore then went on to suggest that the Kiev design was too small to have a world-wide, heavy weather capability, and a new class of larger VTOL ships would probably follow in the near future. He saw the role of the Kiev class as political in peacetime and anti-submarine in war. It was also suggested that since the USSR holds the view that war in Europe and general war at sea are inseparable, Soviet mobilisation of her navy might be a better warning of premeditated land attack in Europe than troop movements. The speaker thought that such an attack could be preceded by extensive naval exercises, however, which would effectively mobilise the fleet without raising western suspicions.

It was further suggested that there was a clear discrepancy between the political rhetoric espoused by the USSR in support of National Liberation Movements and the fact that her armed forces had little capability in this role. The role of the naval infantry was then discussed and whether these troops were only relevant in the Baltic or had roles elsewhere. Captain Moore pointed out that Gorshkov had been an amphibious force commander during the war, and had resuscitated the naval infantry when he became head of the navy. He considered it possible that the naval infantry might be used in an intervention role, though not necessarily in Norway, as was suggested by one participant.

REFERENCES

John E. Moore (Captain R.N.), *The Soviet Navy Today* (London, 1975)
Jane's Fighting Ships (ed. John E. Moore,). Annual publication (London, Macdonald & Jane's)
Soviet Oceans Development (US Government Printing Office, Washington, October 1976)
V.I. Achkasov and N.B. Pavlovich, *Sovetskoe voenno-morskoe iskusstvo v Velikoi Otechestvennoi voine* (Moscow, Voenizdat, 1973.)
N.A. Brusentsev, *Voenno-morskaya aviatsiya*, (Moscow, Voenizdat, 1976.)
S.G. Gorshkov (Admiral of Fleet SU), *Morskaya moshch' gosudarstva*, (Moscow, Voenizdat, 1976)
V.M. Grishanov (Admiral, ed.), *Voina okean chelovek. O moral'no-politicheskoi i psikhologicheskoi podgotovke sovetskikh voennykh moryakov* (Moscow, Voenizdat, 1974)
I.N. Potapov, *Razvitie voenno-morskikh flotov v poslevoennyi period* (Moscow, Voenizdat, 1971)
Spravochnik starshiny i michmana VMF (Moscow, Voenizdat, 1976)
V. Sysoev (Admiral), '150 let Voenno-morskoi Adademii', *Morskoi Sbornik* (1977), No. 1, pp. 7–12.
S.E. Zakharov (Admiral), *Istoriya voenno-morskogo iskusstva*, (issued under the auspices of Glavnyi Shtab VMF) (Moscow, Voenizdat, 1969)

5 The Soviet Air Force

Alexander Boyd

Under the aegis of Air Chief Marshal Pavel Stepanovich Kutakhov's Military Air Forces (*Voenno-vozdushnye sily SSSR*) fall three of the five components of Soviet air power: Frontal (Tactical) Aviation (*Frontovaya aviatsiya*) whose air armies support military district ground forces or the groups of Soviet forces based in Germany, Poland, Czechoslovakis, and Hungary; Long-Range Aviation (*Dal'naya aviatsiya*), which has at periods in the past enjoyed more overt autonomy under direct subordination to the Ministry of Defence or its equivalent as a separate command; and Military Transport Command (*Voenno-transportnaya aviatsiya*). The air elements of the Soviet Navy and the National Air Defence Force or PVO (*Protivovozdushnaya oborona strany*) form part of the commands presided over by Admiral Gorshkov and Marshal Batitsky, having been operationally detached from the Military Air Force (VVS) Command respectively shortly before and during the Great Patriotic War of 1941–45.

These last two extraneous elements can only be briefly dealt with in this short survey. Clearly, the Soviet Naval Air Force's improved and improving anti-submarine warfare and anti-shipping strike capabilities allied to recent ventures in building a carrier fleet are in line with Admiral Gorshkov's dynamic new naval policies. At the same time, an effective carrier-borne strike capability is still lacking – at least for the present. Marshal Batitsky's PVO Fighter Aviation under Colonel-General Borovykh has been equipped with an impressive armoury of constantly up-dated surface-to-air missiles and interceptor fighters. But while some sixty per cent of Borovykh's force consists of recent single-seat MiG-25 (Foxbat) and Su-15 (Flagon), and multi-seat Tu-28p (Fiddler) and Yak-28p (Firebar) fighters, it would appear for the moment that they still lack an effective look-down, shoot-down system.[1] It can be safely anticipated that the PVO Command will spare no effort to make good this particular deficiency. The five air elements have some three-quarters of a million men, of which 490,000 are under Kutakhov's command.

Air Chief Marshal Kutakhov, Commander-in-Chief VVS since March 1969, wears the red star of Hero of the Soviet Union won as a squadron leader flying with the 19th Guards Fighter Regiment in 1943. Appointed First Deputy C-in-C VVS in July 1967 under the late Chief Air Marshal Vershinin, Kutakhov has introduced vigorous new offensive potentials for his air forces in marked contrast with those pursued by his post-war predecessors. Chief Air Marshal Vershinin, who held war time commands on the Southern and Caucasian Fronts (the latter during the perilous winter of 1942–43) and commanded the 4th Air Army, and Chief Air Marshal Zhigarev with whom he alternated commands and whose effective operational experience was largely restricted to the Far East, both placed prime importance on frontal air cover and basic close support, whereas Kutakhov's energetic and more adventurous policies indicate a return to the strategic panache of the mid-1930s when 'special aviation armies' were formed with the primary role of supporting rapid and wide-scale offensive thrusts by the Red Army.

The present shop-window capability of Kutakhov's Frontal Aviation is exemplified by over a thousand tactical machines supporting the Group of Soviet Forces in Germany and representing something in the order of a fifth of the Soviet Union's first-line tactical air strength.[2] The air divisions supporting GSFG have increased by an estimated forty per cent since 1974 their total of combat aircraft – a significant proportion of which are fitted for tactical nuclear strike roles in combination with ground army missile units' . . . for the purpose of destroying the means of mass destruction and defeating the basic enemy groupings on the axis of the main strike of advancing troops'.[3]

While Soviet air regiments are being rapidly and methodically re-equipped with the latest MiG-21 SMT (Fishbed-K), MiG-23 (Flogger-B), MiG-25 (Foxbat), MiG-27 (Flogger-D), Su-17 (Fitter-C), and Su-19 (Fencer) fighters and fighter-bombers, such close attention to the up-dating of combat equipment can be attributed to the bitter price of delayed modernisation paid in June 1941. The Soviet air forces today are unlikely to overlook that particular error. Indeed, some of the aircraft these new machines are replacing are undoubtedly obsolete if reports of MiG-17 (Fresco) fighters remaining in front-line service with GSFG air regiments until 1975 are correct.

There are, however, causes for concern implicit in Soviet tactical air modernisation on this accelerated scale since intensive updating allied to established numerical superiority cannot but affect the air balance between the Warsaw Pact Forces and those of NATO. The NATO Alliance, with somewhat less then 3,100 land-based tactical aircraft for the defence of western Europe, is confronted by over 5,300 tactical aircraft attached to the Warsaw Pact Forces, of which admittedly the 2,900 Soviet machines deployed in eastern Europe and the western military districts of the USSR represent the most threatening and modern component.[4] The significance of Europe as a crucial battleground for tactical air dominance has not diminished in Soviet eyes since the demise of Hitlerite Germany. As in 1941 numerical superiority is seen as a necessary counterpoise to presumed technological advantage, although the reluctance of the western democracies to commit expenditure to defence consolidation, research, and development may stimulate Soviet confidence in technical parity and moderate this policy within at least the next decade.

When 'Operation Barbarossa' was unleashed, the Red Air Force had 6,850 tactical combat aircraft in thirty-five air divisions deployed in the western frontier military districts, backed up by four heavy and long-range bomber corps, the naval air forces of the Black Sea and Baltic Fleets, the fledgling Air Defence (PVO) fighter divisions and contingency reserves in the interior military districts – a mighty array which served initially to intoxicate the *Luftwaffe* in its role as Bolshevik giant-killer. The Red Air Force in the Far East was established in the 1930s in response to Japanese expansionist ambitions, and its consolidation continued from 1943 when units transferred to the western campaign zone were replaced and replenished with the fruits of the resurgent boom in Soviet aircraft production assisted by generous deliveries of combat aircraft from the Allies. When the Soviet Union eventually went to war with Japan in August 1945, the three tactical air armies in the Far East contained over 3,500 aircraft backed by PVO fighters and the 1,500 aircraft of the Pacific Fleet Air Force. Yet this concentration was achieved without any substantial transfers from the tactical air armies in the west, which then contained in the order of 16,000 aircraft, and without calling on the two reserve air armies held in the interior which were never committed to battle.

It is not difficult to understand the *Luftwaffe*'s dawning dismay and eventual despair when faced with the seemingly inexhaustible funds of combat aircraft which the Red Air Force was able to hurl against it. For despite the devastation of 22 June 1941, the *Luftwaffe* was able to enjoy sheer numerical superiority only briefly during 1942. In the spring of 1943 the *Luftwaffe* had lost this advantage irrevocably and by the eve of the fateful Battle of Kursk the Red Air Force was able to field 8,300 combat aircraft and to build up massive air concentrations once more.

More significant in the present age is the increasing offensive capability of the large tactical air forces maintained by the USSR. Deployment vulnerability and tactical 'on-call' capability have been improved with the introduction of the variable-geometry Su-17 (Fitter-C) and MiG-23/27 (Flogger) fighter-bombers, the emphasis on maintaining air superiority over the battle zone confirmed by the wide-scale introduction of the MiG-25 (Foxbat), multi-role developments evolved from the MiG-25 (Foxbat) and, more widely, from the MiG-23 (Flogger), and a new low-level high-speed ground-attack penetration ability gained with the service introduction of the two-seat variable-geometry Su-19 (Fencer) from 1974. All this has been developed in parallel with close attention to improved range, armament load, avionics and ECM and ECCM facilities.

The widening period separating the present-day Soviet Air Forces from the Red Air Force of 1941–5 should not be allowed to persuade us that the Soviets feel they now have nothing to learn from combat experience gained over three decades ago. On the contrary, as emphasised by frequent references in Colonel Timokhovich's recent treatise on the relevance of the air war against the Third Reich to the nuclear situation today, the attention of Soviet air force officers at schools, colleges, and academies is consistently directed towards an analysis of the successes and failures of Soviet wartime air operations.

> The radical changes which have taken place in aviation technology and in the means of waging war since 1945 have facilitated a new qualitative leap-forward in the development of the operational art of the Soviet Air Forces. We have gained more than a little of our knowledge from the experience of the Great

Patriotic War. The lessons and conclusions drawn from the experiences of Soviet air operations in that period, a careful analysis of our failings in the first days of the conflict and the errors overlooked in the pre-war preparations of our air forces can serve to strengthen the Soviet Air Forces of today and enable us to improve their combat readiness and capabilities.

Taken as whole, the wartime experiences of the Soviet Air Forces allow us to become more deeply acquainted with the contemporary problems of their operational art and to approach them on a more informed basis.[5]

To summarise broadly, the Red Air Force in the latter half of the Great Patriotic War was successful in the massing of air power for frontal air superiority, for the development of robust close-support aircraft and unflagging attention to their optimum battlefield effectiveness and in working conscientiously on effective air-ground liaison with immediate battlefield air surveillance exercised via advanced air control posts informed by air liaison officers attached to ground force headquarters. To offset these developments, there remained largely unremedied weaknesses in air defence with poor early-warning and frequently tardy reaction to manifestly large-scale enemy air attack. There were failings in planning and contingency awareness, often as a result of untutored reconnaissance or the inexpert processing of its results to provide the latest information on the state of mobile battle. Most persistently and frustratingly, the Red Air Force was unable to carry out operations in depth behind the enemy front during almost the entire course of the war except by using relatively small groups of bombers operating by night – most widely against railway communications or in preparation for ground offensives. While Soviet nocturnal air activity over the front remained at a high level from late 1942 onwards, it took the form of nuisance raids over the enemy lines by light or obsolete machines which equipped the night-bomber regiments of the frontal air armies. Even in 1944–5 when the Red Air Force had gained a considerable degree of air superiority over the front by day, the frontal air armies still maintained an average strength of a thousand light night-bombers between them.[6]

The seventies have certainly witnessed a new determination to achieve night and all-weather offensive penetration in depth with the introduction of the Su-19 (Fencer) strike aircraft into tactical air service and the acquisition by Colonel-General Reshetnikov's

Long-Range Aviation of the controversial Tu-(26?) (Backfire) variable-geometry bomber. Both machines give the Soviet air forces a deeper and more flexible offensive strike capability than ever before. Quite apart from the implications of its strategic threat to the American mainland, Backfire will remain a potent threat to western Europe, given that a rapid seizure of that area in the event of war would be greatly facilitated by strikes in depth to neutralise NATO airfields, communications, and command centres, and by the denial of bases for airlift reinforcements from the USA.

In addition to their deep-penetration strike responsibility against enemy land and sea targets, the aircraft of Long-Range Aviation and the Naval Air Forces, which have traditionally enjoyed a high degree of commonality in the long-range and strike aircraft which they operate, have been obliged to develop a more sophisticated capability for electronic reconnaissance and target acquisition. Clearly, this is a role of value to General Tolubko's Strategic Rocket Forces as well as to the Soviet army and navy. Tactical reconnaissance types have not been neglected and now include the MiG-25R (Foxbat-B) to augment the earlier MiG-21R (Fishbed-H) and Yak-28 (Brewer-D) machines; specially evolved ECM variants of the Yak-28 (Brewer-E) and the An-12 (Cub-C) are also in service.

Target acquisition and destruction at an early stage of hostilities before the deployment and dispersal of nuclear weapon launching vehicles have been effected is clearly an advantage, and it is in this context that Sidorenko has commented that, 'an important quality of aviation is its capability to discover independently and immediately destroy the enemy's means of nuclear attack'.[7] Such search and attack autonomy – an innovation in the mass-regimented tactics of the Red Air Force – was introduced by Chief Air Marshal Novikov, Commander-in-Chief of the Red Air Force between 1942 and 1946, with the development of 'free hunt' (*svobodnaya okhota*) units to engage targets of opportunity. On the whole, emphasis then was placed on road and rail transport, but a contemporary extension to take in nuclear delivery weapon sites and vehicles is a logical up-dating of Novikov's wartime concept. Once enemy nuclear weapon deployment has been effected, then collection, collation, and analysis of target data will be of paramount importance. Fixing, timings, and modes of strike will need to be calculated swiftly and surely – a factor stressed by General Shtemenko in his survey of the new challenges implicit in highly mobile tactical nuclear warfare.[8]

Whereas doubts still remain as to the place of Long-Range Aviation in the overall inter-continental strategic doctrines of the Soviet military, the significance of the youngest element of Kutakhov's VVS, the Military Transport Command (VTA) under Lieutenant-General Pakilev, has been more clearly defined and its capabilities developed with energy and purpose.

The development of airborne and paratroop forces was undertaken by the Soviet Union from the early 1930s but affected by politico-military conflicts and their effective consolidation retarded. A sudden determined expansion on the eve of the Great Patriotic War proved too late to guarantee the effectiveness of the Paratroop Forces (VDV) in operations. Lack of training, experience, proper equipment, transport aircraft, inept reconnaissance, and poor strategic co-ordination combined with inadequate air cover to undermine and largely frustrate combat success, except apparently during the brief campaign against the Japanese forces in 1945.[9] In the immediate postwar years, while training and exercises continued, the persistent lack of suitable transport aircraft enforced reliance on the twin-engined Li-2 and Il-14 machines towing gliders and promoted a low assessment of Soviet airborne capability by the West.

The introduction of the four turboprop An-12 and An-22 transports – and more recently the four turbojet Il-76 (Candid) – able to convey vehicles, tanks and tracked rocket launchers, has given the VTA an important role in any nuclear campaign. Lomov has commented on the value of 'the use of airborne forces in developing the success of nuclear strikes against supporting or reserve enemy echelons – these missions being carried out simultaneously with the defeat of the first enemy operational echelon', and Sidorenko similarly on, 'the use of airborne troops to exploit rapidly the results of nuclear strikes by landing in the depth of the enemy positions'. Savkin has stressed that, 'there is no doubt that the use of airborne landings for purposes of consolidating the results of the employment of nuclear weapons is one of the main ways to increase rates of advance'.[10] Other tasks possibly allocated to the VDV could include the seizure of enemy nuclear weapon launching sites and stores and the crossing of contaminated zones temporarily obstructing the wholescale passage of ground forces. The VTA has an advantage in that its aircraft can be almost entirely equipment rather than troop-carrying aircraft as *Aeroflot* itself represents an immense auxiliary fleet of potential troop-carriers, and one soon to be joined by the new 350-seat wide-body Il-86 transport which first flew in prototype form in December 1976.

Heightened importance has also been given to the development of combat helicopters, not merely for the delivery of troops to assembly areas in the vicinity of the front but also to ensure battlefield domination. In the latter role successive developments of the Mi-24 (Hind) armed assault helicopter first noted in service with GSFG in 1974 have evolved the basic design into a formidable gunship armed with a four-barrel Gatling-type machine-gun under the nose and anti-tank missiles carried on four wingtip launchers. Soviet military writers have indicated that this kind of machine 'may turn out to be the means of fundamental change in the nature of ground combat'[11] operating in roles which are not merely battlefield cover or assault-landing but which include new concepts in air-armour tactical co-operation and possibly combined units.

This brief survey of new equipment and applications would be incomplete without at least some reference to the role of the Air Force Command (*Glavnyi shtab VVS*) itself. In this context, Colonel Timokhovich's definition of the wartime association between the Armed Forces' High Command and the Air Force Command is succinct and illuminating:

> The *Stavka* of the Supreme Command defined the general tasks of the air forces in their relationship to the developing situation, the aims of campaigns and strategic operations; it allocated air forces to strategic sectors, organised air force co-operation with other arms, implemented measures to equip the air forces and develop their structural organisation and the forms and methods of its control and took decisions regarding the planning of independent air operations. The immediate executive organs of the *Stavka*'s orders and directives in all these matters were the General Staff and the Red Army Air Force Staff. The Commander-in-Chief of the Red Air Force and his Staff, as the organs of air force strategic control, organised co-operation between the groups and formations of frontal and long-range air forces, evaluated combat experience and disseminated this to air units, groups and formations, worked out principles for the use of air forces over the battlefield, directed questions of operational training, material and other aspects of facilitating combat operations, planned and directly organised independent air operations, and directed the

training of cadres, the formation of air reserves and replacements for machines and aircrew after operational losses.[12]

There is little cause to doubt that the essential framework of this wartime relationship has been preserved to provide a structure for the strategic direction of Soviet air power today. Novikov, with his Deputy C-in-Cs Falaleev and Vorozheikin and his Chief of Air Staff, Khudyakov, spear-headed the executive planning of major air operations with the assistance of other members of the Red Air Force Staff in accordance with the overall strategic objective as laid down by Stalin's *Stavka*. Today Kutakhov is backed up by a team whose operational experience, while necessarily dated, was closely in touch with the actualities of air combat. His First Deputy C-in-C, Marshal Efimov, was twice decorated as a Hero of the Soviet Union flying *shturmoviks* with Vershinin's 4th Air Army, and his Chief of Air Staff, Marshal Silant'ev, won his Hero of the Soviet Union while flying with the 160th Fighter Regiment in December 1941. Ultimately, it is on these men as much as on the manpower and technology of the Soviet Air Forces that Kutakhov must rely for his new air force to play its new decisive, hard-hitting role planned for it as the seventies progress.

SUMMARY OF DISCUSSION

Dr Boyd's central thesis of the close relationship between the experiences of Great Patriotic War and the doctrines of the contemporary Soviet air force was queried by a number of speakers. It was argued that very few people with experience of that war remained in the Soviet air force, and that the nature of new aviation technologies exercised a much greater influence upon contemporary Soviet leaders than historical experience. The Soviet air force had become obsessed with US (and UK) nuclear bomber threats after 1945, and concentrated its energies and equipment upon the air defence role. It was only in the late 1960s with the relative diminution of the bomber threat that increased resources were allocated to the role of support or the ground forces, thus creating the illusion of an historical continuum.

The apparent contradiction between the Soviet belief and investment in air defence, and their new emphasis on aircraft with the range to reach western static air defences was also raised. It was suggested that this might lead the Soviet air force to have a low opinion of its capability of penetrating these western defences. This was a new role for them, and it was uncertain whether they were capable of training their personnel in the equipment necessary to carry out successfully such long range, low-level penetration missions.

NOTES AND REFERENCES

1. A new Soviet interceptor with a 'look-down' radar has been reported, though it remains to be seen what role it will be assigned in view of plans to cancel the series production of the US B-1 bomber. (See *International Herald Tribune*, 29 June 1977.)
2. This formation is *16th Air Army* presently commanded by Colonel-General (Air) A. Babayev: it should also be noticed that alone of all non-Soviet Warsaw Pact forces the East German air force (LSK: *Luftstreitkräfte und Luftverteidigung*) has subordinated its aircraft to the joint supreme command controlled by the Soviet Union, thus adding some 280 MIG-21MF/Fls, 80 Su-7s, and 35 MiG-17s to Soviet strength. the LS also comprises two air-defence divisions (Northern and Southern).
3. Lomov, N. A. (Colonel-General), *The Revolution in Military Affairs* (USAF translation of *Nauchno-tekhnicheskii progress i revolyutsiya v voennom dele*, Moscow, Voenizdat, 1973), here p. 150.
4. For a recent and comprehensive order of battle analysis see Colin Gray, 'Soviet Tactical Airpower', *Air Force Magazine*, 'Third Annual Soviet Aerospace Almanac' edition, March 1977, pp. 62–71 (table of Soviet tactical air armies, p. 63).
5. Timokhovich, I. V. (Colonel), *Operativnoe iskusstvo Sovetskikh VVS v Velikoi Otechestvennoi voine*, (Moscow, Voenizdat, 1976) p. 341.
6. On Soviet air armies, see under '*Vozdushnye armii*' – from 1st to 17th Air Army – in *Sovetskaya Voennaya Entsiklopediya* (Moscow, Voenizdat, 1976), (Vol. 2), pp. 291–8. See also P. Kutakhov (Air Chief Marshal), 'Voenno-Vozdushnye Sily v zavershayushchem periode voiny', *Voenno-istoricheskii Zhurnal*, 1975, No. 4, pp. 27–34; and E. Simakov (Colonel), 'Boevoi i chislennyi sostav VVS v tret'em periode voiny', *Voenno-istoricheskii Zhurnal*, 1975, No.7, pp. 74–7 (see tables).
7. See A. A. Sidorenko (Colonel), *Nastuplenie*, (Moscow, Voenizdat, 1970), (also USAF translation, *The Offensive*, Washington, D. C.), here p. 136 (translation) on aviation tactics.
8. S. M. Shtemenko (Army General), in his foreword to *Ideya, Algoritm, Reshenie* (Moscow, Voenizdat, 1972), (USAF Translation, *Concept, Algorithm, Decision*, Washington, D. C.)
9. See for example, A. Novikov (Air Chief Marshal), 'Voenno-vozdushnye sily v Man'chzhurskoi operatsii', *Voenno-istoricheskii Zhurnal*, 1975, No.8, pp. 66–71; see also under '*Vozdushno-desantnye voiska*', *Sov. Voen. Entsiklopediya, op. cit.*, Vol. 2, pp. 286–9.
10. Savkin, V. E. (Colonel), *The Basic Principles of Operational Art and Tactics* ('Soviet Military Thought series, Washington, D.C. n.d.). USAF translation of *Osnovnye printsipy operativnogo iskusstva i taktiki* (Moscow, Voenizdat, 1972)
11. *Ibid.*, p. 184.
12. I. V. Timokhovich, *op. cit.*, p. 266.

Part III
The Men

6 The Soviet Soldier: Behaviour, Performance, Effectiveness

Chris Donnelly

Today every Soviet commander has the term 'effectiveness' – *effektivnost'* – on his lips, understandable enough in a military establishment which has not seen active, full-scale operational service since 1945. We have already investigated some of the properties of the Soviet system at large and Soviet misgivings about overall 'effectiveness', or performance: it is extremely difficult to find an exact translation for *'effektivnost'*, which suggests in turn efficiency, effectiveness, and performance in the round. But what of the Soviet soldier himself? Here effectiveness and performance assume a critical aspect and it should be said at once that it is impossible to evaluate performance in these terms – the individual Soviet soldier – without some consideration from the outset of those features of Russian and Soviet society which have acted to shape the Soviet citizen as he is today and in the process conditioned his attitude to military service. The most important aspect in this context is undoubtedly the attitude of Soviet man to authority at large, an attitude shaped by centuries of demanding and singular historical experience.

Since the Mongol invasion and conquest of the thirteenth century, the inhabitants of what became the Russian Empire and is now the USSR have lived under an autocratic form of government. Indeed it has often been stated, but is none the less true, that because of the difficulties occasioned by her great size, lack of defensible frontiers, sparse population, diverse nationalities, and severe climate, Russia could not have survived as a country except under a centralised autocracy of some kind. In the main, the

Russian people have accepted, and still accept, dictatorship without too much complaint because it has been an effective form of government in dealing with those problems which the people themselves have considered important.

A citizen of the USSR today accepts autocratic interest, interference, and direction in all spheres of life and throughout every stage of his development. The system functions in much the same way as any army – an overall authority, in this case the CPSU (Communist Party of the Soviet Union), exercises a parental discipline, demanding strict obedience to its dictates and chastising those who do not conform exactly to the plan which it has prepared for every individual. On the other hand it provides quite well for those who do conform and relieves them of the onerous burden of making decisions for themselves. Every school and college throughout the country inculcates a uniform, traditional discipline in each of its pupils; the whole of industry and agriculture is run according to a disciplined plan; and the military parallel is accentuated because the authorities even employ military jargon to exhort the people to work harder, for example, they 'storm' difficult labour tasks, and award medals to 'Heroes' of Socialist Labour.

This overall disciplined upbringing goes some way towards counteracting the basic Russian characteristics of laziness, procrastination, and natural lack of discipline, and utilises to the full the Russian's propensity for working for short periods at an extremely intensive pace, and then relapsing into an equal or greater period of inactivity. This attitude is one which any military training programme must reckon with, and in no small measure it dictates the style which the Russians bring to the running of their army.

Another feature of the Soviet system which grooms the civilian for military service is that a Soviet citizen from his earliest days is subject to considerable social pressure, backed by propaganda, deliberately designed to have a militarising influence on him. It would be no exaggeration to say that the whole of Soviet society today is maintained in a state of permanent semi-mobilisation, reminiscent of a country actually at war. In addition to a disciplined and centrally controlled economy, civil defence, military skills, and physical fitness are taught to the entire population through the medium of mass organisations. The overt military relevance of this is underlined in the propaganda campaign constantly being waged glamourising the Red Army's military exploits. Wherever one goes in the USSR, one's attention is invariably drawn to massive memorials of the 1941–5 war and the victory over Fascist Germany. Everywhere the armed forces are in evidence and everywhere they receive official praise and glory. This military omnipresence takes a practical form in that serving military personnel hold important posts on all influential governmental bodies, right down to local levels, and in all state industries the military branch has undisputed priority.

It would be wrong to think of this state of affairs as a Bolshevik innovation, borne in on the tide of the October Revolution of 1917. The predominance of state interests over the civilian was always a feature of Imperial Russia, both in industry and in public services. If differences exist between Imperial Russia and the USSR, they are of detail and degree rather than of principle and in the modern Soviet state there is the added impetus of a planned economy, to increase centralised authority, and Communist ideology, to strengthen the traditional Russian national pride, the traditional sense of moral superiority over the west, and the traditional fear of foreign hostility and the determination to be prepared to resist it.[1]

The young Soviet citizen is well accustomed, therefore, to the idea of military service; but he is in many cases also well *trained* for it before he actually becomes eligible for conscription. From the age of nine, his membership of the Pioneers, and later the Komsomol (the Communist Party's youth organisations), will have involved him in visits to Army Units as a high point of summer camps. At school, all physical training is done under a programme entitled 'Be ready for labour and defence', when physical training activities are directly linked to military skills.[2]

In addition, since the reduction in the length of national service by one year in 1968, all young men between the ages of 14 and 18, whether at school or at work, have been obliged by law to undergo 140 hours of basic military training to prepare themselves for military service.

The ideal of a nation in arms has always been dear to the communist heart, and military training as part of the school curriculum was an accepted feature of Soviet life in the 1920s and 1930s. Following the reduction in size of the ground forces in 1960, the percentage of those eligible men who were actually called up for national service declined steadily as the youth population outstripped the army's need for conscripts. Though this was never truly a problem, it was not ideal that the burden of defending the homeland should fall on only 40 per cent of the population. Furthermore, it left over half of the male population without effective military training and therefore with no mobilisation potential. In view of the possibility, however remote, of a war with China, this, too, was less than ideal. Finally, the system of taking men at the age of 19 or over for three or four years, as was the case before 1968, was not beneficial to their careers and therefore bad for the national economy. Consequently a new law, which came into effect in 1968, made provision for a two-year conscription period in the ground forces, air forces, KGB and Border Guards and MD, and three years in the ocean-going navy, marine infantry and KGB coastguard, as well as 140 hours compulsory military training before conscription.

While many senior officers, to judge by articles in the military press, were rightly concerned that the change in the system would result, at least temporarily, in a fall in combat effectiveness, the author has found little evidence to support the theory that the military as a group was opposed to the new law. For in addition to strategic, economic, and social benefits, the new system promised a reduction in the demands on the military budget (as the cost of pre-service training was to be borne by the institution providing it) and would mean that conscripts, arriving at a unit twice-yearly instead of once a year and already having basic training, would enable the unit to maintain a higher state of combat readiness.

In practice, however, the upheaval caused in the military training system was enormous, and it has taken many years to resolve the problems. Most of the difficulties appear to have been caused by the usual Soviet practice of trying to get a quart out of a pint pot. School, factories, and farms, already working to tightly stretched budgets or struggling to achieve norms, were unwilling to allot sufficient of their funds or personnel to do the pre-conscription training properly. Military units, responsible as they were, and still are, for conducting all basic and special-to-arms training, were not geared to coping with training in the reduced time available. Moreover, the greater complexity of new equipment arriving in increasing quantities in units demanded more effective training than before. Whereas with the longer period of service enough time has been available to train conscript NCOs to help run the sub-units, the new system meant that no sooner was a conscript NCO-trained than it was time for him to leave. Thus an even greater training burden fell on regular NCOs and junior officers and made their careers less attractive just at a period when the civilian economy and standard of living was beginning to show a marked increase. This had undoubtedly contributed to the fall in the popularity of the army as a career choice during the 1960s and the new law did little to help matters.

Since 1971 co-ordination and supervision of pre-conscription training has been the responsibility of regional military commissariats. To improve the effectiveness of pre-conscription training, the Komsomol were charged with helping school, farm, and factory authorities to provide facilities for training and the DOSAAF organisation was given increased responsibility for assisting with the actual training programmes.

DOSAAF (The Voluntary Organisation for Co-operation with the Army, Air Force and Navy) is the latest in a long line of voluntary organisations that seek to provide expert training for those interested in pursuing sports which have a military value.[3] This type of organisation has always been of great value to the Soviet military system because not only does it give young people valuable military training such as parachuting and shooting, but, as recruitment is on a voluntary basis, it also seems to identify the enthusiastic amongst young people and encourages their enthusiasm, making personnel selection for various arms of service on conscription easier. By involving DOSAAF in pre-conscription training on a larger scale, the Soviet authorities have made logical use of an existing and effective youth training organisation. The size and influence of DOSAAF has increased greatly as a result of this extension of its reponsibility. It now offers a greater number of training courses for early school leavers in military technical skills such as electronics, flying, and HGV driving. This is in addition to any pre-service training the man might receive. DOSAAF personnel have been responsible for developing new military sports such as 'hunting the fox' (*lysolov*) an orienteering-cum-direction finding exercise using portable transmitters and receivers; and for introducing and popularising intensive and specialised physical training apparatus, such as the *loping*, a kind of revolving swing now used for training parachutists.

It is now over nine years since the introduction of the pre-conscription programme. In its initial stages, it had great difficulty in meeting the demands put upon it, and for the first five years it is probably no exaggeration to say that well over half of those conscripted had not received effective pre-conscription basic training. This would appear to be no longer the case. Whilst there are still complaints that some conscripts have not had sufficient pre-conscription training, particularly in country areas, this is getting rapidly rarer and is clearly now the exception rather than the rule.

The pre-conscription training system, therefore, would appear to be close to fulfilling what was demanded of it in terms of giving basic military training to young people. It is however, probably a greater overall gain to the system that, under this impetus, the last nine years have seen a striking increase in the militarisation of youth generally. Before 1968, only two-fifths of young men did military service; the DOSAAF sports programme was much more restricted; and the Pioneers and Komsomol had only slight military involvement, and (in the author's own experience) reserve officer training and civil defence training at universities were not treated over-seriously by a great many students.

Today, however, the percentage of young men conscripted is well over two-thirds, and most of those not conscripted will have done pre-conscription training and possibly an ROTC course as well. The Pioneers and Komsomol have much more military involvement. Military training is given in all schools as part of the normal curriculum, and there has been a substantial increase in the scale of DOSAAF work. By 1972/3 the recruitment figures to military colleges had improved, probably as a result of the valuable recruiting agencies that military organisations in schools turned out to be. Thus in an age of the increasing sophistication, awareness and adventurousness of youth, the CPSU has effected, through these military and para-military agencies, a great increase in the level of militarisation amongst young people, and has consequently maintained in some measure their suitability for military service, in marked contrast to the tendency in western countries for young people to become increasingly anti-military.

The effectiveness or otherwise of a conscript's pre-service training, rather than any civilian skill, seems to be the main criterion on which he is selected for choice of arm (DOSAAF specialist training is, of course, also taken into account here). There undoubtedly exists some system of priorities of posting based on degrees of élitism between different arms of services and different units;[4] this subject will be touched on later.

Deferment from conscription can be obtained on grounds of health, hardship (for example, where the conscript is working to support infirm parents), and continuation of education. Nationalist sentiment or a religious belief, which might be thought a danger to security, would not exempt a man from conscription, but would dictate where he served. For example, such a person would be unlikely to be posted to the KGB border troops which offered the possibility of defection; an ethnic German would be unlikely to be sent to GSFG, etc. The construction troops, working as they do unarmed on heavy-labour projects such as the BAM, are an ideal place to send people of dubious reliability.

Studying at a college of higher education would seem to be no longer the safe way of avoiding conscription. One of the justifications given for the shorter national service period was that the increased standard of education made training in a shorter time possible. The converse is certainly true, that the shorter time available for training means that, for the increasing number of technical jobs to be filled in the army, a higher standard of education is necessary. The wider conscription base that followed as a result of the 1968 law has come to include more well-educated personnel, and the recent changes in the law have been specifically designed to enable the armed services to draw on the better educated.[5] Male university students who obtain deferment from national service are obliged to do a part-time officer training course at university, and are commissioned as junior lieutenants into the reserve. On leaving university, students are posted to their first job: usually only those doing exceptionally well are allowed to choose their posting. In the author's experience, in the late 1960s very few students felt that there was any danger of being posted to the military for one to three years 'short service'.

It would appear however that the shortage of well qualified officers during the early 1970s has caused the authorities to draw on the university graduate more and more, and probably as many as 10 per cent of young officers are now serving under this scheme.

The processing of conscripts and the recruitment of officer candidates is the responsibility of the Military Commissariat system, which has offices in every major town to serve the surrounding region. All army units are, in practice, training units, and each will replace 25 per cent of its conscripts every six months. A unit will thus be able to plan at least a year in advance how many conscripts it will need, and with what preferred pre-conscription training specialities.

The regimental, or perhaps the divisional, requirements will probably be passed on, either via the Ministry of Defence or directly, to one or more Military Districts. The District Commissariat is responsible for fulfilling the quota and distributing the best-trained and most promising conscripts as well as it can. If this is an accurate assessment of how the system works, then it would provide a structure for maintaining élitism (that is, in effect, a quality differential between various arms and units).

Though bureaucracy, and especially Soviet bureaucracy, is notoriously inefficient, and there is often complaint that commissariats make a poor and wasteful distribution of special skills, this does not invalidate this argument.[6] For example, if a regiment or division in, let us say, the Group of Soviet Forces in Germany is instructed to submit its bids for its conscript requirements to the Transbaikal Military District, that unit or formation is bound to have a higher percentage of non-Slavs amongst its quota than a unit which bids to the Moscow Military District. Whilst a Tartar or Uzbek may be just as good a fighter as an ethnic Russian, the odds are that on linguistic grounds and grounds of educational opportunity he will be less valuable for technical tasks because of the extra time that would be needed to train him. The numbers of national groups found in Military Districts vary enormously. It may be, therefore, that bidding is co-ordinated at formation level and split between more than one Military District to ensure a more even distribution of national groups, for security reasons allowing no preponderance of any one non-Russian nationality in any sub-unit.[7] The redistribution of populations in the USSR does mean that a representative sweep of virtually any Military District will produce more Slavs than any other single national group, but the proportions differ. A perusal of illustrations of exercises in the Soviet military press will demonstrate that the proportion of Asiatic faces varies in different units, and, though this is clearly a shaky basis for conclusions, it does seem to be highest in rear service and construction units and some Motor Rifle units.

The worker/peasant distribution in the armed forces also bears on this problem. It is now fully appreciated in the West that the Soviet army is not a peasant army, and has not been so since even before the war. The power base of the Communist Party has always been the urban proletariat, and it was from the major Russian cities that the core of the Red Guard and later of the Red Army was drawn. 'Guards' is a title of honour given to a unit or formation for exceptional performance in the last war, and it is significant that most of the units so honoured appear to have been raised in the urban areas of the Russian heartland.

Today, when only 38 per cent of the entire population works in agriculture, an evenly distributed conscription programme would mean that more than three out of five conscripts come from towns. Further factors however complicate the issue. First, the average age of a town dweller is considerably lower than a country dweller; therefore, though the chief cause of this age difference is a deficiency in the middle age bracket, particularly in men due amongst other things to wartime losses, there is still a smaller proportion of young men who fall into the conscript age bracket amongst agricultural workers than amongst town dwellers. (According to the 1971 census 10 per cent of the urban population fell into the 15–19 age group, but less than 8 per cent of the rural population did so. This means that between 1971–4, less than one-third of young men reaching conscription age level lived in the countryside.) Secondly, the lower standards of education in the countryside mean that the peasant conscript is less attractive to the more technically orientated arms, and the lower standard of pre-service training available in the countryside likewise makes for certain problems. Consequently, the burden of conscription might naturally, and without a deliberate policy decision, fall less heavily on the agricultural population. To strengthen this tendency, agricultural authorities are concerned about the drift of young people, particularly the better-educated, away from the farms.[8] Extended service in the army has always been one way for a collective-farm peasant to obtain a passport, a valuable skill, and the chance to obtain work in a town (and hence to achieve a higher standard of living). The attention that has been given in the press to this problem of loss of talent from the farms is bound to have exerted pressure on the commissariats to consider more favourably applications for deferment which come from agricultural workers.

Though in the absence of accurate statistical data it is very difficult to be precise, it is probably a reasonable deduction to say that the percentage of conscripts with peasant background is somewhere around 25 per cent. Statistics relating to young officers which are available seem to bear this out. In a survey of newly commissioned lieutenants, published as long ago as 1969,[9] it was shown that only 15 per cent came of families engaged in agriculture and, of these, less than a third (4.6 per cent) had actually worked on a farm, whereas of the remaining 85 per cent who were children of factory workers or white collar workers 27 per cent had actually held factory jobs. Thirty-five per cent of all those questioned had come straight from schools or colleges, and 20 per cent had transferred from national service. Of this 55 per cent, if the overall statistical proportion of farm workers to town dwellers were maintained in the officer corps, we should expect fully a third to be drawn from the countryside. In fact, the figure is less than one-fifth.

Though it would be misleading to transpose this percentage to conscripts without amendment, especially in view of the increasing importance of sophistication and etiquette as qualities desirable in officers, qualities for which farm workers have never been renowned even in the USSR, it does demonstrate the effect of the lower educational standard in the countryside on military recruitment. As nowadays the trend is to increase the intake of well-educated conscripts (this is evinced by the amendments to the law, see note 5 above), it is yet a further indication that the percentage of countrymen in the armed forces as a whole is likely to be disproportionately low.

There would appear, therefore, to be quite a considerable basis for differentiation in the conscript composition of various army units. A little imagination will allow us to link this to what we know of unit élitism, and therefore unit potential effectiveness and performance. In élite terms, the Rocket Troops (Strategic and Air Defence) and the Airborne Forces top the league. Both require a high degree of security and reliability which would indicate a good standard of political training and a reduced non-Slav element. The Rocket Troops require full pre-conscription training, the Airborne Forces take predominantly volunteers, preferably with DOSAAF special training. All are factors which will in practice reduce the percentage of non-urban conscripts in those arms. Artillery and engineer units, though they require a large number of technically qualified officers and well trained technically-minded men, also need no small numbers of conscripts with brawn rather than brain, due to the nature of their combat tasks. Consequently one could except a balance of town and country conscripts in these arms.

Of the basic combat arms, i.e. Tank and Motor Rifle Troops, Tank forces undoubtedly have the greater prestige; and, as a much higher percentage of personnel in these units is engaged in technical tasks, they will clearly have a greater need for the better educated and well trained conscript than will Motor Rifle units. In the case of

'Guards' units, although they are clearly taught to think of themselves as a cut above the rest, it is difficult to establish whether or not they are still genuinely élite (and whether they are still recruited with an urban bias). The author feels that this probably still *is* the case but he is unable to substantiate his feeling except in the case of certain specific formations such as the Taman Guards Motor Rifle Division of the Moscow Military District, which is clearly one of the Soviet Army's model divisions.

If certain arms get a higher proportion of the better conscript than at the other end of the scale, someone must be missing out, and it seems most likely that line Motor Rifle units, particularly those without 'Guards' titles and stationed in less important areas of the Soviet dominions, will have a disproportionately large percentage of the less well educated, the peasant and the non-Slav.

To judge by articles in the military press (see note 4 above) it is the rear services and construction troops, however, who get the least promising material in educational terms. Because of the lack of glamour of these units, this may be true in terms of officers as well. Yet the rear services will have a particularly taxing job in any future war; and however much equipment is provided for their use, if the human material is unable to cope with it and cannot deliver the fuel and arms on time, it will nullify the efficiency of the most élite combat units. This has been a constant theme in rear service magazines for several years now. Though it is clear that the rear services are being given increasing quantities of modern equipment, this has, if anything, increased the demand for more capable handlers.

In contrast to the above, a study of physical fitness requirements shows that the various arms are interested in it in the following order:[10]

(1) Airborne forces
(2) All artillery (including mortar and rocket) troops; marine infantry
(3) All ground forces units (except those listed elsewhere); all civil defence units
(4) Tank, transport and engineer units
(5) Air defence missile troops
(6) Strategic missile troops
(7) Ships' crews
(8) Air defence radar troops; technical troops

The airborne forces' requirement is twice as high as any other arm.

The military commissariats have the unenviable task of reconciling these often conflicting demands and getting the right conscript to the right unit. Improvement in conscript processing will undoubtedly be a great help in reducing unit training loads and consequently increasing performance. The regular exhortations to this end which appear in the press constitute one more example of the Soviet authorities' constant attempts to 'tune up' the system and eliminate wastage, in this case of personal skills.

With the reduction of training time from three to two years in 1968, the system of promoting national servicemen to junior NCO ranks in their last year became unsatisfactory. Consequently, a system has developed whereby military commissariats select personnel of above average ability and training and dispatch these direct to training units. Here they do a six-month special-to-arm course before going to a field unit as a junior NCO, where they serve their remaining 18 months as section commander or equivalent, in some cases rising to platoon sergeant. This is yet one more demand for the commissariat to reconcile.

The tendency in the last few years has been for more and more platoons, at any rate in combat arms, to be commanded by ensigns (*praporshchiki*). This Imperial Army rank was revived in 1972 to identify a new class of serviceman; a well-trained, well-qualified senior NCO, the ensign will play much the same role in the armed forces as a British staff sergeant or 'warrant officer' (which latter term is often used to translate '*praporshchik*'). The lack of such a person in the Soviet system was made particularly noticeable by the general shortage of young officers and the sudden difficulties of the conscript NCO system that followed the introduction of two-year service. Extended NCO service had always tended to attract soldiers with a poorer educational background, particularly from the country; i.e. those to whom the army offered a better standard of living than they could expect in a return to civilian life. With the increasing complexity of military equipment and tactics, and the increasing level of conscript education and sophistication, such an NCO was not really capable of shouldering his full share of the training burden, which, as a consequence, fell ever more heavily on the shoulders of the already overworked young officer.

Initially the intention seems to have been to upgrade all regular NCOs to ensigns, but this has not been possible. Consequently ensign rank is now established as an intermediate grade between extended-service NCO and officer, carrying considerable prestige and the chance of eventually attaining a limited commission. It is open to sufficiently qualified extended-service NCOs or conscripts on completion of their conscript service. The ensign rank was designed to attract technical specialists or those above average in command ability and intelligence. It also offers the retired NCO with appropriate qualifications the opportunity to re-enlist. Ensigns now hold a great many technical and organisational posts previously held by overqualified officers, and they are increasingly coming to relieve the company officer of much of the routine training. From the Soviet army's point of view, therefore, while there have been certain institutional problems connected with the introduction of a new rank, the innovation must on the whole be considered a success. This timely move has gone some way towards reducing pressure on the sub-unit officer, a man who is, in many ways, the linchpin of the Soviet command and control system.

Let us now turn to the Soviet officer and look at one or two less obvious developments which are likely to have an effect on his performance. Since the 1930s, the Soviet army has been gradually returning to the ceremonies and traditions of the Imperial Russian Army (though without actually acknowledging the fact openly). One of the most striking examples of this has been the growth of the hereditary tradition in officer service. The commendable tradition of 'military families' is often mentioned in the press. The ten Suvorov academies founded to train military orphans during the war, and which now predominantly cater for the sons of serving officers, are known to be one of the best springboards for a military career.

This hereditary professional trend is not unique to the armed forces in the USSR: the children of CP members tend to become members also; the sons of diplomats become diplomats in their turn. If this trend is allowed by the Party to develop further in the armed forces, and there is every sign that this will be so, then it will undoubtedly make for an increase in the stability of the armed forces and an increase in the morale and sense of committedness of the officer corps. Furthermore, if it is coupled to an increase in educational standards of officers generally, as seems to be happening, it cannot but help to increase military professionalism. We can, of course, expect to see a high level of Party activity in the officer corps to counteract any tendency on the part of the officer corps to develop an independent line of thought. It will be interesting to see if there develops a wider social gulf between the regular officer and the reservist, between the officer of an élite unit and the officer from a more humble arm of service.

The officer corps as a whole has, over the past few years, been subject to a campaign to get it to increase its professionalism in the interests of military effectiveness. The demands that modern warfare make on officers, particularly at the junior level, have increased in scope as well as in quantity. Overtasking is characteristic of the Soviet system as a whole, on the sound quartermaster's principle that if you ask for sufficient to give a comfortable safety margin, you might actually get just enough to do the job. However, if taken to extremes when making demands on personnel, this can be counterproductive.

In the case of the young officer, he receives an average three or four years' intensive training to equip him with all the knowledge necessary to take him up to battalion command or its equivalent. A battalion is a sub-unit in the Soviet system, usually a major's command. However, so rapid is the development of military service that by the time the officer attains this rank and appointment in, say, his early thirties, tactics and equipment have changed radically,[11] and much of his knowledge is out of date. So heavy are the demands on a sub-unit officer's time, responsible as he is for keeping his men up to a strict training schedule, that he has not been able to keep up to date. This has resulted, in extreme cases and particularly in technical services,[12] in newly supplied and highly efficient equipment not being fully utilised, because no one was able to instruct soldiers in its use.

Furthermore, such is the dynamism of modern war, very much more independent command responsibility is likely to fall on the sub-unit commander. Deep offensive operations into the depths of the enemy territory will require a greath breadth of knowledge on the part of, amongst others, the battalion commander who finds himself commanding not just 31 APCs in a straightforward attack but an additional tank company, artillery battery, sapper platoon, recce section, and logistic tail, all of which must be controlled and co-ordinated with great precision and speed, possibly in and NBC environment. There can be no doubt that exceptionally heavy demands will be made on officers in a future offensive war. To cope with the modern battlefield, an officer must not only be well-trained in his speciality, but most develop what the Soviets term *'shtabnaya kultura'* and *'initsiativ'*.

This 'culture' which the military authorities are trying hard to develop in the modern officer amounts to a broad, wide-ranging education, not just in military matters but in general matters too. His professional knowledge should not be limited to specialities but encompass an understanding of other arms and services. Only if this is so will he be capable of adapting to a rapidly changing battlefield. A thorough knowledge of what is going on around him and an ability to appreciate the overall battle picture will enable a sub-unit officer to make correct military decisions and act on them in *anticipation* of orders, when such orders have not actually got through because of the chaos of the battlefield. An officer in such a position, who anticipates correctly what the orders would have been had they got through, and carries out the 'orders' successfully and with a certain flair, is said to have acted with *'initsiativ'*, that is, the Soviet version of initiative.

It is hard for a western officer to appreciate what a difficult concept this is to reconcile with a normal Soviet upbringing. There has never been a native Russian word for initiative. The idea of an individual initiating unilateral action is anathema to the Soviet system. The Soviet army has always considered as one of its strengths its iron discipline and high-level, centralised command system combined with a universal tactical doctrine. The run-of-the-mill officer, particularly a sub-unit officer, has never had to do other than obey orders. But the modern battlefield now threatens disruption of formations and their communications, and threatens the flow of orders. The success of an entire operation, the Soviets hold, may depend on speedy reaction to enemy moves, sudden weaknesses and unexpected counter-attacks. The battalion group commander who waits immobile, because no orders have been received, will at best make no contribution to the success of the operation; at worst he will be quickly destroyed by enemy ground or air forces, perhaps opening up the flank of the main forces to enemy counter-attack.

Yet the Soviet army can only conceive of functioning on rigidly disciplined lines, and therefore the need for initiative and strict obedience to orders are in conflict. The problem is much discussed and argued in the military press in terms of the extent to which initiative must or must not be permitted, and the need or otherwise of showing leniency when an officer tries to use initiative and makes the wrong move. It would appear that the authorities believe that grounds for a solution do exist: their conclusion could probably be summed up as follows.

An officer must never act except in obedience to orders, and according to the regulations and the principles of Soviet tactical doctrine; in the dynamic conditions of the modern battlefield, slow response to a change in the battle situation may jeopardise the whole operation; in the fog of war, orders may not get through in time; in such a situation, therefore, an officer must be prepared to act without orders. But, unless he does what the senior commander requires, and therefore contributes to the success of the main effort, his independent actions are useless and may actually hinder the senior commander. Therefore, an officer must develop his 'staff culture', that is, his ability to visualise the general situation, appreciate the principles of operation governing both other arms and services and his superior commanders, and at the same time be able to out-think the enemy. Any action he undertakes must be strictly in accordance with existing tactical doctrine so that his superior commander will know what pattern of action is likely to be taken. The crux of the matter is that only if an officer has got this good all-round professional and general education will he be able to make a correct assessment of the situation and undertake the correct action. An officer who is capable of filling this bill has got *'initsiativ'*.

The fact that taking the wrong course of action leads to severe penalties has, it seems, dissuaded many young officers[13] from attempting to develop their initiative. However, the development of an officer 'caste', the gradual lowering of the age of commanders, the increasing sophistication of the officer corps, and the inculcation of a traditional military etiquette is bound to help the growth of professional self-confidence.

Over the last ten years, both from the drift of articles in the military press and from personal accounts related to the author, it is clear that, though he may not have initiative in the true western sense, the young Soviet officer *has* become more capable of reacting rapidly to unexpected situations and *is* prepared to act without definite orders if he has some idea of how to handle the situation. The problem that now faces the military authorities is how to equip their junior officers with the knowledge to make the correct decisions and the expertise and means to carry out the subsequent complex military operation. To refer back to our example of the battalion group commander, he may know what should be done, and have the courage to attempt it, but will he have the technical means of control available, the staff and the skill to do it? The answer to this latter question is, at this moment, probably no. This may appear to be a rather sweeping statement, but in view of the many articles in the military press exhorting officers to try to achieve this ideal, and expressing concern at the inability of some to do so, I do not think that it is unjustified.[14]

It is significant that, as far as is possible to ascertain, experiments with command structures to try to improve unit flexibility and rapid response seem to have concentrated on *reducing* the age of commanders, not increasing their age and experience. An example is in the already quoted Taman Guards Motor Rifle Division, where the vanguard regiment of this division (i.e. the regiment where rapid response and maximum use of initiative is most desirable) is commanded by a 'young officer', probably a major; its battalions are commanded by captains,[15] and its companies by lieutenants.

It will be interesting to see if such a rejuvenation is carried to all regiments. Already by 1971, 65 per cent of regimental officers in the ground forces were under the age of thirty.[16] The young commander of the regiment quoted above, we are told, had just graduated with honours from the Frunze Staff Academy. Officers of various rank attend the staff courses at this prestigious Academy, captains and majors being the most numerous. On graduation they go to regimental staff or command appointments at a level dependent on age, experience, and ability. To judge from comments made to the author by a delegation of instructors of this academy who visited the UK early in 1977, the average age of students has been falling gradually over the past few years, and quite a few senior lieutenants are now admitted to the course.[17]

If appointing such young officers to unit and sub-unit commands is successful in imbuing the Soviet military system with flexibility and responsiveness, and can be achieved without forfeiting essential professional ability, then no major reorganisation of officer training and career structure will be necessary to achieve it. If, on the other hand, it fails, then the Soviets may well be faced with the prospect of rethinking their command structure, and appointing much more senior and well trained officers to command battalions.[18]

One of the main things which has prevented the young officer from broadening his education has been the extent to which he is committed to running a necessarily rigid training programme for the conscripts under his command. The military officer is responsible for all aspects of training, including political education, and at subunit level he must personally conduct, or at least supervise, a very large percentage of this training. Considerable use is made of conscripts in their final term to train new arrivals, but this is not wholly satisfactory. Soviet military educators define three phases of a conscript's life,[19] the first six-month period, when he is gauche and disorientated, and overawed by the difficulties of military life and the strict discipline; the middle twelve months, when he has learnt to live with the system and extracts a great deal of satisfaction from team activities and mastering his military skills; and his final six-month period when he is bored with his work and his main concern is his rapidly approaching demobilisation. Clearly a conscript in his last six months can often adversely affect a new arrival by his cynical 'time serving' approach to military service, and thus his use as a trainer, while obvious, is limited, and must be subject to supervision. The introduction and spread of the 'ensign' rank has gone some way to alleviating the young officer's training burden, but it is still heavy. Once again, overtasking is to blame.

Anyone acquainted with the Soviet system knows full well the pressure in all quarters of society to improve output and efficiency and meet deadlines, whilst reducing consumption and material demands. In the armed services the problem is particularly acute, especially in respect of a shortage of time and training aids. Training materials and supplies are always in short supply, and 'thrift' campaigns[20] feature constantly in unit political instruction periods. In itself, this does not constitute a problem, and it is a fact of life which armies in many countries have to contend with. Moreover, two years would also appear to be ample time to train conscripts who have, as is the case in the Soviet system, not only a reasonable educational standard but also a fair degree of acclimatisation to a militarised way of life, and already possess the rudiments of military knowledge and awareness.

It is a combination of factors however which make for a genuine training problem in the Soviet army. Soviet military doctrine calls for 'the main aims of a war to be achieved in its initial period without additional mobilisation',[21] and an important tactical and operational principle requires commanders 'to ensure the preservation of the combat effectiveness of their troops by seeing that they are properly prepared and efficiently organised'[22] at the very start of a campaign. 'Today troops are expected to be ready in minutes or even seconds.'[23]

Thus a Soviet commander must maintain his unit at the peak of combat readiness, trained and prepared to go at a moment's notice; yet at the same time he must run it as a training unit, with a constant and rapid turnover of conscripts, when all the time the volume and complexity of equipment is increasing, and an increasing amount of time must be devoted to physical training and political education. Moreover, gone are the days when it was sufficient for the soldier to do one job and one job only. Now he must be able to perform not just his own battle skill, but at least two related skills,[24] so as to reduce sub-unit vulnerability to losses when no reinforcements are available. In addition, the unit must take part in large-scale exercises to train staff command and control and traffic procedures, which interrupt the sub-unit training schedules.

It is when added to these features that the shortage of training material becomes a real problem. In true Soviet fashion, units are encouraged to produce training equipment from their own resources, and to develop technical and procedural means of increasing training effectiveness in the ever shortening time available. This has led to a plethora of training simulators – not the complex electronic gadgets found in small numbers in western armies but a mass of simple machines or articles which initiate the basic motions of a weapon or vehicle. A good example of homemade simulators to provide basic training for tank crews is given in *Voennyi Vestnik*, 4, 1974, p. 70. Such simulators not only save wear on valuable equipment and increase the value of limited periods of training time, but they allow for training according to schedules, which would have been interrupted in the field by adverse weather conditions. Examples are often given in the press of training time wasted on getting to exercise areas, preparing vehicles, etc.[25] Simulators will help to avoid this wastage.

A disadvantage of simulators is that men learn to operate simulators well, but not the actual equipment in field conditions. This factor is recognised and it is stressed that a reasonably high degree of true field training with realistic battle conditions (live ammunition, explosives, active radioactive materials, etc.) must be maintained. Nevertheless, if the attention given in the military press is representative of the actual state of affairs, more time is being devoted in units to improving the technical proficiency of troops at the expense of realistic battle acclimatisation exercises.

The Soviet army training programme runs on a loosely co-ordinated training 'year' of six months. Themes for each training year are suggested and receive good coverage in the military press. Such themes (for example, fighting in built-up areas) do not appear to be mandatory on units and are certainly not meant to be exclusive, but merely to act as a focus for training; and articles in the military press act as an aid to unit commanders.

At the end of each month, the training performance of each sub-unit within a unit, and each individual within a sub-unit, is assessed competitively. Both individuals and units are given marks for performance over all and for specific tasks, sporting achievements, or exercises; and rewards are issued to those with the highest marks. This system of 'socialist competition' between sub-units and units serves to maintain the pressure of training, as well as being another means of engendering enthusiasm; officers have a vested interest in ensuring that their units do well in competitions, because the results affect their promotion prospects.

The basis of a unit training programme is the training day. The basic guidelines, such as the overall time each day to be given over to sleep, training lessons, the intervals between meals, etc. are laid down in field regulations (an example of a timetable drawn up in accordance with the new regulations was published in *Voennyi Vestnik*, 1, 1976, see Figure 6.1.) Formation commanders may issue guidelines for subordinate units, detailing training themes, or establishing co-ordination of activities to make best use of shared training accommodation. Adapting the formation commander's timetable and tailoring it to suit the unit's training needs is the responsibility of each unit commander. Articles on this subject are always at pains to point out that there is never enough time to get everything done at an easy pace. It is the responsibility of the unit commander to allot training priorities and arbitrate between conflicting requirements.

One feature of the new regulations is that they permit the unit commander to leave the organisation of the whole morning of each training day to company commanders, allowing them wide scope for organising training in their own way. The co-ordination of afternoon training between sub-units, enabling them to train together, means that fewer officers and ensigns are required to conduct the training and consequently the rest could have time off, either for leisure or to improve their own knowledge. In this way, the new regulations make for an improvement in the working conditions of the regular staff.

As is the case with all Soviet enterprises, military units and

Figure 6.1 **Training day timetable**

1	Reveille	0600–0605	5 mins
2	P. T. (cleaning quarters)	0610–0630	20 mins
3	Washing and bed-making	0630–0650	20 mins
4	Political interpretation of latest news and morning inspection	0650–0720	30 mins
5	Breakfast	0725–0755	30 mins
6	1st lesson	0800–0850	50 mins
	6th lesson	1300–1350	50 mins
7	Dinner	1400–1440	40 mins
8	After-dinner rest	1440–1510	30 mins
9	Care of personal weapon and equipment	1510–1530	20 mins
10	(a) Political education (Monday, Thursday)	1530–1830	3 hrs
	(b) Maintenance of technical equipment (Tuesday, Friday)	1530–1830	3 hrs
	(c) Team sports or communal activities (Wednesday, Saturday)	1530–1830	3 hrs
11	Individual tuition or study	1830–1940	1 hr. 10 mins
12	Supper	1940–2010	30 mins
13	Free time	2010–2140	30 mins
14	Evening walk and roll call	2140–2155	15 mins
15	Lights out	2200	

formations are subject to spot checks,[26] either by superior staffs or special Ministry of Defence teams, to ensure that the required state of readiness is maintained, and that the unit is being efficiently run. If serious faults or failures, such as falsification of competition results, come to light, the responsible unit's staff officers are likely to be at best severely reprimanded and, at worst, replaced.

Unfortunately, it has not been possible to obtain details of the new (1976) Soviet Field Regulations; but from those references which have appeared in the open press, it would appear that, whilst material rewards for good performances have been substantially increased, so have disciplinary measures. 'Standards of discipline are increasing as the importance of the time factor increases. Complete readiness to repel a surprise attack and successful action to destroy the enemy are only possible when there exists a high level of discipline and organisation. . . .'[27] Attacks on such breaches in discipline as the fashion for soldiers to 'style' their uniforms by tapering the trousers or making fancy scarves,[28] etc., is evidence that the authorities are not going to tolerate any 'softening up' of discipline in the army, and are keen to prevent effete civilian habits from diluting the moral strength of the army.

In other words, the authorities' model for improving military efficiency is to increase the amount of initiative which junior commanders are to be allowed to exercise, and thereby to create a more flexible and responsive training system, whilst on the other hand tightening up on individual discipline so as to prevent flexibility from becoming laxity and to prevent the engendering of a tendency to question orders.

An increasingly important role in the maintenance, improvement, and supervision of military efficiency is being given to the political organs within the armed forces. GLAVPUR, the Chief Political Administration for the Armed Forces (that is, the Communist Party's political education corps among the military), now has officers down to company level. Their job is to relieve the commander at each level of much of the burden of his duty to maintain the political educational level of his men. Their duty is to strengthen morale, discipline, and ideological awareness, and thereby to encourage obedience to the commander and an enthusiastic approach to training. More and more, the Party is reverting to Imperial Russian traditions and conventional soldierly virtues as a foundation for moral and psychological training. These are not by way of replacements for communist ideology, but rather practical and effective supplements to it, though they have on occasion necessitated a slight adaptation or evolution of the ideology to accommodate them. Self-sacrifice and heroism is a constant theme, and it is the task of the Communist Party members or active Komsomol members in sub-units, under the organisation of the political officer, to provide a practical lead in this respect. Being a Communist Party member in the ranks in wartime can be a risky, if glorious, business. Though Party members numbered far fewer than a fifth of the armed forces in the 1941–5 war, they won almost three-quarters of all awards for gallantry of 'Hero of the Soviet Union',[29] a very high percentage of which were conferred posthumously. Detachments chosen for particularly difficult missions were always stiffened with a high number of communists, and this principle is still adhered to.[30]

Particularly difficult problems for the political officer to overcome will be achieving the mental adjustment in the minds of the troops necessary in a sudden transition from peace to war; and maintaining morale and moral conviction in the face of a high casualty rate in operations such as fighting in towns where small sub-units will be operating in isolated conditions, and on a battlefield where weapons of mass destruction are used.

In addition to this military-political task, the political officer performs the important Party function of carrying the Party word to the soldiers. Military service provides the Party with an ideal opportunity to instruct a large captive audience of young men at a formative stage in their lives in the Communist ideal. Political instruction given in the armed forces is an important contribution to creating the 'New Soviet Man', and in the past year, there has been a marked increase in the amount of ideological agitation devoted to this theme.

As an additional political duty, the political staff are charged with the supervision of the armed forces to ensure their political loyalty and reliability. This is in the broadest terms; identification of actual counter-espionage and subversion is the responsibility of the KGB section in each Division.

In order to get his political and moral message across, it is not sufficient for the political officer merely to organise lectures; he must involve unit personnel in work of a socially active nature, and use all sorts of extra-mural activities to convey his message: 'Brains-trust' type quizzes; amateur theatricals; wall newspapers; company libraries; propaganda displays; and cultural visits to local sights, war memorials, and battlegrounds, etc.

The ideal is that up to 50 per cent of the sub-unit personnel should be involved in 'social work' of some kind. A breakdown in a typical company gives:[31]

Party Secretary	1
Komsomol Secretary	1
Komsomol group organisers	3
Lenin room committee	5
Platoon agitators	3
Wall newspaper editors	5
Satirical wall newspaper editors	3
Ad hoc leaflet producers	3
Voluntary sports instructors	4
Sports competition organisers (including choir, Soviet-GDR friendship circle, music circle, etc.)	10
Company librarian	1

The two afternoons per week allotted to political training will involve at least some formal lectures, so most of the above activities will have to take place outside training hours, i.e. in the soldier's 'free time'. One sometimes gets the feeling that high on the list of communist proverbs there must be one which reads: 'An idle mind is the capitalist's workshop'.

In addition to his purely political role, the political officer has come to be responsible for a whole range of fringe tasks and even specific military tasks, to the extent that political officers are sometimes called to task for subordinating their Party duties to purely military requirements. On the whole, however, the political officer's military involvement and expertise serve to increase his credibility in the eyes of the men and also to improve his understanding of, and therefore his value to, the system. To his lot has fallen much of the responsibility for supervising the soldiers' welfare and dealing with their personal problems. The political officer is usually given the task of running the unit's socialist competition programme and distributing rewards. He carries direct to troop level the latest Party directions to the army, such as campaigns to reduce wastage of bread or misuse of clothing. He is tasked with identifying and bringing to light abuses in the system, e.g. inefficient use of manpower skills, or injustices in the application of regulations.[32] This, however, is the limit of his authority to interfere in military activity. He may offer his suggestions for military solutions to problems, but the unit commander has absolute overall authority in military matters. In many ways, the political officer has become a very valuable general dogsbody and factotum for the sub-unit commander in battle. If a liaison officer is needed, the political officer can be sent; if a duty roster needs working out, the political officer can do it; when night falls on the battlefield, and the commander has been too busy to work out identification signals, the political officer can be asked to do so. Why are supplies not getting through? Send the political officer to find out.

While there will undoubtedly be conflicting demands on the political officer's time and loyalties, his position in a unit and sub-unit seems to have evolved reasonably satisfactorily; and while there is some evidence to suggest that many officers would prefer to see rather less training time given over to political instruction, the author has found no evidence to suggest that there is nowadays any significant friction in the ground forces between political and military staff at unit level. This must be because the political officer appears to fulfil a useful function, not only in Party but also in professional military terms. There can be no doubt that, on balance, the institution of the political staff is of great value to the army, and contributes to its military efficiency rather than detracts from it.

In conclusion, a word of caution is not misplaced. It must not be assumed that even the most serious of those constraints on the performance and behaviour of the Soviet soldier to which I have referred above will in practice nullify the effectiveness of the Soviet army as a whole. If the political decision to go to war had been taken the fact that, for example, one quarter of a division's troops may at the time in question be virtually untrained raw recruits will definitely *not* prevent that division from being flung into battle; nor will it excuse that divisional commander for failure to carry out his orders. When in the past the Soviet army has gone to war, it has always done so whilst suffering from certain imperfections, either in equipment, training, or organisation. Soviet commanders at all levels have traditionally overcome these imperfections by the exercising of a considerable amount of ruthlessness and brutality in the running of their units. The high casualty figures that Soviet commanders were prepared to accept in the course of operations during the last war is a well-known example of this. At the troop level, it was not considered extraordinary for a Soviet officer to shoot a soldier as a matter of 'company discipline' during the last war.[33] The author has heard it confirmed by reliable and well-informed Czech sources that during the Soviet invasion of Czechoslovakia in 1968, no small number (the most conservative estimate quoted a figure of one hundred) of Soviet soldiers were summarily shot by their officer as a disciplinary measure.

Consequently, whilst imperfections in the system undeniably cause the Soviet High Command no little concern and may well alter or in some way affect their decisions as to *how* to plan the waging of a war once war has begun, there can be no doubt that the lesson of history as far as the Soviets are concerned, is that, when the chips are down, the adverse effects of a great many imperfections can be greatly reduced by a rigidly enforced discipline.

SUMMARY OF DISCUSSION

In the brief discussion that followed this paper Mr Donnelly was asked if there was any sign that the Russian army was professionally prepared to fight a war other than a massive confrontation with NATO, particularly in view of the fact that some Russian commentators were no longer as sure as they had been that this was the kind of war the Soviet Union was most likely to have to fight. Mr Donnelly felt that the training and attitudes inculcated in the Red Army were still overwhelmingly directed towards a large-scale engagement with NATO. They might serve equally well in a war with China, where there was a clear national enemy of a different colour. On the other hand, the Soviet forces might well find it difficult to take on, for example, Yugoslavia, another Slav socialist country well-versed in guerilla tactics, and this was one reason why the Soviet Union was unlikely to take military action there. The question of the balance between Great Russians and other non-Slav nationalities in the Soviet armed forces was raised, particularly in view of the demographic trends favouring the latter. Mr Donnelly saw no major problem arising except in the very long run. There were no barriers to the rise of non-Russians in the military hierarchy, provided they completely accepted Russification and foreswore any ethnic nationalism. On the other hand, those who did not speak Russian well were liable to be treated as second-class citizens. The lecturer was finally asked about drunkenness and crime in the Soviet forces. He felt that the former was a big problem, but that it became, as a rule, the cause of disciplinary action only if it interfered with the performance of a soldier's duties.

NOTES

1. For a very good seventeenth-century illustration of this, see Oliphaunt, *The Russian Shores of the Black Sea*: (Edinburgh, W. Blackwood, 1855).
2. For example, the current norms (i.e. level of achievement to be met) which are listed at the back of every schoolchild's yearly report book, require that 15-year-old boys be able, amongst other things, to throw a 500-gramme hand grenade 25 metres.
3. For an excellent review of the development of DOSAAF and its predecessors, see W. Odom, *The Soviet Volunteers*, (Princeton University Press, 1973).
4. Compare, for example, references in the following articles:
    (a) *Krasnaya Zvezda*, 10 November 1976, by Col. Gen. Gordakov stating that all conscripts to the Rocket Forces nowadays have complete pre-conscription training;
    (b) *Tyl i Snabzhenie*, September 1975, p. 29 and p. 32, making reference to the poor level of pre-conscription training in rear service personnel and giving details of methods for developing ability in unpromising conscripts in a transport platoon.
5. The Decree of the Praesidium of the Supreme Soviet of the USSR, issued on 25 February 1977, and amending the USSR law of 12 October 1967 on Universal Military Service, has made provision for conscripting men with *higher* education for 18 months to the army and two years to the navy.

6. See *Krasnaya Zvezda*, 16 April 1971, quoted in H. Goldhamer, *The Soviet Soldier* (Crane, Russak & Co. Inc., New York, 1975).
7. During the 1941–5 war, there were only 10 nationally recruited formations formed. These were an Estonian corps, 3 Guards' Kazakh divisions, and Latvian, Lithuanian, Azerbaidjam, Bashkir, Georgian, and Armenian divisions. M. Ruban, *The Soviet School of Courage and Warcraft* (Moscow, Progress Publishers, 1976), p. 19.
8. For a particularly graphic illustration of this problem, see a satirical sketch in *Krokodil*, No. 11, 1972, pp. 8–9.
9. *Krasnaya Zvezda* 5 April 1969.
10. *Krasnaya Zvezda* 9 February 1977, giving details of 1977–80 military sports classifications.
11. See *Voennyi Vestnik*, 10, 1971, p. 44 for a consideration of the problem of major changes in equipment and techniques every five years, and the necessity of retraining instructors.
12. See, for example, *Tyl i Snabzhenie* 6, 1974, p. 76.
13. *Voennyi Vestnik* 12, 1971, p. 36, gives a dramatised example of initiative gone wrong, bringing down punishment on the head of the offending officer.
14. See, for example, *Voennyi Vestnik* 12, 1971, p. 21. and 12, 1974, p. 35, emphasising the difficulties of co-ordination and control at battalion level; and *Voennyi Vestnik* 8, 1976, p. 35 on instilling initiative in student officers at a Guards Higher Tank Command College.
15. M. Ruban, op. cit., p. 101.
16. Ibid., p. 45.
17. An interesting and not wholly irrelevant point is that one of the most common questions posed by memcers of this same delegation to British student officers was concerned to establish whether or not the British officers came from families with military traditions.
18. For an example of a battalion in the advance guard commanded by a lieutenant colonel, *Voennyi Vestnik*, 4, 1975, pp. 55–9, also stressing the requirement for initiative and broad-based training.
19. A. M. Danchenko, et al., *Voennaya Pedagogika* (Voenizdat, Moscow, 1973), pp. 103–9.
20. For example, see *Tyl i Snabzhenie*, 8, 1976, p. 51, referring to a campaign to save bread, and 12, 1975, p. 31, referring to fuel and vehicle economy.
21. Sokolovskii, *Voennaya Strategiya* (3rd edn.) (Voenizdat, Moscow, 1968), p. 370.
22. V. E. Savkin, *Osnovnye Printzipy Operativnogo Isskustva i Taktiki*, (Voenizdat, Moscow, 1972), pp. 339–49.
23. M. Ruban, op. cit., p. 21.
24. See for example, *Tyl i Snabzhenie*, 1, 1976, p. 40.
25. *Voennyi Vestnik*, 6, 1974, p. 34.
26. See, for example, *Tyl i Snabzhenie*, 9, 1975, p. 67.
27. M. Ruban, op. cit., p. 21.
28. *Tyl i Snabzhenie*, 8, 1976, p. 90.
29. M. Ruban, op. cit., p. 61.
30. See Shovkolovich et al., *deistvye motostrelkovogo batal'ona v gorode* (Voenizdat, Moscow, 1971), pp. 47–8.
31. M. Ruban, op. cit., p. 129.

32. For an example of unjust application of regulations concerning overcharging officers for equipment losses and damages, see an article in *Krasnaya Zvezda*, 14 November 1976, 'When Something Breaks Down'.
33. H. J. Berman and M. Kerner, *Soviet Military Law and Administration* (Harvard University Press, 1955), p. 146.

7 The Soviet Army as the Instrument of National Integration

Teresa Rakowska-Harmstone

(with assistance from Captain Raymond Sturgeon, Canadian Forces)

> Our Army is brought up in the spirit of deep loyalty to the Socialist Motherland, to the ideas of peace and internationalism and to the ideas of the friendship of the peoples. This is where the Soviet Army differs from the bourgeois armies; this is why the Soviet people love their Army and are proud of it.
>
> *Secretary General Leonid Brezhnev, reporting to the 25th Congress of the CPSU, 24 February, 1976*

In the multi-ethnic Soviet society the Soviet army is undoubtedly one of the most important instruments of national integration, but the model to which Soviet soldiers are assimilated is basically that of a Russian soldier. The still predominantly Russian character of the Soviet armed forces reflects the demographic realities (the Russians, in 1970, constituted 53 per cent of the Soviet population), the military traditions of the Tsarist army that have continued strongly to influence the Soviet army's character, and the qualitative hegemony the Russians enjoy in the Soviet political life and in the society at large.[1] In the Soviet theory and practice the Russians are considered to be 'the leading nation', and the one organisation where this is demonstrated most clearly is the Soviet army.

The Soviet army's ethnic base is wider than that of the old Imperial army, which excluded 45 nationalities from the draft.[2] All

TABLE 7.1 USSR. Major Ethnic Groups (according to the 1970 Census)

Ethnic group	Absolute figures (millions)	Percentage of the total
USSR Total	241.7	100
Russians (1)	129.0	53.3
Ukrainians (1)	40.8	16.9
Uzbeks (4)	9.2	3.8
Belorussians (1)	9.1	3.7
Tatars	5.9	2.4
Kazakhs (4)	5.3	2.2
Azerbaijani (2)	4.4	1.8
Armenians (2)	3.6	1.5
Georgians (2)	3.2	1.2
Moldavians	2.7	1.1
Lithuanians (3)	2.7	1.1
Jews	2.2	0.9
Tadzhiks (4)	2.1	0.9
Germans	1.8	0.8
Chuvashi	1.7	0.7
Turkmen (4)	1.5	0.6
Kirgiz (4)	1.5	0.6
Latvians (3)	1.4	0.6
Mordvinians	1.3	0.5
Bashkirs	1.2	0.5
Poles	1.2	0.5
Estonians (3)	1.0	0.4
All Others	8.9	3.4

SOURCE: *Itogi Vaesoiuznoi Perepisi Naseleniia 1970 goda* (Moscow, 1973,) v. IV

Note: The 1970 Soviet Census enumerated 102 national groups, in addition to the 'other' category. The Soviet Union is a federal state with 15 union republics; the national groups which have union republics are in italics above. Other national groups have lower level autonomous units: autonomous republics, autonomous regions, autonomous provinces, and autonomous districts, depending on size. Some major groups do not have an autonomous status – Jews, Germans, and Poles; either because they are dispersed (an autonomous unit created for the Jews in Eastern Siberia attracted only a few of them), or because they have their own state outside the USSR (Poles), or as a punishment for an alleged collaboration with the Germans in the Second World War (Germans and Crimean Tatars, the latter a part of the general Tatar group).

The key: (1) – Slavs
          (2) – Caucasians
          (3) – Baltics
          (4) – Central Asians

the Soviet nations and nationalities (102 were listed in the 1970 Census) are subject to universal military service. Twenty-one of them, in addition to the Russians, number more than one million people; of those the Ukrainians are the most numerous, with 40 million people and 17 per cent of the Soviet population, followed by the Uzbeks and the Belorussians, each nine million strong (see Table 7.1).

Soviet military historians divide the history of the Red army into three basic periods, four, if the pre-federation period is counted:[3] a preliminary stage between the Revolution and the formation of the USSR; stage one between the military reforms of 1924 and 1938; stage two, started in 1938 which continued, roughly, until the mid-50s; and the current stage, which is said to have begun with the consolidation of the military might of the socialist countries in the Warsaw Treaty Organisation, when the Soviet army assumed a new role, that of defending the 'world socialist system'. The accommodation of the ethnic factor in the military organisation and indoctrination has been of importance at each stage.

Following the October Revolution, Red army units were formed in Russsian areas as well as on the territories of newly established non-Russian socialist soviet republics in the western borderlands: Ukrainian, Latvian, Lithuanian-Belorussian, and Estonian military formations came into being. But in the chaos of the Civil War and Allied Intervention, these national formations, particularly in the Ukraine, concentrated on pursuit of their own national objectives, and by early 1919 the Bolshevik leadership concluded that an integration of military effort was imperative. Soviet sources quote a telegram by Lenin to the Ukrainian Soviet government, reproaching the Ukrainians for 'playing a game of independence', and ordering them to co-ordinate military activities with the Red Army command, even if this 'temporarily weakens the military situation in the Western Ukraine.[4] An April Resolution of the Central Committee of the Communist Party(Bolsheviks,RKP (b)), called for an unconditional unity of action between the Soviet republics in the conduct of war. This was followed by a May 4 Resolution, instructing the Communist Parties of the non-Russian republics to subordinate their military activities to the Russian Federation;[5] it directed that the territory of each republic should form a military district subordinated to the Revolutionary Military Council of the Russian Federation, and that republics should place their military command structures under the orders of the Council.[6]

Appropriate resolutions were passed by the governments of the Ukrainian, Lithuanian-Belorussian, and Latvian socialist republics in May,[7] and on 1 June the Central Executive Committee of the Russian Federation adopted a decree on political and military unity of the Russian Ukrainian, Latvian, and Lithuanian-Belorussian soviet socialist republics, 'for the struggle with world imperialism'. The decree established a unified Red Army command and single agencies for recruitment and supply, and integrated the republics' national military formations into an overall operational and command structure of the RSFSR's Red Army.[8] In 1920–1 the system was extended to Turkestan and to Caucasus. In an exchange with Lenin in 1920, Mikhail Frunze—then in command in Turkestan—advised against a creation of a separate Moslem army and staff and recommended instead the formation of local regiments to serve along with Russian regiments in a single army. A similar principle was adopted in the Caucasian Federation in 1921.[9] It should be noted, however, that in Kazakhstan and in North Caucasus it was not until 1928 that the indigenous nationalities, previously exempted from the draft, were called into military service for the first time.[10]

The establishment of an integrated command structure heavily dominated by the Russians introduced an element of ethnic conflict as the minorities resented the Russification imposed on them during army service. The problem came up at the 12th Congress of the RKP (b) in April 1923 in the context of overall discussion of national relations, and was articulated most strongly by the Ukrainians. Mykola Skrypnik, one of the Ukrainian leaders, complained that the Army was 'an instrument for the Russifying of the Ukrainian and the whole non-Russian population',[11] a complaint echoed by another Ukrainian delegate:

> ... the Red Army is objectively not only an instrument for educating the peasantry in a proletarian spirit, it is an instrument of Russification. We transfer tens of thousands of Ukrainian peasants to Tula and force them to grasp everything in Russian. ... Here is the inertia of the Great Russian command structure; our top command is overwhelmingly Russian ... [12]

The Congress debates on the national problem (of which the Red Army question formed only a small part) resulted in a compromise which provided for safeguarding of national rights within the framework of overall socialist unity and and the promotion of the policy of *korenizatsiia*, which meant education and promotion of non-Russians in all walks of life into positions of eventual equality. In reference to the Red Army the Congress resolved to increase educational work there 'in the spirit of the development of ideas of friendship and brotherhood of the Soviet nations', and to take steps to organise national military formation 'taking all necessary measures to secure full military preparedness of the republics'.[13] A Central Committee resolution of June 1923 provided for translation and publication of political and specialised literature for the national military units in their languages.[14]

The formation of the USSR and the military reform of 1924 officially ushered in the first stage in the development of a unified Red Army. Defence was placed under All-Union jurisdiction; national military formations were continued under a unified command, in line with the decisions of the 12th Congress. The military reform included a five-year plan for the formation of such units, to be organised on a pattern following that advocated by Frunze earlier.[15] In line with the policy of *korenizatsiia* an effort was also made to train non-Russian officer cadres for service in territorial national regiments.[16]

There is no information on the extent of the implementation of the *korenizatsiia* policy in the armed forces, but the limited data on the ethnic composition of the officer corps (see Table 7.2) indicate

TABLE 7.2 USSR. Soviet Army Officers, Ethnic Breakdown, 1943

Ethnic group	Basic officer ranks	Senior artillery officers
Ukrainians	28,000	6,000
Belorussians	5,305	1,246
Armenians	1,079	240
Tatars	1,041	173
Georgians	800	129
Chuvashi	405	–
Mordvinians	383	99
Ossetins	251	–
Moldavians	–	49
Kazakhs	–	25
Bashkirs	–	22

SOURCE: Col. P. Rtishchev, 'Leninskaya natsional'naya politika i stroitel'stvo Sovetskikh Vooruzhennykh Sil', *Voenno istoricheskii Zhurnal*, No. 6, June 1974, p. 7.

that, except in the case of the Ukrainians, little progress was made. The change in the political climate by the late twenties and the early thirties, the abandonment of *korenizatsiia* in favour of accelerated integration; and the renewed emphasis on the leading role in the Soviet Union of the Russians, because they were 'most progressive', were the key factors in the non-implementation of the principle of national equality in the army as well as in other areas. While the national formations continued *de jure*, in practice the Russian hegemony continued.

The second stage in the development of the Red Army was ushered in by the military reform of 1938. This abolished the national military formations and replaced them with the principle of individual recruitment *kadrovyi printsip* into ethnically-mixed Russian-language basic units.[17] The explanation offered for the change stated that in view of the progress made in the construction of socialism the national military units had become obsolete; all Soviet citizens served in the Red Army which was recognised by the working people as the defender of all the Soviet nations and nationalities, and overall cultural progress and voluntary study of the Russian language made it possible for non-Russian recruits to serve in ethnically-mixed Russian-language units. Moreover, the technical reorganisation of the armed forces and the increase in international tensions made the continued existence of territorial units detrimental to the needs of defence preparedness.[18] Commenting on the disbanding of the national units in 1939 Marshal Klimenti Voroshilov, the USSR Commissar of Defence stated:

> The Red Army is the sole army of the Soviet state on a common and equal basis. For this reason the existence of separate, small national military formations, permanently tied to their own territory, contradicted the fundamentals of the Stalin Constitution and the principles of the extra-territorial recruitment of our army.[19]

The Red Army entered the Second World War with units newly reorganised on a multi-ethnic basis, but in the heat of battle national formations were resurrected in some cases, because of 'the urgent need to form battle-worthy units in a short time'.[20] These included two Kazakh Guard divisions, Latvian and Estonian infantry corps, the Georgian, Azerbaijani, Armenian, and Tadzhik divisions, the Lithuanian and Uzbek infantry divisions, the Bashkii and Kalmyk cavalry divisions, and other national formations: these were composed 'mainly of officers and men of one nationality'.[21] At the same time a heavy emphasis on Russian patriotism in defence of the Motherland all but obliterated the 'internationalist' appeal of the Soviet state. In retrospect the performance of national divisions in the war and heroism of individuals of various nationalities are much praised; but the Red Army also has had to cope with mass defections by non-Russians. With the end of the war the temporary national formations were disbanded and the Red Army returned to the 1938 principle of mixed units and individual recruitment. The 12 October 1967 military law, which reduced the length of military service from three to two years, also restated the principle of compulsory military service for all male citizens and the ethnically-mixed basis for all units.[22] Military districts are drawn without regard to national republican boundaries and there are no provisions for local representation in their command structures.

The third period of development of the Soviet Army is said to have begun with its assumption of a new role as the defender of socialism not only within the USSR but for all the socialist countries grouped within the Warsaw Treaty organisation:

> Following the emergence of the socialist world system and the establishment of the Warsaw Treaty political and military organisation, the Soviet Army entered the third stage of its development. The Soviet Armed Forces have been confronted with new responsible missions. Today the task of defending socialism includes the defence of the gains not only of the peoples of the USSR, but of the other socialist countries as well.[23]

The assumption of the new role, the commencement of which is not dated precisely, began to be emphasised in the late sixties and early seventies, following the 1968 Warsaw Pact troops invasion of Czechoslovakia, and as a part of the new thrust toward the integration of eastern Europe with the Soviet Union on the basis of 'proletarian internationalism'.[24] In a general way its role now is reminiscent of the role played by the Russian Federation's army vis-a-vis the military formations of the other republics in the pre-1924 period. It may be worth noting here that the Soviet experience in the development of armed forces in a multi-national state is considered by Soviet sources to be 'of major significance for the strengthening of co-operation between the socialist countries on the basis of the Warsaw Pact.'[25]

The role of the Soviet army in furthering the goal of *national integration* is not only explicitly acknowledged but is also considered to be of primary importance, the emphasis which complements professional training. John Erickson observes that 'preserving the army and the armed forces as a national-ideological school of the nation seems to be on the point of becoming almost counterproductive. . . . '; he acknowledges, nevertheless, that the army's political role forms an essential part of an 'Army-Party' compact.[26]

The party sees the army as the school of the nation, and political education, individual recruitment base, ethnically-mixed units, and the training programme, are all designed to mould the multi-ethnic manpower into a unitary product, a soldier imbued with the spirit of 'Soviet patriotism', with undivided loyalty to the Soviet Union, to the Party, and to the ideas of 'proletarian internationalism at home and abroad.[27] The value of such indoctrination for the Soviet army's combat effectiveness is obvious; as one Soviet general put it, it serves 'to knit soldiers together into a monolithic combat group to be reflected in enhanced combat readiness.[28] The no less important byproduct is the educational and hopefully value-forming experience each conscript takes with him into civilian life after army service. This is particularly important in the case of non-Russians.

Leonid Brezhnev, Secretary General of the CPSU central Committee describes the Soviet army as 'a special kind of army in that it is a school that fosters feelings of brotherhood, solidarity and mutual respect among all Soviet nations and nationalities.'[29] Mixed units and as individual recruitment programmes are considered necessary for the success of integration efforts; and internationalist education is the key task to be carried out by the armed forces:

> The Communist Party has always considered, and still considers that the military units mixed from the national point of view, are the basic organisational form of the armed forces, the form which follows from the international nature of the Soviet power. The mixed units are the best way to educate the personnel in the spirit of friendship of the Soviet peoples.[30]
>
> The entire mode of life of the Soviet Army and Navy promotes cohesion and friendship among the fighting men of different nationalities. At the same time the internationalist education of

the personnel constitutes one of the key tasks facing the commanders, political bodies, Party and YCL (Young Communist League) organizations in the units. Realization of the role played by the USSR today evokes in Soviet servicemen a feeling of legitimate patriotic pride, a readiness to defend their multinational Motherland . . .[31]

The potential recruit is first exposed to the integration impact of military service in the one year of pre-induction training. Established in 1967 as a substitute for the reduction in length of military service, the pre-induction training is carried out at the *rayon* (district) level at schools, factories, and collective farms by regular army instructors (many of whom are in reserves) under the overall supervision of the Ministry of Defence. While formal political instruction is not included in the training, there is a strong emphasis on the so-called 'military-patriotic education' (with the YCL prominently involved) and on elements of social control, such as discipline, and patriotism.[32] For non-Russian youths (educated in the local language schools) pre-induction training may be the first exposure to instruction in Russian. The level of pre-induction training, however, varies from area to area, and instruction in Russian in the national areas may not always be available.

The recruit really becomes immersed in the 'international' environment with the moment of induction, when he enters, from a recruit depot onwards, the ethnically-mixed Russian-speaking milieu. For a Russian the change is minimal, but a member of an ethnic minority, particularly if of peasant origin, finds himself in an alien environment and facing a loss of ethnic identity. By virtue of sheer numbers Russians form a majority in the mixed units, but other national group members find few, if any, co-nationals there. The Russian language is the working and the social language of the armed forces. This is logical as Russian is not only the majority language but also the Soviet *lingua franca*, and in the context of Soviet national relations it has always been considered the key instrument of national integration. Under the USSR Constitution the non-Russians have, in their national areas, the right to education, publication and cultural pursuits in their national languages, with Russian taught as the second language and in many cases learned badly or not at all (see Table 7.3). But in the armed forces, where any concessions to ethnic autonomy ended with the reform of 1938, the Russian language is the sole medium 'in which

TABLE 7.3 USSR. Fluency in Russian and Urbanisation of Major Ethnic Groups

	Percentage of Ethnic Groups Which Claim Russian as Mother Tongue	Percentage of Ethnic Groups Which Claim Fluency in Russian as a Second Language	Percentage of Urbanisation
Ukrainians	14.2	36.3	49
Belorussians	19.0	49.0	44
Moldavians	4.1	36.1	20
Azerbaijani	1.3	16.6	40
Armenians	7.5	30.1	65
Georgians	1.3	21.3	44
Kazakhs	1.6	41.8	27
Uzbeks	0.5	14.5	25
Tadzhiks	0.6	15.4	26
Turkmen	0.8	15.4	31
Kirgiz	0.3	19.1	15
Lithuanians	1.5	35.9	47
Latvians	4.6	45.2	53
Estonians	4.4	29.0	55
Tatars	10.0	62.5	55
Germans	30.0	59.6	46
Chuvashi	13.0	58.4	23
Mordvinians	2.3	65.7	36
Bashkirs	4.7	53.3	27
Ossetins	5.4	58.6	53
Jews	78.2	16.3	98
Poles	20.7	37.0	45

SOURCE: As cited in Table 7.1, pp. 9, 10, 20, 27 and 28.
1: The Ossetins are a much smaller group in numbers (488,000 in 1970), but are included here because they are visibly present in the armed forces.
2: USSR percentage of urbanisation in 1970 was 56 per cent.

instruction and education in the Armed Forces are conducted', and is seen as 'an important means of strengthening the international ties uniting Soviet fighting men'.[33] All military publications, from high-level professional journals to unit newspapers and training manuals are printed in the Russian language. The exclusive use of Russian, places an additional burden on a minority soldier whose knowledge of the language is poor. Soviet sources report that such soldiers are being helped by their fellows;[34] but considering the known killing pace of basic training and additional time consumed for political indoctrination, the amount of such assistance, even if freely given, cannot be extensive. There are no indications that any formal instruction in the Russian language is provided for soldiers who need it.

The environment thus created is in itself a potent force for integration. This is then reinforced by an extensive and all-pervading system of political indoctrination to which men and officers are exposed. The system is directed by the armed services Main Political Administration (MPA) and constitutes also one of the main responsibilities of the Party and YCL organisations in military formations. Professional officer cadres also are supposed to assist. As Marshal Grechko has instructed the 1974 graduating class of military academies, one of their tasks—to be conducted under guidance of the Party and the YCL—is to inculcate in the soldiers 'the high communist principles, feelings of Soviet patriotism and proletarian internationalism and a constant readiness to defend the achievements of socialism'.[35] National integration forms one of the main themes in the political education system. As a prominent Tadzhik scholar and propagandist, and an ex-high Party official put it:

> During their term of active service representatives of different peoples pass through an excellent school of internationalist education. The process of the nations drawing closer together is developing rapidly and tempestuously in the Armed Forces as in the country as a whole.[36]

There are three keynotes in the national integration theme. 'Proletarian Internationalism' emphasises the unity based on common working-class consciousness of the Soviet peoples under the leadership of its vanguard—the Communist Party. 'Soviet Patriotism' inculcates loyalty to the socialist Motherland; and the 'Friendship of the Peoples' formula describes an alleged process of the Soviet nations and nationalities 'ever growing closer together', the process whereby their common features grow and particularistic features gradually disappear. These concepts have formed a steady diet in military political education endeavours, but in the early seventies they began to receive an exceptionally strong emphasis, reflecting the Party's perception of the growing problem of ethnic nationalism,[37] and appearing also in connection with the celebrations of three relevant anniversaries: the 50th anniversary of the formation of the Soviet Union, Lenin's centenary, and the 25th anniversary of the victory in the 'Great Patriotic War'.

The Resolution of the Central Committee of the CPSU adopted at the 50th Anniversary of the formation of the USSR specifically instructed the Ministry of Defence of the USSR and the Main Political Administrations of the Soviet army and the navy to issue orders to commanders, MPA units, and party organisations to prepare a broad-scale educational campaign and a programme of mass political work in the armed forces designed to 'further strengthen the friendship and fraternal relations among soldiers of all nationalities, fostering in them a pride in the achievements of our Motherland, and strengthening their sense of the community of socialist countries and their readiness to defend the revolutionary gains of the peoples'.[38]

Examples of national integration indoctrination campaigns may serve to illustrate the themes, the scope, and the forms and methods used. In the Transcaucasus Military District, for example,[39] the plans for a campaign on the national integration theme were prepared by the District's Military Council and approved in a joint session between the MPA and the first secretaries of the three republics included in the District: Georgia, Armenia, and Azerbaijan. The topics of the campaign were Lenin's theory of national relations, the Party's nationality policy, 'achievements of fraternal Soviet republics in communist construction, the Party's revolutionary, combat and labour traditions, and the people and the Army'. In the course of the campaign officers were directed 'to study Lenin's theoretical legacy systematically and in depth in order to acquire a profound Leninist understanding of the national question and . . . the meaning and purpose of the Party's struggle for its solution'. A number of garrisons held theoretical conferences on the subject. Indoctrination of soldiers and non-commisioned officers was carried out in political study groups, the main subject of which was 'the theme of Friendship and Troop comradeship—the Most Important Military Tradition in the Soviet Armed Forces', as well as 'questions of national relations and Leninist ideas of friendship among peoples'. The campaign was not limited to internal activity within the military, but included also the local population in mutual interaction with military personnel. Throughout the District, meetings were held explaining to the soldiers the sources of unity between the three republics ('joint struggle by workers of the Caucasus in indissoluble friendship with the Russian workers'). Local veterans of the communist movement addressed many of them. Lectures and speakers were exchanged between the military and the localities (units in Armenia heard 800 lectures by civilian speakers in 1969–70), and cultural personages of the republics addressed officers' clubs. At the same time 'hundreds of servicemen' gave talks in local enterprises, schools, and collective farms. Local press carried appropriate articles, and arts festivals were held by the military with the local artists.[40]

A similar campaign was also described in the Kiev Military District.[41] This was mapped in a series of conferences between the MPA and the Ukrainian party and YCL leaders. Its *leitmotiv* was 'the ideal of Soviet patriotism and the internationalist duty to defend socialist achievements. Here also Lenin's theory of national relations was a subject of independent study. At thematic evenings dedicated to 'friendship of the peoples' and achievements of the union republics, soldiers of appropriate nationality told others how their national areas 'flowered' under the Soviet rule. One such evening featured nationalities of North Caucasus; another a Chechen-Ingush, an Ossetin, a Belorussian and Ukrainian. 'Days of the Republics' were also held, when soldiers returning from short leaves at home addressed groups of their fellows. The study of Russian was given 'a significant amount of attention', and special study groups were formed for soldiers who were not fluent in Russian. An interesting aspect of this campaign was that part of it was devoted to the new 'internationalist' role of the Soviet army. 'A great deal of Party attention' was directed at educating 'privates and sergeants in the spirit of love and respect for peoples and armies of socialist countries', with special emphasis on the 'essence of proletarian internationalism', on 'propagandising experience gained in joint military actions waged by soldiers-internationalists', and on 'the goals and tasks of the Warsaw Treaty Organisation'.[42]

Before evaluating the impact which service in the Soviet army has on the integration of non-Russians into the prevalent 'Soviet' model within the army and in subsequent civilian life, it is useful to assess the extent to which the ethnic composition of the armed forces and its officer corps reflects the ethnic composition of the population. Self-perception in terms of relative standing is important in attitude formation and in the soldiers' willingness to identify themselves with the required model.

Hard data on the subject of the *ethnic composition* of the Soviet armed forces are rarely available, but projections can be made on the basis of the figures given and ethnic analysis of names. The

Tsarist army was ethnically predominantly Russian, particularly in its officer corps, and, as noted above, excluded many subject nationalities from the military service. While some influx of minority recruits into Red army units undoubtedly took place during the Civil War, by the end of it the army was still three-fourth Russian and 95 per cent Slav in ethnic composition: figures given for the end of the Civil War list 77.6% Russians, 13.7% Ukrainians, 4% Belorussians, and 4.7% Latvians, Tatars, Bashkirs, and others among Red army personnel.[43] In 1972 Marshal Grechko reported that at the time of the formation of the Soviet Union (1924), the non-Russian army personnel constituted only 25 per cent of the total, as compared with their 47 per cent share in the total population.[44] No ethnic breakdown is available for the officer corps in the period, but at the beginning of the *korenizatsiia* campaign (where minorities were encouraged to enter officer schools), the army–navy schools in Petrograd had 2,354 cadets in training, of whom 83% were Russians, 4% were Ukrainians, and 3% were Jews; with Latvians, Estonians, Poles, and Germans each accounting for approximately 1%; the remaining 6% were Tatars, Bashkirs, and others.[45]

No comparable figures are available for the current period. In view of the universal military service, however, it may be assumed that the ethnic composition of Soviet servicemen by and large reflects the ethnic composition of the population, particularly in the ground forces. Technical services are known to receive a higher proportion of educated youth, and thus their composition is undoubtedly biased in favour of the Russians and national groups which are relatively better educated and more economically developed. No information is available on the NCOs, but there also a similar bias is likely to be present, enhanced by the voluntary nature of enlistement.

The officer corps, by all indications, is heavily dominated by the Russian cadre, but includes members of other ethnic groups, primarily other Slavs; Marshal Grechko himself is of Ukrainian ethnic origin. Recruitment into the officers corps requires high educational qualifications and fluent Russian, which exclude most members of some national groups, such as Central Asians. It is also voluntary and thus depends on attitudes: preference for a military career, perception of status, and expectations of advancement. Ukrainians and Belorussians meet these criteria; also some Asian groups settled within the Russian Federation (RSFSR), who are relatively bilingual (see Table 7.3) and have traditionally entered military service. These are represented in the officer corps: the Tatars, the Chuvashi, the Mordvinians and, among smaller groups, the Ossetins.

Figures for the non-Russian officers in the army and the air force basic officer ranks (*osnovnaia massa ofitserov*) were given for 1943 (see Table 7.2). Assuming that the total number of officers was approximately half-a-million,[46] the figures indicate that during the war ethnic Russians constituted over 90 per cent of the officer corps. The other two largest groups were the Ukrainians (approximately 5 per cent) and the Belorussians (approximately 1 per cent). A similar ethnic breakdown for senior artillery officers for the same year (see Table 7.2; no figures are available for the total), also indicates that the Ukrainians and the Belorussians were the second and third group among officers. Thus during the war the Soviet officer cadres were overwhelmingly Slav. Other nationalities listed included the Tatars, Georgians, Armenians, Mordvinians, Chuvashi, and the Ossetins, in the artillery also Bashkirs, Moldavians, and Kazakhs. The breakdown is interesting not only because of the groups included, but also for the omissions. With the exceptions of a few Kazakhs, there are no Central Asians (the Uzbeks were then the fourth largest national group in the population) and no Azerbaijanis. The absence of the Balts is understandable, as the three Baltic republics were not part of the Soviet Union prior to the Second World War.

There is no information on the ethnic composition of the junior officer corps in the post-war period. Some approximate guesses can be made on the basis of a social origin survey of a sample of 1,000 junior lieutenants, lieutenants, and senior lieutenants, carried out by the army newspaper, *Krasnaya Zvezda*, in 1969.[47] This reveals that 82.5 per cent of the lieutenants came from factory and office workers' families, and only 17.5 per cent from the collective farms, and that one in four had a higher education. Urban social origin of the majority indicates a bias in the sample in favour of more modernised nationalities. Of the sample's national origins it is said that it included members of 30 nationalities; those listed include all of the union republics' national groups, except the Turkmen.[48]

Ethnic characteristics of senior officers are never discussed, but an analysis here is made easier because lists of general officers are commonly available. In most cases names indicate the bearer's ethnic origin.[49] Three representative samples were used here to estimate ethnic origins of the Soviet armed forces high command: a list of all the 'generals of the army' appointed between 1940 (when the rank was established) and 1975 (59 names), a list of general officers, members of the 1974 USSR Supreme Sòviet (55 names), and the list of general officers who were elected members of the CPSU Central Committee at the 23rd Congress in 1971 (36 names). Among the generals of the army 91 per cent were Slavs (60% Russians, 20% Ukrainians, 4% Belorussians, 7% Slavs who could have been members of either group and including two Poles) and 8 per cent were of non-Slav origin (two names were Turkic, two Jewish).[50] Of general officers, members of the USSR Supreme Soviet, 95 per cent were of Slav origin (80% Russians, 15% Ukrainians), 5 per cent were of other ethnic origins;[51] 94 per cent of general officers, members of the CPSU Central Committee, were Slavs (61% Russians, 25% Ukrainians, 8% Belorussians); of the remaining 6 per cent, one was an Armenian and one was a Jew.[52] The Central Committee contingent included the Minister of Defence and his deputies, commanders-in-chief of all the services, commanders of most military districts, heads of main political administrations in the key services, and a few distinguished veterans such as Marshals Voroshilov and Budenny.

As shown in the above analysis, the Soviet army's high command is composed almost exclusively of Slavs, mostly Russians. The Ukrainians and Belorussians, and the few others who 'made it', are, for all practical purposes, Russified. All the evidence also indicates that the Slavs have a higher share in the general officer corps than in the population at large. This is not surprising if, in addition to their weight in the population, one considers traditions of military service which go back to Tsarist times, and their relatively high degree of urbanisation and educational standing. Members of other groups present also reflect their group's degree of assimilation, relative economic standing and attitudes. Among those absent, or at least invisible, one should note Central Asian Moslems (20 million strong in 1970) and members of the Baltic nations which, while small, stand highest in the Soviet Union on the scale of education and economic development. Also, with a few exceptions, there are no Jews.

In evaluating the impact of service in the Soviet army on the national integration of military personnel it should be noted that the problem does not arise in the case of ethnic Russians who form the backbone of the service. In a very real sense it is 'their' army in traditions, organisation and over all *esprit de corps*. For them, the thrust of indoctrination on the theme of the 'friendship of the people' (as distinct from general political indoctrination which is not the subject of this paper) is designed to develop the acceptance of the non-Russians as comrades-in-arms and to imbue them with a sense of responsibility for helping minority members to become good Soviet soldiers, i.e. to carry out their 'leading role' in the Soviet 'fraternal family'. It is difficult to judge how effective this is. The concept of 'Soviet patriotism' presents no special problems to a Russians soldier as it is largely equated with the old concept of Russian patriotism and loyalty to Mother Russia.

In discussing the impact on other ethnic groups a distinction should be made among members of the professional cadres—officers and NCOs—and ordinary servicemen. The professional cadres—men who voluntarily chose a military career as a profession—have already made a conscious decision to integrate on entering the service, and to pay the price of Russification necessary for advancement in what is still basically a Russian army. On the face of available evidence this seems a fair assumption. Since their integration into a prevalent model is largely a *fait accompli* this group will not be further considered in this section.[53] It might be added here, however, that the officer cadres (like professionals in general) tend to resist fine points of ideological indoctrination and to resent the time consumed by political education in the service (excluding the officers in the MPA). There is some evidence also that the younger officers, like educated Soviet youth in general, tend to be more cynical and more questioning toward the official Party line, and in some cases may be vulnerable to appeals by civil rights–national dissidents.[54]

The effect service in the army has on the integration of non-Russian servicemen should be assessed in its two different aspects: first, the servicemen's functional integration; secondly, a change of their national attitudes. In terms of functional integration, the question to ask is to what extent military service enhances a non-Russian soldier's ability to function effectively in an integrated environment and to use the Russian language, the ability that, after the service, makes him socially and geographically mobile. In terms of attitudes it is important to assess to what extent the service undermines ethnic nationalism, develops the man's identification with the goals of the political system and his loyalty to the Soviet Motherland. In both cases the impact differs for members of different groups depending on their cultural background and the degree of assimilation.

There is little doubt that army service has a major impact on functional integration of non-Russians. It breaks down their ethnic insularity and exposes them to contacts with the Russians and other national groups on a daily basis. It also, willy-nilly, forces them to acquire at least a rudimentary working knowledge of Russian. Many tend to settle in urban-industrial areas after military service, and there is evidence that some marry Russian girls and/or leave their national area altogether. The denationalisation impact of army service on non-Russian conscripts, particularly the Ukrainians, is decried by a Ukrainian national dissident:

> Now we cannot even speak of minimal safeguards for the most elementary national interests of Ukrainian youth (as well as for the youth of other Republics) in the Army. Millions of young Ukrainian men come home after several years' service nationally disorientated and linguistically demoralized and become in their turn a force exerting an influence for Russification on other young people and on the population at large. Not to mention that a considerable number of them do not return to the Ukraine at all. It is not hard to imagine how tremendously damaging all this is for national development.[55]

Western experts also agree that the integration impact of the army is strong even in the case of Central Asian Moslems, the least assimilated group among non-Russian nations:

> ... it is the army which is the principal instrument of the russification of the Muslims. ... Military service is for many young Muslims, and particularly those coming from the country, their first direct contact with foreigners. For some it is the only chance they have of becoming acquainted with the Russian language, of which previously they knew nothing. Sometimes it is a decisive experience which affects a Muslim's whole life by breaking down the cultural barriers separating him from the Russians.[56]

At the same time, given the universal character of military service and the many years in which it has been operating, the impact, as revealed by statistics of urbanisation, bilingualism (see Table 7.3), settlement patterns, and intermarriage seems rather small. The incidence of inter-ethnic marriages is growing, but is largely confined to urban areas and is still rather low.[57] The ethnic settlement pattern in 1970 reveals that with the exception of the Russians, and to a lesser extent Ukrainians and Belorussians and diaspora nationalities, only a fraction of the population of major national groups reside outside their national republics, and even those outside tend to remain in their contiguous areas.[58] In the case of major ethnic groups, the bilinguals still only rarely exceed more than a half of their total numbers. In terms of linguistic assimilation, in 1970 13 million non-Russians declared Russian as their mother tongue (14% of the non-Russian population).[59] Given the period of time passed since the Revolution this can be seen either as a great achievement, or as a rather meagre result of a sustained effort of more than 40 years, depending on one's point of view. Undoubtedly army service has played an important role in the popularisation of the language. On the evidence of Soviet ethnographers, army service ranked third, behind Russian-language schools and work contacts, as the factor instrumental in the learning of the Russian language by non-Russians.[60]

The impact of army service and its political education programme on ethnic attitudes is more difficult to assess. It would be unrealistic to expect that a national conditioning developed from childhood can be overcome in a period of from two to three years. This seems especially unlikely in an environment where, despite lip-service to the 'fraternal Soviet family of nations' the Russian predominance hits a non-Russian soldier squarely in the face. Exposure to indoctrination which is as crude as it is endlessly tedious, tends by its very repetitiveness and fictitious assertions to be counterproductive. Soviet sources include references to nationalist and religious prejudices in the service (the latter most frequently applied to Moslem soldiers), and manifestations of 'nationalist conceit'. Commanders are said to underestimate or ignore harmful nationalistic prejudices among servicemen,[61] and it is admitted that nationalist survivals continue to exist in 'the minds of some people', with the blame assigned to 'imperialist propaganda' and 'right' and 'left' opportunism.[62] A Soviet lieutenant colonel, very aptly, called the Soviet army 'a mirror of contemporary Soviet society', a statement which perhaps best reflects the limits of the army's impact on attitude formation:

In the general conditions of the social environment in which Soviet troops live and serve there are examples of the social and class distinctions inherent in our society; differences in the standards of organization and discipline of the representatives of the two allied classes of workers and collectivized peasantry, differences between manual workers and those doing brain work, and also special national traits.[63]

In Soviet society at large the evidence is strong that ethnic nationalism has been growing among union republic nations; at the same time a trend towards assimilation into the surrounding Russian majority has been noted among most national groups with area of settlement within the RSFSR, and among diaspora groups.[64] Both trends seem to be reflected in the Soviet army by the visible presence of the national groups in the professional cadres, and in the apparent impact (or lack thereof) military service has on their integration into the Soviet society. Evidence available is inadequate to draw any definitive conclusions, but it seems that, with one significant exception, army service has little impact on the national integration of groups, among whom ethnic nationalism is on the increase, but that it is a potent factor in furthering integration of groups which are already on an upward assimilation curve. It can be hypothesised further that, in the case of unassimilated and less modernised national groups, functional integration promoted in the period of military service may actually serve to strengthen the ranks of their national élites which have acted as spokesmen for the new ethnic nationalism, as in the case, particularly, of the Moslems of Central Asia.

The one significant exception is the Slavs—Ukrainians, Belorussians and Poles—the first the most numerous and the most important among the non-Russian ethnic groups in the Soviet Union. Because of the close cultural affinity to the Russians, the Slavs are highly vulnerable to Russification, a vulnerability of which the Ukrainians particularly are very much aware, as seen in statements quoted above. For the Slavs service in the Soviet army seems to be a powerful factor in furthering their integration into Soviet society and advancing their Russification, both in functional and attitudinal terms. This is reflected by their considerable representation in the officer corps and in the command structure. Among the Slavs the Ukrainians are a special case, not only because of their numbers. The Ukraine, more than any other of the Soviet republics, has experienced, in the post-Second-World-War period, a strong upsurge of ethnic nationalism and in recent times (as also in the twenties), has been the focus of the ethnic conflict in Soviet national relations. At the same time, however, the Ukrainians, outside their republic, are assimilating to the point where they are second only to the Russians in promoting Soviet national integration among other ethnic groups.

In the case of other major union republic nationalities little evidence exists that service in the Soviet army has played any role in their attitudinal integration; Georgians and Armenians and the three Baltic nations are all historical nationalities with a strong sense of separate national identity and all have shown signs of growth of ethnic nationalism. For them, also, the functional integration role of army service is less important, because they all have high educational quotients and a relatively high degree of economic development (Latvians and Estonians stand highest on the Soviet scale). The two Caucasian groups, particularly the Armenians, are represented in the officer corps (as they are also in the All-Union service), but there is little evidence of their denationalisation. The Baltic nations—probably because of their small numbers as much as because of their attitudes—are not represented. For Central Asian Moslems and the Azerbaijanis army service is very important in terms of functional integration, as mentioned above, but it seems to have had no impact on their attitudes, and indeed may, in the long run, contribute to the growth of ethnic nationalism in their republics, by facilitating the transition of Moslem youth from the insularity of their villages to their republic's political arena. Their absence from the officer corps, despite their significant share in the Soviet population, seems to be a function of cultural attitudes as much as of their still relatively low level of modernisation.

In summary, the Soviet army plays a significant role as an instrument of functional integration of all the Soviet non-Russian nations and nationalities and appears to be effective in attitudinal integration of autonomous and smaller nationalities and, in part also, of the Slav groups. But army service seems to have had little effect in counteracting ethnic nationalism of major union republic nations. The fact that national integration in the armed forces is for all practical purposes synonymous with Russification may be a strong contributing factor to this failure.

Because of the relatively small size of non-integrated groups (except Central Asian Moslems) and their absence in the officer corps (except the Ukrainians) this failure in attitudinal integration does not seem to be at present an important variable in the combat effectiveness of the Soviet armed forces, although in the long run it may become a major problem if Central Asian and Ukrainian nationalism continues to grow.[65] It is however, perceived as a weakness in the army and in society at large, and is a matter of major concern. In the armed forces this concern is reflected in the emphasis on integrated organisation and training and in the importance attached to political indoctrination.

NOTES AND REFERENCES

1. See Yaroslav Bilinsky, 'The Rulers and the Ruled', *Problems of Communism*, Vol. xvi, No. 5 (September-October, 1967), pp. 16–26; Serweryn Bialer, 'How Russians Rule Russia', Ibid., Vol. xiii, No. 5 (September-October, 1964), pp. 45–52; and Teresa Rakowska-Harmstone, 'The Dialectics of Nationalism in the U.S.S.R.', Ibid., Vol. xxiii, No. 3, (May–June, 1974), pp. 1–22.
2. Col. P. Rtishchev, 'Leninskaya natsional'naya politika i stroitel'stvo Sovetskikh Vooruzhennykh Sil', pp. 3–9, *Voenno-Istoricheskii Zhurnal*, No. 6, June 1974, p. 3.
3. Some sources count the preliminary period as stage one. In line with other sources, however, such as Col. A. Korkeshkin, 'Strength of the Soviet Army', *Soviet Military Review*, No. 11, 1972, pp. 58–60, it was decided here to count as stage one the period beginning in 1924.
4. Rtishchev, op. cit., p. 5.
5. I. Z. Zakharov, 'Sovetskie Vooruzhennye Sily na zashchite natsional 'nykh i internatsionnal'nykh interesov narodov SSSR', pp. 103–118, *KPSS-Organizator Bratskoi Druzhby Narodov SSSR, Uchenye Zapiski Kafedr Obshchestvennykh Nauk Vuzov Leningrada; Istoriya KPSS*; Vol. xiii (Leningrad, 1973), p. 5. The Resolution of the Central Committee of the RKP (b) stated that it was shown by experience that 'the tendencies of the separate socialist republics to keep their military operations, inclusive of operational aspects, within their national boundaries, led, in practice, to repeated clashes between their local and national objectives and the military tasks of the Socialist Revolution as a whole'. Ibid.
6. Col N. Pankratov, 'The Militant Union in the Making', *Soviet Military Review*, pp. 11–13, No. 9, September 1972, p. 12.
7. Ibid., p. 13.
8. Korkeshkin, op. cit., p. 59, and Zakharov, op. cit., pp. 106–7. It may be remembered that it was also in April 1919, at the 8th Congress of the RKP (b), that the Party programme established the principle of the unitary character of the Party, denying autonomy to its branches based in national territories. The principle, which is still in force, provides that all the national branches of the Party are subordinated to its Central Committee on the basis of democratic centralism.

The Soviet Army and National Integration 151

9. Rtishchev, op. cit., p. 5.
10. Zakharov, op cit., p. 110.
11. Ivan Dziuba, *Internationalism or Russification?* (London: Weidenfeld and Nicolson, 1968), p. 136.
12. Ibid.
13. Quoted in Zakharov, op. cit., p. 108; also in Rtishchev, op. cit., p. 6.
14. Rtishchev, op. cit., p. 6.
15. Ibid.
16. Zakharov, op. cit., p. 109.
17. The 7 March 1938 Decree of the Central Committee of the All-Union Communist Party (Bolsheviks, VKP (b)), and the Council of National Commissars of the USSR, provided that national units and formations, and military schools, be reorganised into All-Union units, and be staffed in extra-territorial manner, and that all citizens of national republics and provinces should be called for military service on the same basis as all other nationalities of the USSR. Quoted Ibid., p. 111.
18. Rtishchev, op. cit., p. 7.
19. XVIII Sezd Vsesoiuznoi Kommunisticheskoi Partii (b) Stenograficheskyi Otchet, 1939, p. 191. Cited in Robert Conquest, *Soviet Nationalities Policy in Practice* (London: The Bodley Head, 1967), p. 52.
20. Rtishchev, op. cit., p. 8.
21. *Ibid.*; also Korkeshkin, op. cit., p. 59 and Marshal A. A. Grechko, 'Sluzhim Sovetskomu Soiuzu', pp. 7–25, in *Armiia Bratstva Narodov* (Moscow, 1972).
22. Rtishchev, op. cit., p. 8; see also John Erickson, 'Soviet Military Manpower Policies', pp. 29–47, *Armed Forces and Society*, Vol. 1, No. 1 (November 1974), p. 35.
23. Korkeshkin, 23 Korkeshkin, op. cit., p. 60.
24. See Teresa Rakowska-Harmstone, 'Proletarian Internationalism – A New Stage in the Development of Eastern Europe', *Survey* (98), Spring 1976.
25. Rtishchev op. cit., p. 9.
26. Erickson, op. cit., p. 43.
27. The meaning of 'proletarian internationalism' is all-embracing; it postulates a unity based on the class principle which overrides ethnic, racial, and other loyalties; this in turn postulates the acknowledgement of the leading role of the Communist Party – as the vanguard of the working class – (in the Soviet usage, this means the Communist Party of the Soviet Union (CPSU), and the acceptance of the principle of democratic centralism, which is the Party's operational principle. See A. K. Azizian, *Leninskaia natsional 'naia politika v razvitii i deistvii*, (Moscow, 1972).
28. Col. Gen. S. Kurkotkin (Commander of the Transcaucasus Military District), 'In the Spirit of Friendship of Peoples', *Kommunist Vooruzhennykh Sil*, No. 16, August 1970, pp. 23–9.
29. Quoted in Col. K. Spirov, 'The Soviet Army – A School of Internationalism', pp. 23–5, *Soviet Military Review*, No. 10, October 1974, p. 23.
30. Rtishchev, op. cit., p. 4.
31. Spirov op cit., p. 24.
32. Erickson, op. cit., pp. 35–6.
33. Captain A. Skrylnik, 'Our Strength is in the Friendship of the Peoples', *Soviet Military Review*, pp. 2–5, No. 7, July 1972, p. 5.

34. Ibid.; and Kurkotkin, op. cit.
35. 'Priem v Kremle v chest vypushnikov voennykh akademii', *Krasnaya Zvezda*, 2 July 1974, p. 1.
36. B. G. Gafurov, (an interview with) 'Nations: Flourishing, Drawing Together', pp. 2–5, *Soviet Military Review*, No. 10, (October, 1972), p. 5. Gafurov is a noted historian, an ethnic Tadzhik, and, for 10 years (1945–56) was the first secretary of the Tadzhik Communist Party, Since 1956 he has been with the Academy of Sciences of the USSR, acting as the leading Soviet representative in relations with the Third World.
37. Teresa Rakowska-Harmstone, 'Recent Trends in Soviet Nationality Policy', N. T. Dodge, ed., *The Soviet in Asia*, Proceedings of a Symposium sponsored by the Washington Chapter of the American Association for the Advancement of Slavic Studies and the Institute for Sino-Soviet Studies, George Washington University, May 19–20, 1972 (Mechanicsville, Md., 1972), pp. 7–17.
38. Resolution of the Central Committee of the CPSU 'O podgotovke k 50-letiiu obrazovaniia Soiuza Sotsialisticheskikh Respublic', pp. 3–13, *Partiinaia Zhizn'*, No. 5, 1972.
39. Kurkotkin, op. cit.
40. Ironically one of them was an Armenian poetess, Sylva Kapoutikian, who has been under strong criticism for nationalist deviations.
41. V. I. Bukhalo, 'Some Forms of International Education for Army Youth (Based on Materials from the Red Flag Kiev Military District 1966–1970)', *Ukrains 'kyy Istorychnyy Zhurnal*, October 1974, pp. 58–65.
42. The 'internationalist' theme in its application to relations between socialist countries obviously is considered important in the Soviet army's political indoctrination. A detailed programme of lectures on the subject, for example, was discussed by Capt. A. Starovarov, 'The Armed Forces of the Socialist States and their combat cooperation; a guarantee of the peace and security of the peoples', *Kommunist Vooruzhennykh Sil*, No. 17, September 1970, pp 61–8.
43. Korkeshkin, op. cit., p. 59.
44. Marshal A. A. Grechko, 'Armiya Sotsialisticheskaya, mnogonatsional' naya', *Kransnaya Zvezda*, 17 December 1972, pp. 1–2.
45. In December 1923. Zakharov, op. cit., p. 109.
46. It is reported that during the Second World War some two millions Soviet officers were trained, at a rate of 400,000–500,000 annually, and that the rate of annual replacement equalled total annual input of new trainees, because of the extremely high casualty rate. Peter Kruzhin, 'Soviet Military Colleges', *Analysis of Current Developments in the Soviet Union*, Institute for the Study of the USSR, (Munich), No. 610, 28 July 1970. The figure of 500,000 was therefore used here as an approximate base figure for the officer corps in 1943. This, compared with data in Table 2, gives the figure of approximately 460,000 Russian officers, i.e., 92% of the total. The strength of the Soviet officer corps in the 70s was estimated at approximately 685,000 (20% of the armed forces of 3.4 million). See Herbert Goldhamer, *Soviet Military Management at the Troop Level* (Santa Monica: Rand Corporation, 1974), p. 11.
47. Col F. Khaturin, Lt. Col. A. Shchelokov, 'Lieutenants; Sociological Portrait', *Soviet Military Review*, No. 9, September 1969, pp. 2–7.
48. Russians, Ukrainians, Belorussians, Moldavians, Latvians, Estonians, Lith-

The Soviet Army and National Integration 153

uanians, Kazakhs, Armenians, Georgians, Azerbaijanis, Tadzhiks, Kirgiz, Uzbeks, Tatars, Mordvinians, Chuvashi, Mari, Bashkirs, Kalmyks, Kabardinians, Ossetins, Komi, and others. Ibid.

49. Ethnic analysis of names is not an exact method but it has proved to be generally accurate. In most cases, ethnic origin can be deduced from a name, if given name, family name, and patronymic are included. The drawback of the method is that it is sometimes impossible to distinguish between names of related ethnic groups, as in the case of Slav names (although some Ukrainian, Belorussian, and Polish names are quite distinct), or Turkic names. Slav and Moslem names, however, are quite distinct, as are Armenian and Georgian names, Lithuanian names, and names of Germanic origin (the latter frequently in Latvia and Estonia).
50. The list in Peter Kruzhin, 'Soviet Generals of the Army', *Radio Liberty Research*, RI 89/75, 28 February 1975.
51. P. Kruzhin, 'Predstavitelstvo Sovetskikh vooruzjennykh sil v Verkhovnom Sovete SSSR 9-go sozyva', *Radio Liberty Research*, No 205/74, 10 July 1974.
52. List in Peter Kruzhin, 'Military Representation in the Party's Top Organs', *Analysis of Current Developments in the Soviet Union*, Institute for the Study of the USSR (Munich), No. 654, 8 June 1971.
53. Within a narrower, more specialised, and more explicitly Russian setting the army professionals are a counterpart of Party and state functionaries in the All-Union service, the 'Feds' as it were, who run the USSR. This group is also heavily dominated by the Slav (mostly Russian) element, and non-Russians among them tend to be Russified and, in some cases, to be 'more Catholic than the Pope.' As in the officer corps Ukrainians are second to the Russians also in this group, and it includes individuals of other ethnic origin who 'made it' in the federal service. B. G. Gafurov, quoted above, is an example.
54. In May 1969, the naval officers Gavrilov, Kosyrev, and Paramonov were arrested by the KGB and accused of founding a 'Union to Struggle for Political Rights in the USSR.' See Peter Reddaway, *Uncensored Russia: Protest and Dissent in the Soviet Union*, (New York: American Heritage Press, 1972), p. 175.
55. Dzyuba, op. cit., p. 137.
56. Alexandre Bennigsen and Chantal Lemercier-Quelquejay, *Islam in the Soviet Union*, (New York: Praeger Publishers, 1969), pp. 199–200.
57. Intermarriage between Slavs and between Slavs and Jews is fairly common, but it is less frequent between other groups and between them and Slavs. For Moslems, exogamous marriages are still quite rare. See Ann Sheehy, 'Intermarriage in Central Asia and Kazakhstan', *Radio Liberty Research*, RL 149/75, 11 April 1975.
58. *Tsentral' noe Statisticheskoe Upravlenie pri Sovete Ministrov SSSR, Itogi Vsesoyuznoi Perepisi Naseleniya 1970 goda*; Vol IV, *Natsional 'nyi Sostav Naseleniya SSSR, Soiuznykh i Avtonomnykh Respublik, Kraev, Oblastei i Natsional'nykh Okrugov* (Moscow, 1973) Tables 1–3, pp. 9–19.
59. Ibid., Table 4, p. 20.
60. S. I. Bruk and M. N. Guboglo, 'Faktory rasprostraneniia dvuiazychiia u narodov SSSR', pp. 17–30, *Sovetskaya Etnografiia*, 1975, No. 5, p. 25, and for Moldavia, Tables 7 and 8, p. 26. It should be noted that in most ASSRs the instruction in the native language in phased out by the 6th grade and is replaced, in higher grades, by instruction in the Russian language. This is not

the case in the union republics where national language instruction in national language schools continues through secondary education.
61. Kurkotkin, op. cit.
62. Rtischev, op. cit., p. 9.
63. Quoted in Yuri V. Marin, 'Call for More Militant Patriotism Among Soviet Youth', *Analysis of Current Developments in the Soviet Union*, Institute for the Study of the USSR, No. 536, 18 February 1969, p. 2. The quote is from Lt. Col. P. Proshutinskii, 'The Social and Political Nature of Discipline', *Kommunist Vooruzhennykh Sil*, No. 22, 1968, p. 44.
64. See George W. Simmons, ed., *Nationalism in the USSR and Eastern Europe in the Era of Brezhnev and Kosygin* (to be published by Detroit University Press); also T. Rakowska-Harmstone, 'Dialectics . . . , op. cit.
65. Central Asian Moslems and the Azerbaijanis alone among the Soviet nationalities have the fertility rate exceeding 30 per thousand of population. See G. Baldwin, et. al., 'Projections of the Population of the USSR and Eight Sub-Divisions, By Age and Sex: 1973 to 2000', *International Population Reports*, U.S. Department of Commerce, Social and Economic Statistics Administration, Bureau of the Census, Ser. P-91, No. 24, June 1975.

Part IV
Strategic Perspectives

8 Arms Control and Soviet Strategic Forces: The risks of asking SALT to do too much

Richard Burt

Few diplomatic enterprises in the postwar era inspired as much enthusiasm in the West and especially the United States as the Strategic Arms Limitation Talks (SALT) with the Soviet Union. Despite occasional criticism, during the early 1970s the view that the negotiations offered an important and promising means of reducing the risk of East-West nuclear war and of engaging the Soviet Union in a more generalised process of detente became widely-shared. This consensus – which, for the most part, still exists – reflected several deeply-felt beliefs. These were that in an era of strategic parity (*a*) the political utility of nuclear weapons had declined; (*b*) the military contingencies in which the use of nuclear weapons could be credibly threatened had correspondingly been reduced in number; (*c*) a conceptual framework for working out a stable super-power strategic relationship existed; and (*d*) efforts by either side to achieve some vaguely-defined position of strategic 'superiority' was counter-productive and perhaps dangerous. These sentiments were reinforced by the successful efforts of US and Soviet negotiators to agree on the terms of accords limiting ballistic missile defences and ballistic missile deployment in 1972.[1] Although the so-called SALT I accords, particularly the five-year Interim Agreement controlling land- and sea-based missile deployment, contained several imperfections, the very fact that they were reached demonstrated to many in the West that the Soviet leadership shared, or at least was sensitive to, prevailing western notions of deterrent stability and nuclear 'sufficiency'.

However, over the last five years, much of the optimism generated by the early experience of SALT has been dissipated. This is partly due to the sheer complexity of the follow-on negotiations: governments have found it difficult to grapple with the difficult conceptual problems and sensitive political issues posed by attempting to extend the SALT formula to new categories of weapons systems.[2] But an equally important problem, has been created by the Soviet Union's strategic weapons programme. While the Soviet Union remains publicly committed to further progress at SALT, it has become increasingly apparent that western assumptions concerning Soviet arms control objectives and strategic procurement policies are badly in need of revision. Recent Soviet behaviour cannot be easily reconciled with what were earlier seen to be the dominant 'lessons' of SALT. Three aspects of the contemporary Soviet strategic weapons programme seem especially disconcerting:

(i) *The continuing momentum of Soviet weapons procurement.* Having deployed over 1000 intercontinental ballistic missiles (ICBM) and 650 submarine-launched ballistic missiles (SLBM) between 1967–75, the Soviet Union is justifiably able to claim super-power status. Yet her strategic requirements seem open-ended: three new, high-payload ICBMs are entering the Soviet inventory as well as two new ballistic missile submarines and a new SLBM. New ICBMs and SLBMs – for possible deployment in the 1980s – are also reported to be under development.[3] Keeping in mind the fact that it is enormously difficult to characterise precisely the overall state of the super-power strategic balance (especially using such 'static' indicators as numbers of warheads, deliverable payload or total megatonnage), it is still difficult to resist the conclusion that the Soviet Union has not adopted the western concept of parity.

(ii) *The 'defensive' emphasis of Soviet strategic deployment.* Despite the willingness of the Soviet Union to limit severely the construction of ballistic missile defences in the ABM treaties of 1972 and 1974, there is little indication that the Soviet leadership is prepared to rest deterrence on mutual vulnerability.[4] The continuing importance placed on the maintenance of a large and redundant air defence establishment can be explained by the possible threat to Soviet territory posed by conflicts on her periphery. Yet the apparent emphasis placed on civil defence planning, together with a vigorous programme of research and development on advanced ballistic missile defence technology, indicate that the Soviet Union has placed high priority on limiting damage in the event of nuclear war. When these developments are coupled with the counter-force potential of the new family of ICBM now undergoing deployment, it seems perfectly legitimate to wonder whether the Soviet Union believes she can actually wage and win a nuclear conflict.

(iii) *The manipulative approach to arms control negotiations and agreements*. Despite references to SALT as a super-power dialogue, the experience of negotiation has not been overwhelmingly positive. Contrary to earlier expectations on the part of many, the talks have failed to evolve into a seminar for strategic 'enlightenment', where each side would come to understand better the military and political preoccupations of the other. For a start, the United States quickly learned that important issues could only be resolved in direct talks with the high-level Soviet leadership. More importantly, the Soviet Union has shown a curious insensitivity to western expectations concerning the implementation of agreements. By exploiting the terms of the 1972 accords to their fullest, the Soviet Union stands accused of violating the 'spirit', if not the precise language of these agreements.[5] The Soviet Union also appears bent on exploiting the structure of existing East-West negotiations, by rapidly modernising those forces – especially delivery systems targeted against western Europe – that are not subject to limitation at SALT or by the force reduction talks under way in Vienna.

How to interpret recent Soviet procurement decisions and negotiating behaviour is, of course, the crucial question facing western governments. If the Soviet Union does not accept the basic tenets of western strategy, are efforts at arms control futile? Are the two sides therefore locked into a continuing and dangerous process of strategic arms competition? In attempting to answer these questions, it is important to recognise that there are several competing explanations for why Soviet practice has failed to match western expectations. The growing popularity of the organisational perspective in governmental decision making has led many analysts to conclude, despite a paucity of information, that the Soviet military establishment—especially élite and budgetarily-favoured service arms like the Strategic Rocket Corps—is essentially geared (to borrow Khrushchev's phrase) to 'turn out missiles like sausages'. Thus, the size and posture of Soviet strategic forces, it is suggested, may bear little resemblance to present-day Soviet notions of what strategic forces are good for and how they might be used.[6] Similarly, observers sensitive to the 'politics' of Soviet defence decision-making point out that like the United States, the Soviet leadership in the early 1970s did not have an entirely free hand in embarking on Secretary General Brezhnev's 'peace programme' with the West; Brezhnev, it is maintained, had to win military acquiesence to arms control with the United States by making certain guarantees concerning defence spending and perhaps the deployment of specific systems.[7] There is also the more fundamental argument which springs from the western model of 'arms race' behaviour: this is simply that from the Soviet perspective, 'worst' case analysis suggests that recent procurement decisions are appropriate responses to what are viewed as threatening developments in the West – for example, the elaboration of more discriminating targeting strategies or the improvement of missile accuracies.[8]

These approaches, to a varying degree, are all useful in fitting the troubling aspects of Soviet strategic behaviour into some comprehensible pattern. At the same time, they all seem to suffer from the same weakness: they impose western standards of rationality (or with some bureaucratic models, irrationality) on Soviet actions. The problem, then, may lie as much with western expectations as with Soviet behaviour. The inauguration of the SALT process and the 1972 agreements may have led western governments and observers to conclude that a greater degree of consensus between East and West on strategic issues existed than was actually the case. In other words, notwithstanding detente or the emergence of strategic parity, the Soviet Union may rationally view important political and military advantages accruing to the continuing accumulation of strategic arms.

If this is true, then the implications for SALT and American strategic force design are enormous. But the task of formulating a workable model of Soviet strategic behaviour is clearly difficult. To the extent that it exists, the Soviet strategic 'debate' is muted and is often conducted in a manner that provides little insight into real Soviet concerns. Doctrinal pronouncements are plentiful, but western analysts have approached them with understandable wariness: as John Erickson has pointed out, military doctrine has been formulated by and for military men.[9] As such, it possesses an educative and morale-building function and cannot thus be understood to provide a fair representation of Soviet thought. Soviet strategic doctrine, moreover, for years appeared to be out of joint with Soviet capabilities; the oft-noted emphasis in Soviet writings on 'warfighting' did not, during the 1960s, appear to offer any realistic chance of success. But the steady augmentation of offensive and defensive capabilities has brought Soviet strategic doctrine and the forces themselves into greater congruence. This, together with the questionable applicability of Western models, makes it profitable to place US-strategic competition into the context of Soviet experience, military doctrine and political objectives.

NUCLEAR DIPLOMACY AND MILITARY DOCTRINE

The starting point of any examination of Soviet thinking about nuclear weapons is probably to recognise that for much of the postwar period the Soviet Union believed herself to be in a position of overwhelming strategic inferiority. It is debatable whether the United States, in the immediate aftermath of the Second World War, consciously sought to use the US nuclear monopoly to impede the process of Soviet consolidation in eastern Europe. As critics of these arguments have rightly pointed out, if the Truman Administration did engage in 'nuclear diplomacy', it surely wasn't effective. But whether or not the US 'nuclear monopolists' of the late 1940s recognised the impact of nuclear weapons is a very different question from whether the Soviet Union was sensitive to western nuclear potential. The procurement by the United States during the 1950s of several hundred nuclear-capable bombers and their deployment in forward bases encircling the Soviet Union was inevitably understood by the Soviet Union as jeopardising the hard-fought gains of the war. After essentially establishing a buffer zone in eastern Europe to protect the regime from external threats, the Soviet Union found that the US Strategic Air Command (SAC) ruled out the possibility that she could remain immune from attack in the event of major East-West conflict.

It is, of course, difficult to calculate the actual psychological impact on the Soviet leadership of American strategic superiority during the Cold War period. Until the Soviet Union possessed a credible nuclear delivery capability (and a regional one at that), the political and military relevance of nuclear weapons was publicly denigrated in the late 1940s and early 1950s in terms similar to Chinese statements a decade later. Despite this, Soviet leaders during the 1950s and 1960s were made acutely aware of the existence of American superiority. Nuclear weapons were woven deeply into the fabric of western defence doctrine and the United States sought political value from her expanding strategic weapons arsenal at the several critical junctures during the period. But to argue that the Soviet Union 'learned' the value of strategic nuclear power from observing American behaviour is not persuasive in itself. Its major flaw is simply that Soviet writing and behaviour over the last decade has not reflected the growing perception in the West that nuclear weapons possess declining political utility and that strategic 'superiority' is an illusory goal. In fact, just the opposite seems to be the case. Whether, as many observers suggest, the Cuban missile crisis had a decisive impact on Soviet strategic thinking is unclear. But it is probably true that Soviet sensitivity to the drawbacks of inferiority was more acute than American appreciation of the advantages this created. The options opened for the United States by strategic superiority were, for the most part, taken for granted. In American debates over nuclear weapons in the 1960s strategists focused on conflicts and contingencies like Vietnam where strategic power seemed to offer few, if any, solutions. The options closed for the Soviet Union, on the other hand, were surely felt more keenly.

The impact of US strategic superiority on Soviet perceptions was reinforced by geography and ideology. Geography has literally 'brought home' the meaning of war to the Russians. In the postwar era, the fact that the Soviet Union lay adjacent to the central theatre of East-West conflict lent to Soviet strategic thinking a quality of realism lacking in much American theory. Central strategic war, according to Soviet literature, is not likely to stem from mechanistic instabilities within the super-power military relationship, but from real and enduring differences between competing political systems and national interests. But the Soviet view of the political roots of conflict is not a detached one. The two super-powers are not, as Paul Warnke characterised them, 'apes on a treadmill', doomed to act out a futile drama that neither is able to understand nor control. Instead, the Soviet accumulation of power has the positive function of protecting the state (and its socialist gains) in a hostile world. Seen in this light, it is not possible for Soviet weapons deployment to be definitionally 'destabilising'. Soviet strategic power makes attack from the West less likely and thus forces would-be aggressors to adjust themselves to the reality of the

Soviet presence, the changing 'correlation of forces' and the legitimacy of Soviet prerogatives.[10]

It is difficult to deny that the Soviet Union view of the political function of strategic power has not been borne out by recent experience. The doctrine of the declining utility of strategic power very much reflects an American accommodation to the realities of nuclear parity. The Soviet Union, on the other hand, has been handsomely rewarded during the last decade by the decision of her leadership to embark upon and to sustain a nearly continuous process of strategic modernisation. Militarily, the attainment of parity has served to accentuate her non-nuclear capabilities, especially her conventional capabilities in central Europe and to diminish the credibility of US ultimatums over Soviet military intervention in the Third World. Perhaps more important, however, are the political gains flowing from parity. From the Soviet perspective (as well as others), it is her expansion of strategic power that makes the process of detente possible, if not irreversible. The United States suggested several approaches to strategic arms limitation during the 1960s, but none were acceptable to Soviet leaders because they would have frozen the Soviet Union into a permanent position of inferiority. In essence, the arrival of nuclear parity forced the United States to take the Soviet Union seriously; for the Soviet Union, the very inauguration of the SALT dialogue constituted an important political victory. SALT conferred upon the Soviet Union super-power respectability and provided external proof that a change in the balance of power had indeed taken place.

Although SALT has been assigned a special priority by the Soviet leadership, its function seems to differ in many important respects from the dominant American conception. While both sides view the exercise as essentially concerned with reducing the likelihood of conflict, there is no consensus over what the causes of such a conflict might be. Western strategic theory stresses inherent characteristics of the strategic relationship, i.e., some postures are more stable than others. It also takes a detached view of developments that could threaten super-power strategic stability. Deterrence models, for example, talk of 'Country A' and 'Country B'. This tendency towards strategic 'aloofness' can be discerned in the arguments of influential US policy-makers: Former Secretary of Defence Robert McNamara often argued during the 1960s that a larger number of Soviet strategic weapons would reduce American incentives for pre-emption and would thus lower the risk of nuclear conflict. Similar views are difficult to find in the Soviet literature. To the extent that Soviet statements reflect a coherent model of strategic interaction, there seems to be nothing inherently dangerous about increases in Soviet capabilities. Even those systems, however, that pose little threat to the survivability of Soviet means of retaliation, like SLBM, are seen to pose grave threats to stability when they are deployed by the West. There is thus no internal inconsistency between Soviet interests in SALT and the continued modernisation and expansion of strategic forces. For the United States, the maintenance of some rough balance in strategic capabilities is a prerequisite to success at SALT. Without 'bargaining chips' in the form of new weapons systems under development, it is maintained that the Soviet Union would have little interest in engaging in arms control. The modernisation of the American inventory – or at least the threat to modernise – is seen a necessary 'tactical' accompaniment to negotiations. As I have argued, the Soviet approach appears to be different. Just as the expansion of strategic forces was a necessary prerequisite for the founding of the talks, improvements to the Soviet posture are integral to the negotiations themselves: they are to some extent what the negotiations are all about.[11]

At the same time, the present Soviet leadership appears to take a realistic attitude towards what can be achieved in superpower arms control. Despite SALT's importance as a mechanism for recognising Soviet strategic gains, recent Soviet statements seem to recognise that there are limits to what can be achieved. Strategic 'superiority' is not ruled out as an ultimate objective, but out as a practical outcome of existing super-power strategic competition. Unlike much western strategic writing, which views the concept of strategic superiority as 'meaningless' in an era of assured second-strike forces or alternatively, dangerous if either side could succeed in denying the other side a second strike capability, the Soviet position seems simply to be that while 'superiority' would be politically useful for the Soviet Union, she is unlikely to attain it in the near future.[12]

The Soviet concept of 'superiority' – that nuclear advantages can be translated into political influence – reflects a distrust of deterrence that pervades much of what Benjamin Lambeth has called the Soviet 'doctrinal image of nuclear war'.[13] Like super-power strategic arms competition, nuclear conflict is understood as a continuation of the idelogical struggle. In Clausewitzian terms, war – even involving super-power strategic exchanges – is a 'supremely political act' in which the Soviet Union can and, indeed, must prevail.¹⁴ To the extent that doctrine is actually reflected in force posture and operational tactics, this has three important consequences.¹⁵

First, doctrines of deterrence – merely threatening a certain level of assured destruction – cannot be relied upon to protect the state. If conflict occurs, it is likely to result from deep-seated differences between systems and not temporary asymmetries in the US-Soviet balance. Moreover, the act of devastating the civilian and industrial assets of an adversary and then sitting by helplessly while Soviet urban centres are subjected to similar attacks will not in any way guarantee the survival of the Soviet Union. Similarly, concepts for controlling escalation after the nuclear threshold has been crossed are, for the most part, absent from Soviet literature. Both for political reasons (the requirements of victory) and because intra-conflict deterrence would be enormously difficult to manage, *escalation would largely be automatic*.¹⁶ Second, the inadequacy of pure deterrence strategies means that emphasis must be given to 'war-waging'. Many force characteristics that are inimical to deterrence are essential in this context. The ability to launch pre-emptive attacks, especially against military targets, is required. The ability to defend one's own military assets and population against attack is equally important. At any given level of conflict, *the Soviet Union would seek to be dominant*. Third, the ferocity of the Soviet doctrinal image of nuclear conflict ironically imposes a certain caution in Soviet behaviour. American efforts to lower the nuclear 'threshold' (implicit in selective targeting scenarios) are viewed with distrust because they imply that limited East-West nuclear conflicts are possible and can be managed. Because the nuclear threshold in the event of conflict is already low for the Soviet Union (because of the rapidity of escalation), the overall threshold for overall conflict, it would seem, remains high. *The Soviet Union, then, does not intend to stumble inadvertently into war with the West*.¹⁷

ASSESSING THE THREAT

Analyses of Soviet attitudes towards the political and military functions of nuclear weapons are by themselves not terribly useful for pinpointing the specific problems created by the Soviet Union's expansion of strategic forces. However, if Soviet procurement decisions are placed into an evolving doctrinal framework, it is possible to identify the central issue that should concern western defence planners over the coming decade: the growing capability of the Soviet Union to attack US strategic forces and limit damage to its own military and civilian assets in the event of counter-attack. Several different aspects of the emerging Soviet offensive and defensive posture have led some observers to wonder if the Soviet Union, at some point during the coming decade, might be capable of denying the United States a credible means of retaliation in time of nuclear war. The new generation of ICBMs now undergoing deployment in the Soviet Union has particularly generated controversy. These systems alone could not deprive the United States from responding to a nuclear attack with bombers (on alert) and SLBM (at sea), but there is little doubt that the SS-17, SS-18, SS19 ICBMs pose severe problems for the survivability of the existing US land-based missile force.

The new Soviet ICBMs have important advantages over the systems they are replacing: they possess greater throw-weight, they have been equipped with MIRV and, most important, as testing continues and design improvements are made, they will be increasingly accurate. Given the estimated yield of the separately-targetable warheads atop the new ICBM, the attainment of accuracies (expressed in terms of circular error probability) of .25nm will result in single-shot kill probabilities (of warheads) against hardened targets like missile silos ranging from .54 to .99 (see Table 8.1). This means that even in spite of the technical and physical problems inherent in co-ordinating a first-strike against some 1000 missile silos in the United States, the Soviet Union, in theory at least, could be able to destroy over 90 per cent of the US *Minuteman* force with a fraction of her ICBM when she has completed phasing in her new family of land-based missiles in the early 1980s. If, as missile guidance techniques improve, the Soviet Union is successful in reducing warhead accuracy to .2nm or below (purportedly the accuracy of some existing US ICBM), some 1800–2000 MT-range warheads (aboard 300 SS-18 or alternatively, 500 SS-19) could, in theory, threaten the entire US land-based missile force.[18] As some analysts have pointed out, this would not only mean that the United States would lose one component of her retaliatory 'triad' in a first-strike, but that the Soviet Union – even after a US second-strike – would possess a large margin of 'residual' counterforce and countervalue superiority.[19]

The counterforce capability of Soviet ICBM raises troubling

TABLE 8.1 The New Generation of Soviet Strategic Missiles

Category	Type	Max. Range (St. Miles)	Throw-weight[1] (Payload in pounds)	Warhead yield	(SSKP)[2] 1RV	2RV	Numbers deployed (Jan 77)	Comments
ICBM	SS-X-16[3]	3000+	n.a.	n.a.	–	–	T	SS-13 replacement
	SS-17	6000+	4-6000	4X800KT[5]	.54	.78	40	SS-11 replacement
	SS-18[4]							
	Mod 1	6000+	15-18000	18-23MT	.99	.99	50	SS-9 replacement
	Mod 2			8X 1MT+[5]	.57	.81		
	SS-19							
	Mod 1	6000+	6-7000	6X 1 MT[5]	.57	.81	140	SS-11 replacement
	Mod 2			5 MT	.91	.99		
IRBM	SS-X-20[6]							
	Mod 1	3000	n.a.	3X KT range	–	–	T	S- 4/5
	Mod 2	4000+		KT range				replacement

NOTE: Unless otherwise stated, the estimates in this Table are drawn from Table 1 in *The Military Balance 1976-77* (London: IISS), pp. 73-5. T = Undergoing testing

1. These are estimates, see Edward N. Luttwak, 'Strategic Power: Military Capabilities and Political Unity', *The Washington Papers* (Beverley Hills: Sage Publications, 1976), Table 2, p. 25; and Colin Gray, 'The Future of Land-Based Missile Forces', forthcoming Adelphi Paper, IISS, Appendix 1.
2. This is single-shot kill probability (per warhead) against a 1000 psi point target with accuracies of .25 nm CEP. Calculations done with the Boeing Aerospace Company's Vulnerability Assessment Calculator. These are representative figures. The existing CEP of these systems is uncertain, but probably range between .2 – .8 n.m.
3. May be deployed in a mobile mode.
4. A third version of the SS-18 has been tested, reportedly with a single 15 MT warhead.
5. Multiple independently-targeted re-entry vehicles (MIRV).
6. SS-X-20 consists of 2 stages of SS-X-16 ICBM.

questions when seen in the light of other Soviet damage-limiting programmes. The Soviet navy's objective of achieving a so-called 'strategic' anti-submarine warfare (ASW) capability has been well-documented.[20] Unlike western navies, which have tended to view the effort to find and destroy SLBM submarines as either destabilising or too difficult to entertain seriously, Soviet naval doctrine continues to accord a high priority to defending against sea-based forces that directly threaten the Soviet homeland. Naval construction in the Soviet Union appears to reflect this emphasis: 3–4 nuclear attack submarines are, at present, entering the inventory per year and this could increase to 8–10 in the late 1970s when the Soviet Union reaches the SLBM limit provided for by the SALT Interim Agreement and excess building capacity can be allocated to attack (torpedo-equipped) cruise-missile boats. But strategic ASW capabilities should not be assessed purely in terms of attack submarine holdings, for Soviet concepts and techniques of ASW appear to differ, to a large extent, from western approaches. Most importantly, Soviet ASW operations emphasise the role of surface combatants and naval air in co-ordinating the activities of submarines over large areas of ocean space. The result, in theory, is an 'area' approach to ASW with emphasis on the integration of diverse capabilities, including satellite and land-based air and missile forces.[21] In practice, Soviet naval forces are optimised for the strategic ASW mission. Not only are new surface combatants, like the *Kiev* carrier, designed principally as anti-submarine warships, but new generations of missile armament, like the SS-NX-14, are reported to be ASW rather than anti-shipping weapons. Thus, it is difficult to escape the conclusion that despite the enormous difficulties of effectively carrying out the strategic ASW mission, the Soviet navy fully intends to pursue this course in the event of conflict.

The Soviet preoccupation with damage-limitation is also apparent in the air defence programme. While the ABM agreements of 1972 and 1974 left both sides unable to defend against ballistic missile attack, the Soviet Union has retained a strong interest in advanced ABM technologies and has continued to modernise her defences against bomber attack. The vigorous research and development programme for ballistic missiles defence reportedly includes the construction of a new phased-array, transportable ABM radar as well as the testing of new, endo-atmospheric interceptor missiles.[22] Of greater potential importance over the longer term, Soviet interest in laser and charged particle applications for ballistic missile defence has also been reported. However, as long as both sides adhere to the terms of the ABM agreements, the Soviet Union will be unable to translate technological advances into operational ABM capability. This is not the case for bomber defences and the Soviet air defence capabilities are large and redundant, consisting, in aggregate, of approximately 2500 interceptor aircraft, 10,000 surface-to-air missiles (SAM), and 5000 radars. Many of these systems are positioned to counter threats from China and western Europe and older systems are not capable of defending against low-altitude penetration. However, a new generation of low-altitude SAM is entering the Soviet inventory and if the technological problems of achieving a 'look down-shoot down' interceptor system is mastered (as is under way with the development of the US Airborne Warning and Control System—AWACS—by the United States), the air defence environment for existing US strategic aircraft (255 B-52 G/H and 66 FB-111A) could become formidable.

In space, a similar emphasis on defensive measures can be seen in Soviet interest in anti-satellite capabilities. A section of the Soviet air defence establishment was assigned the anti-satellite mission in 1964 and tests of a 'killer' satellite, designed to manoeuvre towards and intercept other space craft, were reported in 1967–71. After this initial series of experiments, little activity occurred in this area until 1976 when at least four satellite interceptors were launched and manoeuvred into close proximity to other Soviet satellites. These tests, which were undertaken at altitudes used by some US reconnaissance and early-warning satellites, coincided with unconfirmed reports that ground-based lasers had been used by the Soviet Union to blind optical and infra-red sensors aboard US surveillance space craft. These developments have led some to conclude that the Soviet Union is attempting to achieve the capability of disabling the US space-based early-warning, reconnaissance, and communications systems in the event of war. But if this is the Soviet objective (and these activities are not directed towards a far less sophisticated adversary, China), it should be noted that Soviet interceptor systems have yet to be tested at altitudes at which many US satellites operate and even at low-altitude interceptions (below 600 miles), the Soviet interceptors have not been observed to possess any kind of 'kill' mechanism.[23]

Finally, Soviet civil defence activities reinforce a picture of a nation that can wage and survive a central strategic conflict. Reliable information on the actual ability of the Soviet Union to afford her industry and civilian population a high degree of protection against nuclear attack is scanty, but there is little doubt that this is an official objective.[24] It has been noted that the Soviet civil defence effort has equal footing with the military service arms and that responsibility for the programme has been placed in the hands of a deputy defence minister. A number of different measures for protecting civilian assets are discussed in official Soviet literature, ranging from short-term plans for the evacuation of urban centres prior to attack, to long-term industrial plans to disperse and relocate industry outside of large cities. Shelter complexes are also emphasised and special attention has apparently been given to constructing an extensive system of hardened command, control and communications centres for the political and military leadership. In the industrial sector, civil defence is said to be not only taken into account in locating new industries but also individual buildings within industrial complexes. There is, of course, a debate in the West over how closely the Soviet Union adheres to various civil defence procedures and, if they are followed, how effective they would be. It has been estimated that an efficient urban evacuation programme would allow over 95 per cent of the Soviet population to survive the immediate effects of attack and that a system could be arranged to allow a large proportion of this group to escape the longer-term effects of fall-out.[25] It is also noted that critical industrial machinery could be protected by such relatively simple techniques as using sand-bags. At the same time, there is little hard evidence that these precautions have been undertaken. In one crucial area of civil defence that can be easily monitored, there is no public information to indicate that the large-scale urban evacuation procedures have been rehearsed in recent years. And without such rehearsals, it is open to question how effective real efforts at evacuation would be in time of crisis.

It is possible, then, to draw some alarming conclusions from Soviet activities in ICBM procurement, ASW, air defence, satellite interception, and civil defence. A scenario could be constructed, for example, in which the Soviet Union, after disrupting US early-warning capabilities, carried out simultaneous attacks on land-based missiles and submarines at sea. Air defence forces would then be assigned the task of defending the Soviet homeland from bomber attack while Soviet civil defences minimised the damage caused by surviving missile and bomber attacks. In assessing this worst of 'worst cases', however, it is crucial to distinguish between intentions and capabilities. As we have seen, in some areas it is doubtful that Soviet forces, now or in the near future, will be able to perform as advertised. In other areas, the technological means exist to counter emerging Soviet threats. This is clearly true for Soviet ASW. To be effective, a Soviet ASW force would have to be able to simultaneously destroy (or at least neutralise) a large portion of the 20 or so US SLBM submarines that are continuously on-station in range of their targets in the Soviet Union. This implies a capability for submarine detection and tracking which eludes existing Soviet forces. While Soviet ASW capabilities can be expected to continue to improve, advances in ASW counter-measures like submarine quieting, and, more importantly, the US deployment of a new generation of long-range SLBM (the *Trident* series) will maintain the relative invulnerability of US submarines at sea.

Soviet anti-satellite capabilities also leave much to be desired. An increasing proportion of US satellites operate at altitudes beyond the reach of the interceptor that has been observed in tests and a large number of counter-measures are available to protect those systems that must operate in lower orbits. Satellites can be 'hardened' to protect them from electromagnetic disturbance; manoeuvrability can be built into US systems to allow them to escape attack and satellites can be 'hidden' from Soviet tracking equipment.

The United States also possesses the means to react to Soviet civil defence activities. First, depending on the nature of the command and control structure (of which virtually nothing is known), attempts to protect high-level political leaders and military commanders are not necessarily threatening; in fact, the loss of central control over nuclear decisions in the early phases of a conflict could be far more dangerous. The ability of the Soviet Union, on the other hand, substantially to reduce the vulnerability of urban and industrial assets to nuclear attack would be an entirely different matter. But it is highly doubtful that this can be easily achieved. Not only does the Soviet programme seem less impressive in practice than it does on paper, but improvements in US missile accuracy as well as efforts to tailor warhead effects more carefully to the nature of targets should be able to offset most civil defence developments.[26]

More vexing questions are raised by Soviet air defence and ICBM capabilities, because these programmes seem much more likely to achieve their objectives and because the technical solutions to the problems they create are expensive. The air defence problem is relatively straightforward: improvements to low-altitude Soviet SAM and interceptor capabilities are likely to make it enormously difficult for significant numbers of existing US aircraft to penetrate to their assigned targets during the coming decade. Because there are good arguments for maintaining a credible manned bomber capability aside from their capacity to inflict damage, the United States is forced to consider bomber modernisation. There are essentially two available options: the procurement of a more capable, low-altitude penetrator like the B-1 or the deployment of long-range cruise missiles abroad aircraft to 'stand-off' from Soviet air defences. Ideally, a future US bomber force would incorporate both penetrating and stand-off aircraft in order to complicate air defence tasks. Yet the estimated costs of either option, not to mention the expense of combining them, are significant. This was clearly the dominant factor that led the Carter Administration to cancel the B-1 programme and opt for the air-launched cruise missile.

The potential capability of Soviet ICBM to destroy a large fraction of the US land-based missile force raises a more complex set of problems. The question is not, as it is in the case of aircraft, whether US ICBM can penetrate to their targets after launch but whether they can survive an attack prior to launch. Thus, ICBM vulnerability creates the classic 'prisoners' dilemma familiar to all western strategists: in a crisis, there is an incentive attached to launching vulnerable weapons before they can be destroyed and, understanding this, there is also an incentive for the attacker to destroy them before they can be launched. Clearly, the incentives attached to Soviet pre-emption would have to be balanced against the potential cost of US retaliation with bombers and SLBM. Yet a highly vulnerable US ICBM force might be viewed as a lucrative target during a severe crisis, especially if the other components of the US deterrent were only able to retaliate against urban and industrial targets. If this were the case, it is possible that the United States might be 'self-deterred' from delivering such a retaliatory blow because of the almost certain knowledge that the Soviet response would be in kind. But even if Soviet planners are unwilling to risk the survival of the Soviet Union to such uncertain mechanisms as self-deterrence, there can be no doubt that the vulnerability of US ICBM to pre-emptive attack will constitute an unsettling factor for US planners in the 1980s.

The problems posed by recent Soviet strategic developments should not be compared, then, to concerns generated in the West during the late 1950s, when Soviet missile developments threatened to make US forward-based bomber forces vulnerable to surprise attack. Under a situation of almost total vulnerability, incentives for pre-emption would be far greater. However, the problem of 'partial vulnerability' inherent with the existing US ICBM posture is still bothersome and in some ways is even more insidious because there is no consensus over its significance. Uncertainty over the meaning of ICBM vulnerability for deterrence and in the event of deterrence failure, of large asymmetries in throw-weight or hard target capabilities following a strategic exchange, complicates the task of finding solutions to the problem. If, prior to or during a conflict, the essential role of strategic forces is seen as merely maintaining the ability to hold Soviet cities and industry hostage, then a simple solution is to phase out US ICBM and place greater emphasis on more survivable elements of the strategic triad-bombers or SLBM. In this way, it is argued, the incentives for both sides to pre-empt would diminish and the Soviet Union is denied a lucrative target for attack.

But the implications of moving from a triad to a diad are unclear. For a start, neither bombers or SLBM are entirely invulnerable to attack. Bombers and existing SLBM are also ill-suited to carrying out limited and discrete nuclear attacks. This could mean, that in the event of war, the United States, without ICBM, might only possess a narrow range of unpalatable escalation options. Ironically, the systems whose accuracy, penetrability, and command and control characteristics are at present best suited for undertaking selective attacks—ICBM—are themselves most vulnerable to attack. Rather than phasing out ICBM, a possible means of coping with the problem would be to improve the accuracy and throw-weight of land-based missiles so that those that survived attack would still be capable of undertaking selective strike operations. At best, this would only be a short-term corrective; as Soviet first-strike capabilities grew, improvements to US ICBM would further increase incentives for the Soviet Union actually to employ them.

In the longer term, if ICBM are judged to be a necessary component of the US deterrent, it will probably become necessary to enhance ICBM survivability through mobility. ICBM deployed aboard mobile ground launchers or aircraft while a costly option, would undoubtedly complicate the task of Soviet pre-emption. But whether the attempt to deploy a mobile ICBM should be combined with efforts to improve warhead accuracy and yield, as is now the case with the MX ICBM programme, is another question and should be approached as such. Oddly enough, the problem of ICBM vulnerability is compounded by the fact that Soviet land-based missiles are themselves potentially vulnerable to ICBM attack. Thus, decisions taken by the United States to enhance the survivability of US ICBM could be perceived by the Soviet Union to jeopardise her own land-based forces. The consequences of this would be unpredictable to say the least. Soviet strategic literature is curiously silent on the subject of ICBM vulnerability. This may indicate that Soviet planners are not convinced that 'partial' vulnerability raises serious strategic problems or is sensitive to political manipulation. On the other hand, a large proportion of the Soviet Union's overall deterrent and war-fighting capability resides in land-based missiles and it seems logical that threats to their survival would reinforce tendencies towards pre-emption.

WHAT CAN ARMS CONTROL DO?

There is no simple or single solution to the many different problems posed by Soviet strategic force modernisation. One thing, however, is clear: the very different historical and doctrinal baggage that the two super-powers have brought to the SALT exercise make it unlikely that formal negotiations can resolve the questions of land-based missile vulnerability, Soviet civil defence, or strategic ASW. For a start, the objectives of the two sides in the talks, whether legitimate or not, are different and reflect contrasting understandings of what constitutes strategic stability. This contrast – in crude terms, between strategies of deterrence and defence – is increasingly evident in the force postures of each side. As Soviet strategic programmes and doctrine become more congruent, arguments that Soviet deployment decisions essentially mirror US behaviour become less persuasive. Certainly, the Soviet Union is receptive to technological and operational concepts developed in the West, but these are often exploited in the service of very different strategies.

The hope, then, that the SALT process can be used to restructure US and Soviet forces to correspond to a highly stylised model of deterrent stability is fading. Not only are individual weapons and the aggregate forces of the two sides diverging, but there exists no common definition of what problems SALT should attack. The political leadership in both countries has emphasised the importance of reductions beyond those set at the Vladivostok summit in 1974. Yet, by themselves, reductions in forces offer few important advantages. The ability of the two powers even to sit down at SALT was in large part based on their possession of large and diverse strategic inventories. In some circumstances, large cuts could jeopardise the survivability of forces and could therefore erode confidence in the mutual retaliatory relationship. Smaller cuts, of the sort suggested by the Soviet Union in negotiations during 1976, would yield only minor cost savings (always an important consideration), and would not address any important problems. Perhaps the most significant reduction measure would be an agreement (of the sort envisaged by the Carter Administration) to reduce numbers of fixed MIRVed ICBM. But the Soviet Union, having heavily invested in these systems in recent years and apparently unconvinced of the magnitude of the vulnerability problem, seems unlikely to agree to such an arrangement in the near future.

SALT not only appears unable to solve certain strategic problems; in some instances, it could exacerbate them. In the case of ICBM vulnerability, the application of separate ceilings for land and sea-based missiles in the 1972 Interim Agreement effectively ruled out the option of moving the US deterrent to sea. (Under the guidelines for a new agreement reached at Vladivostok in 1974, both sides were to be allowed to exercise this option.) Another example is the regional nuclear balance in Europe where arms control efforts have only reinforced the incentives for the Soviet Union to modernise her forces. Because negotiators at SALT have only sought to limit systems of direct strategic relevance to the two super-powers, i.e. weapons able to reach the territory of both, the Soviet Union, in principle, is free to modernise and expand strategic forces, like the new SS-20 IRBM, targeted against western Europe. This is given added significance by the fact that US nuclear forces in Europe – strike aircraft or, possibly in the future, cruise could become subject to arms control constraints, either at SALT or at the mutual force reduction talks in Vienna. This anomalous situation is not only the product of Soviet design, but of geographical circumstances. Still, it is becoming increasingly difficult for western

Europeans to ignore the deployment of the medium-range *Backfire* bomber or the SS-20. But the problems of dealing with these systems at SALT is enormous; as a bilateral channel of super-power communication, SALT is politically unsuited to grappling with the multilateral, Alliance-wide consequences of controlling Eurostrategic deployment.

If SALT can make some problems worse, it can also interfere with efforts to find their solutions. The importance attached to gaining agreement at SALT has naturally led some decision-makers to question the development and deployment of weapons that might complicate the process of negotiation and methods for monitoring compliance. Long-range cruise missiles, for example, have been criticised on the grounds that SALT has become bogged down over the issue of distinguishing between 'tactical' and strategic versions of the weapons. The deployment of mobile ICBM will also complicate verification tasks and, like cruise missiles, arms control proponents have viewed their deployment as a threat to SALT. But under certain conditions, these two systems offer potential technical solutions to problems outlined above: cruise missiles might offer NATO the most efficient and survivable means of responding to improvements in Soviet medium-range capabilities; mobile ICBM, meanwhile, are a promising option for reducing the vulnerability of land-based missiles. If the possibilities raised by these technologies must be foreclosed in order to simplify negotiations, then long-run arms control goals such as saving money or bolstering deterrence could be sacrificed by the more immediate objective of obtaining agreements.

While these arguments point up the limitations of SALT, they do not provide a convincing rationale for abandoning super-power arms control altogether. Despite Colin Gray's thoughtful arguments, we have not yet reached the point at SALT where it is 'time to stop'.[27] In addition to its importance to US-Soviet political relations, SALT does have an important, if often underestimated, strategic function. In setting admittedly crude upper limits on the future capabilities of both powers, SALT can lessen much of mutual uncertainty that adheres to US-Soviet strategic relations. This enables each to work out their separately perceived strategic problems within a common framework of expectation. Although the Vladivostok guidelines give both sides enormous 'elbow room' in decisions of force design and modernisation, if a SALT II agreement is reached both sides will possess a much clearer idea of what the strategic balance will look like in the mid-1980s than would otherwise be the case. As a result, US and Soviet planners should be better placed to distinguish between realistic contingencies and alarmist threats. For example, the limits imposed by the Vladivostok understandings – on total delivery vehicles, delivery vehicles with MIRV, and "heavy" ICBM – greatly facilitate a more accurate portrayal of land-based missile vulnerability. If western governments are careful not to read too much into the successful negotiation of agreements (in terms of Soviet acceptance of doctrinal concepts), SALT can function as a useful tool for military planning.

The fact that the Soviet Union approaches SALT from a different doctrinal perspective does serve to restrict arms control possibilities. But this doesn't mean that the United States should turn down opportunities for agreement simply because the Soviet Union has different motives for engaging in talks. The Soviet Union's willingness to enter into the 1972 ABM Treaty did not, as some hoped, signal her acceptance of the concept of mutual assured destruction. Instead, it more likely than not reflected a calculated desire to head off competition in an area in which the United States possessed a commanding technological lead. But regardless of the reason, the Soviet Union's decision to agree to severe restrictions on ABM deployment did correspond to prevailing US notions of stability and for that reason, the accord was worth having. Thus, the United States should not be averse to entering into arrangements that conform to her own strategic preferences. At the same time, Soviet preferences differ and efforts to formulate a set of mutually-shared grand principles at SALT are likely to be counterproductive. A bigger danger, however, would arise if arms control planning were based on the assumption that such common principles already existed. The ABM case suggests that it is possible for the two sides to satisfy different interests at SALT and that for arms control to work, the perceived benefits of any given measure do not have to be the same, only equal: political equivalence, rather than technical stability, should be the goal sought by negotiators.

Doctrinal differences, moreover, are not immutable. While SALT has not facilitated a convergence in US and Soviet strategic thinking and is unlikely to do so any time soon, it is hard to believe that it has had no impact on the perceptions of the two sides. Because doctrine is so closely intertwined with historical experience and organisational routines, it was naïve (and arrogant) of US negotiators to believe that, once exposed to American ideas, the Soviet leadership would abandon its own conceptions. Still, as former SALT negotiator Gerard Smith has argued,[28] the arms control process has served to familiarise Soviet leaders with the arcane concerns of nuclear strategy and politics and may have also spawned a new group of Soviet civilian 'defence intellectuals'. The impact of this development should not be over-estimated. But the possibility that new perspectives are being brought to the policy-making process at least suggests that Soviet doctrine is susceptible to change, if not always in the direction that western arms controllers might desire.

These considerations lead to the general conclusion that arms control, if placed in the proper perspective, continues to be an interesting option for the United States. There is real danger, however, in asking more from SALT than it can deliver. This runs two risks. First, in asking too much from SALT, expectations are created that cannot easily or safely be satisfied. Witness, for example, the widespread cynicism that greeted the Ford Administration's claim in 1974 that the Vladivostok understanding had placed a 'cap on the arms race'. In the short term, magnifying SALT's importance may seem a necessary means of creating a domestic arms control constituency. Over the longer term, however, this tactic could backfire: exaggerating what SALT can accomplish is bound to make any agreement emerging from the negotiations seem an anti-climax.

Second, the tendency to expect too much from SALT fosters the belief that strategic problems can only be solved through mutual agreement. In fact, because the super-powers are often unable to agree on what constitutes a problem, there may be many cases where unilateral doctrinal and procurement decisions offer more promising solutions. But as we have seen, unilateral solutions to separately perceived problems can often run counter to requirements for negotiation. There is no simple way to reconcile this dilemma. In some cases, it will be preferable to forgo the deployment of weapons that will make negotiations more difficult. But it will be important to recognise that arms control is not just about obtaining agreements and that the objectives sought by arms control can sometimes be achieved more easily by other means. As Soviet behaviour illustrates, arms control is a component of, and not a replacement for, unilateral strategic planning.

SUMMARY OF DISCUSSION

The discussion on Mr Burt's paper began by focusing on the problem of land-based missile vulnerability, and methods of ameliorating it. The speaker pointed out that the land-based missile force was more important to the USSR than to the US, as the former had no equivalent of SAC and appeared reluctant to increase its SLBM forces. To ask the Soviets to limit their heavy ICBM forces was to ask much more of them than, for example, to ask the US to dismantle its Titan force. If the US believed the ICBM force would attract a pre-emptive attack, then the solution was to dismantle it. If it was seen as a political instrument, however, as Schlesinger had suggested, then the advantages of secure command and control and flexibility of targeting were of prime importance, and to dismantle the force was to forgo a range of important political options. The intended functions of land-based missiles were the central issue: if it was believed that numerical symmetry was imperative, both before and after an exchange, then the answer was to deploy a large number of mobile missiles with low accuracies; if they were only needed for limited politically inspired strikes then the answer was to deploy a small number of mobile missiles of low accuracy; if the worry was purely that they were vulnerable, the answer was to get rid of them. To deploy mobile missiles of high accuracy was to incite the Soviets to believe that the US was aspiring to a first-strike capability.

The twin questions of the relationship of SALT to the NPT and the different interests of the US and western Europe in SALT were then raised. The speaker asserted that the link between SALT and NPT was largely spurious, and that, if anything, the ABM part of the SALT agreements made proliferation a more attractive option for potential nuclear powers. Both the US and USSR had a strong interest in preventing proliferation, and the latter especially would be probable second-choice target for many of the current near-nuclear states. The speaker agreed that the decision to exclude Forward-Based Systems from SALT had largely eliminated possible differences of interest within NATO over the content of SALT I, but technology was now making it increasingly difficult to separate US strategic from European tactical weapons in SALT discussions, the cruise missile being a prime example of this trend. The intellectual challenge now presented by the negotiations was how to solve a new class of problems which has arisen because of the difficulty of compartmentalising tactical and strategic issues in the way that had previously been possible.

Mr Burt then went on to argue that the US-USSR arms race reflected a deeper conflict which could not itself be resolved by successful arms control measures. The main utility of arms control negotiations was to give both sides a more accurate and detailed picture of the other's likely military posture a decade ahead. The issue of what was a 'bad' SALT agreement was then raised, with the speaker arguing that although the collapse of SALT might make little difference to military postures, the political cost might be very high. In conclusion, it was suggested that the problem of Forward-Based Systems would have to be faced in any future SALT II negotiations, and the west European states would then have to decide which future military options they were prepared to forgo in order to reach an agreement.

NOTES

1. These agreements are described in detail by Hedley Bull in his 'The Moscow Agreements and Strategic Arms Limitations', *Canberra Papers on Strategy and Defence 15*, (Canberra: Australian National University Press, 1973).
2. For a discussion of the technical problems that have hampered the efforts of the two sides to reach a follow-on SALT agreement, see Richard Burt, 'Technology and East-West Arms Control', *International Affairs*, January 1977.
3. See former Secretary of Defence Donald Rumsfeld's remarks, *Annual Defense Department Report FY 1978*, 17 January 1977, pp. 62–3.
4. In fact, there is plenty of evidence that suggests just the opposite. For what appears to be a criticism of the assured destruction concept, see G. A. Arbatov, 'The Impasse of the Policy of Force', *Problemy Mira i Sotsializma*, No. 2, February 1974.
5. See Colin Gray, 'SALT I Aftermath: Have the Soviets Been Cheating?' *Air Force Magazine*, November 1975, pp. 28–33 and section on 'verification' in *Strategic Survey* 1975 (London: IISS), pp. 111–116.
6. The importance of the internal dynamics of Soviet weapons procurement process are discussed by Edward L. Warner III, 'Soviet Strategic Force Posture: Some Alternative Explanations', in Horton, Rogerson and Warner (eds.), *Comparative Defense Policy*, (Baltimore: The John Hopkins University Press, 1974), pp. 310–25 and Arthur Alexander, 'Armor Development in the Soviet Union and the United States', *Rand Report* R-1860-NA, September 1976, Chapter VIII.
7. For a concise statement of this argument which does not necessarily imply agreement, see Thomas W. Wolfe, 'Military Power and Soviet Policy', in *The Soviet Empire: Expansion and Detente*, pp. 155–7.
8. See, for example, Richard Barnet, 'Promise of Disarmament' *New York Times Magazine*, 17 February 1977, p. 17.
9. 'Soviet Military Capabilities', *Current History*, October 1976, Vol. 71, No. 420.
10. Thomas Wolfe quotes I. Sidelmikou in 'Military Power and Soviet Policy', Ibid., footnote 7: 'The greater the combat might and readiness of the Soviet armed forces . . . the more secure is peace on earth.' Also Herbert Goldhamer's concept of Soviet 'long-term investment' in strategic power, 'The Soviet Union in a Period of Strategic Parity', *Rand Paper* R-889-PR, November 1971.
11. Thomas Wolfe suggests, in fact, that the Soviet Union 'has regarded the negotiations as a means by which it might be compensated for technological and other advantages historically enjoyed by the United States, in lieu of

narrowing such advantages by unilateral effort alone.' 'The SALT Experience: Its Impact on US and Soviet Strategic Policy and Decision-making', *Rand Report* R-1686-PR, September 1975.
12. Even the most outstanding champions of detente and arms control in the Soviet press do not explicitly rule out the Soviet achievement of superiority. See, for instance, G. Arbatov's spirited defence of recent Soviet procurement policies reported in *Pravda*, 5 February 1977. (Reported in *New York Times*, 5 February, p. 1.)
13. 'The Evolving Soviet Strategic Threat', *Current History*, October 1975, p. 123.
14. Ibid., p. 124.
15. These are distilled from some of the excellent studies that have been done in the West on contemporary Soviet military doctrine. See especially Lambeth, op. cit.; Thomas W. Wolfe, *Soviet Strategy at the Crossroads* (Cambridge: Harvard University Press, 1969), Chapters 7 and 8; John Erickson, op. cit., and *Soviet Military Power*, (London: RUSI, 1971).
16. It is interesting here to recall Khrushchev's assertion (to President Kennedy) during the Cuban Crisis: 'If indeed war should break out, then it will not be in our power to stop it, for such is the logic of war.' As quoted in Robert Kennedy's *Thirteen Days*, (New York: W. W. Norton, 1969), p. 86.
17. This cursory glance at Soviet nuclear doctrine, of course, does not do justice to the subject. On the surface, the Soviet emphasis on war-fighting (and winning) seems difficult to reconcile with visions of uncontrolled escalation. In fact, as Soviet conventional and nuclear capabilities have grown and matured, Soviet doctrine seems to place greater emphasis on different phases through which an East-West conflict could pass. This has not led to the recognition of 'thresholds' in war or the elaboration of limited war strategies. It has, however, focused greater attention on three levels of conflict: conventional war in the theatre, nuclear war in the theatre, and general strategic war. On the theatre level, the possibility of non-nuclear conflict has received greater attention in recent years, at least in terms of an initial stage of a war that would very probably go nuclear at some point. Whether or not theatre conflict went nuclear, Soviet writings seem to accept the possibility that it could be limited to – but not within – the theatre. In other words, the defence of Europe might be 'decoupled' from the US strategic deterrent. Thus, if war were to break out, the whole of Europe would constitute the operational theatre, while the homelands of the two super-powers might conceivably be spared. If this 'territorial threshold' were crossed and escalation to central strategic war occurred, the civilian populations and industrial assets need not be immediately struck – the primary targets of Soviet interest would initially be the military targets of the adversary. Although it is a mistake to equate these escalatory phases in Soviet doctrine with contemporary western notions of strategic flexibility and selective response, it is clear that the achievement of strategic parity by the Soviet Union, coupled with her continued augmentation of theatre capabilities, has created a new range of options for Soviet planners. For an illuminating outline of Soviet thinking about the possibility of confining East-West conflict to various levels of intensity and scope, see Joseph D. Douglass, Jr. *The Soviet Theatre Nuclear Offensive*, United States Air Force, USGPO, pp. 99–122.
18. For a useful (but not entirely convincing) discussion of the various problems of

actually conducting a successful first-strike against US ICBM, see John Steinbruner and Thomas Garwin, 'Strategic Vulnerability: The Balance between Prudence and Paranoia', *International Security*, Summer 1976, pp. 138–81.
19. See especially Paul Nitze, 'Assuring Strategic Stability in an Era of Detente', *Foreign Affairs*, January 1976, on the possible implications of post-attack asymmetries in counterforce and countervalue capability.
20. This is primarily due to Michael MacGwire's diligent research. See chapters in *Soviet Naval Developments: Capability and Context*, (New York: Praeger Special Studies, 1973) and *Soviet Naval Policy*: Objectives and Constraints, (New York: Praeger Special Studies, 1975), edited with K. Booth and J. McDonnell.
21. Norman Polmar, 'Thinking about Soviet ASW', *Proceedings* (of the US Naval Institute), May 1976, pp. 110–29.
22. *Aviation Week and Space Technology*, 30 August 1976, pp. 14–18.
23. See Lawrence Freedman, 'The Soviet Union and "Anti-Space Defence"', *Survival*, January/February 1977, pp. 16–23 and 'Military Competition in Space', *Strategic Survey 1977*, (London: 1155), pp. 26–31.
24. The most detailed public discussion of the Soviet civil defence programme – at least that is how it looks on paper – is Leon Goure's *War Survival in Soviet Strategy*, (Washington: Center for Advanced International Studies, University of Miami, 1976). See also 'Soviet Civil Defence', *Strategic Survey 1977*, op. cit., pp. 31–4.
25. T. K. Jones, 'Soviet Civil Defence', Boeing Aerospace Co. (unpublished paper).
26. Rep. Robert Leggett has argued, for example, that 'It is not necessary to strike every industrial target if you can carefully select and destroy the key targets. To use a very simplistic example, if you obliterate steel, rubber or transportation – certainly, if you can obliterate all three – there is no need to target a truck factory. There is no question that we could reduce the Soviet Union to the status of India for many decades, perhaps permanently.' 'Civil Defense: What It Can do and What It Cannot do', *Congressional Record*, 30 September 1976.
27. Colin Gray, 'SALT: Time to Stop', *Strategic Review*, Fall 1976, pp. 14–22.
28. Gerard Smith, 'Negotiating with the Soviets', *New York Times Magazine* (reprinted in *Survival*, May/June 1977).

9 The 'Forward Reach' of the Soviet Armed Forces: Seaborne and Airborne Landings

Peter Vigor

The notion of projecting armed force across large expanses of water is a western not a Soviet military concept. This is so is largely due to the accidents of geography. Britain, for instance, (probably the biggest practitioner in history of the art of projecting military force over distances) soon reached a stage in her development where, if she were going to continue to expand at all, she would have to pursue that expansion across the seas. No part of Britain is even as much as a hundred miles from the coast; and, once that puny interval had been covered, the British people had either to content themselves with the narrow pleasures of cultivating their existing domains, or else devise means of establishing themselves on the far side of the Channel, or of the North or the Irish Seas or the Atlantic Ocean.

A similar choice, at varying stages in their history, confronted the French, the German, the Spanish, the Italian, the Portuguese, the Dutch, and the American peoples. Those of them who had considerable opportunities for expanding by land over neighbouring territories, usually came to seaborne landings comparatively late in their history. The Germans, for instance, did not do so until the second half of the nineteenth century, when they colonised parts of Africa; nor did the Americans make the attempt until 1898, when they annexed the Philippines and invaded Cuba in the course of their war against Spain. Further back in history, Julius Caesar projected military force across the seas when he invaded and conquered Britain, and so did Norman William in 1066. Even the Scandinavians for several centuries employed seaborne landings as a means of territorial expansion, and, in so doing, established kingdoms in Britain and in Russia.

We thus see that the geography of western Europe, and also that of the United States, has compelled the West, whenever in an expansionist mood or whenever impelled by strong considerations of strategy, to project armed force across considerable distances of water, often half-way around the world. The particular purposes underlying these operations may be grouped into three categories:

(i) To seize a distant chunk of the globe inhabited by a militarily less effective people and incorporate their territory into one's own empire. This was done by the British, for instance, in Australia, New Zealand, Africa and so on, and by half a score of other countries, some of which have already been mentioned above.

(ii) To open a new theatre of war in the course of a war that is already raging against a major enemy. Gallipoli in the First World War is a good example of this, as is Overlord in the Second.

(iii) To support an existing operation in a given theatre of war by making a tactical landing in its vicinity. The troops set down on the enemy shore can then act in concert with the other forces, and thus help to ensure the success of the latter's operations. Anzio in the Second World War and the Imchon landing in the Korean War are obvious examples of this.

It goes without saying that all such landings, no matter to which of the categories they belong, have traditionally had to be seaborne. Only very recently has modern technology provided governments with the power to mount airborne landings; and consequently in the historical part of this paper it is almost exclusively with seaborne landings that we shall be dealing.

The geography of the USSR has produced a very different result. The Russians, by contrast with western countries, have not needed to cross oceans in order to expand (at any rate, not until the 1960s); and they therefore have not needed to project force in this particular fashion at any time in their history till the present. It is not that the Russians have never been expansionist: on the contrary, they are one of the most expansionist peoples the world has ever seen; and this is true whether we are talking about Tsarist Russia or Soviet Russia. The increase in the size of Russia from what it was at the beginning of the thirteenth century to what it is today at the end of the twentieth is best demonstrated by a sketch map (see Figure 9.1); and none can deny that the increase has been very considerable.

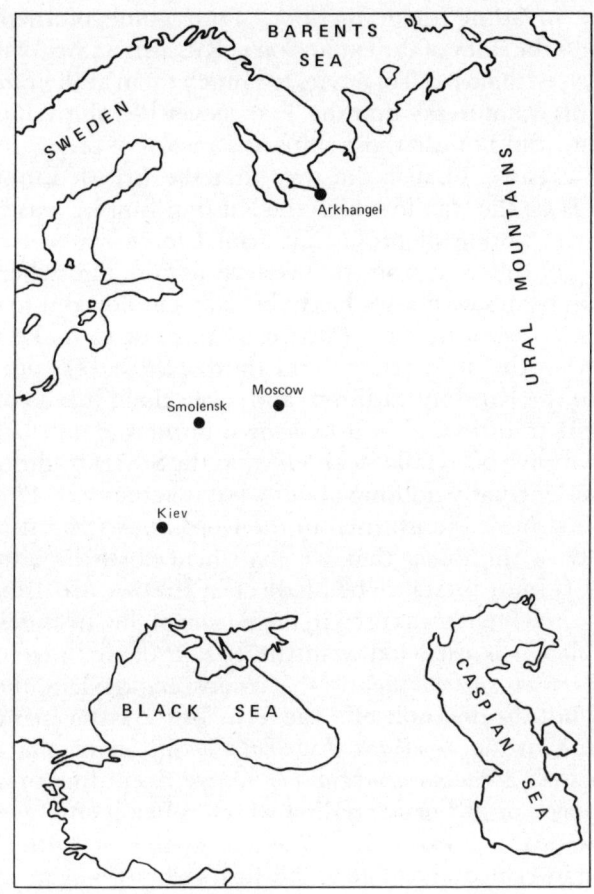

FIGURE 9.1 *Russia as she existed, late thirteenth century*

What concerns us here, however, is not the actual increase in the size of Russia, but the means whereby this increase was brought about. As the map shows clearly, Russia always expanded into contiguous territories; and by 'contiguous' is meant territories into which her infantrymen could march on their flat feet without having to cross the oceans. The armies of Ivan the Terrible, of Peter the Great, of Catherine the Great, of Nicholas I, Alexander II, Alexander III, and Stalin all conquered their neighbours' territories by invading them on foot. True, some of them rode. Nevertheless the story of the expansion of Russia is a story of infantry and cavalry, with no need of navies to launch them at their intended victims. This is not to say that the Tsars never had ships; but it is to say that they did not use those ships as a means of projecting force across the oceans. That is the way that the British Empire was created; it is *not* the way in which the Russian Empire was created.

The Soviet notion of projecting armed force across the sea is therefore very different from the western notion; and whereas the West, as has been said above, has habitually employed it to enlarge its empires, to open up new theatres of war, or to make tactical landings in existing theatres, only the third of these three purposes is common to the Russian tradition; and, even then, it is a comparatively recent tradition, as will be shown in more detail below.

So far, we have been talking about what the Soviet tradition is *not*; we have said virtually nothing about what it actually *is*. The Soviet view of our subject is enshrined in the word *desant*; and it is to the Soviet view of the *desant* that we shall henceforth be addressing ourselves.[1] It must therefore be made clear that we are using *desant* in the sense in which it was used in the Russia of the 'twenties, not in that in which it is used today in the Russia of the 'seventies. In modern Russian, *desant* means the troops engaged in the *desant* operation, not the desant itself,[2] the term for the latter being either the tongue-twisting *morskaya desantnaya operatsiya* or the equally tongue-twisting *vozdushnodesantnaya operatsiya*, according to whether it is a seaborne or airborne landing which is being envisaged. The change of meaning from the 'twenties to the 'seventies passed through an intermediary stage in the 'fifties when *desant* meant both the military concept and also the troops engaged in it.[3] Unfortunately, it no longer appears to do so; and if one wanted to be pedantic one would abandon it. The alternative, however, is to use throughout this paper the much longer phrase *desantnaya operatsiya*, which is not immediately assimilable to the English tongue. In this paper the word *desant* is used to denote the *concept*; while, when it is necessary to refer to the *troops*, expressions like 'amphibious forces', or 'airborne forces' will be used.

To clarify the Soviet view of *desant* further, it must be said that, theoretically speaking, the Russians use the phrase to describe all three of the western versions of it that have been set forth in preceding paragraphs. In other words, if a Russian wanted to talk about the Sicilian Expedition of Ancient Athens or the conquest of Britain by Julius Caesar, he would use the phrase *desantnaya operatsiya* to describe them.[4] He would also use the same expression, if he wanted to talk about Overlord or Gallipoli or the Japanese seaborne landings in the Pacific that were made during the Second World War. Historically, however, neither of these two sorts of operation have ever been mounted by Tsarist or Soviet governments; and their military thinking has therefore always concentrated on the *tactical* use of the *desant*.

In the Soviet view, the main aim of a tactical *desant* is to get one's troops into the enemy's flank or rear; but this must be done in co-operation with one's own main forces which, as a general rule, will be expected to link up with the *desant* not so very long after the latter has been put down. A tactical *desant* is therefore *not* an autonomous operation, but a form of military activity designed to assist the efforts of one's other forces.[5]

It will be noted that a Soviet tactical *desant* is concerned above all to get troops into the enemy's rear, and then to ensure that they link up quickly with the main forces, which are assumed to be advancing in their direction. This is true whether we are discussing *desants* which are transported by ships or aeroplanes or those which are conveyed on the backs of horses or on top of tanks. For, tanks and horses in the Russian view can be just as effective as ships and planes for getting troops into the enemy's rear, which is, as has been said above, the major purpose of a tactical *desant*; and if horses now are no longer considered to be a viable means of transporting troops, the use of tanks for this purpose is still considered valid; and indeed there are signs that their use in this fashion is regaining popularity among the Russians.

But the subject of this paper is the 'forward reach' of the Soviet armed forces, by which is meant the projection of force across fairly considerable distances. Tank-borne *desants* in the last war did not manage to transfer their troops across more than very short distances; and there is no sign that the modern experiments aim at going much further. Fascinating as it would be to discuss in detail the Soviet use of tank-borne or horse-borne *desants*, they clearly fall outside the scope of this paper and must therefore be omitted. It must suffice to say that the job of the tanks (and of the horses too, for that matter, in the old days when they were used) is to get the troops that are riding on them through the enemy's defences as quickly as possible, and with as little fighting as possible; because their function is not to assist in smashing the enemy's resistance by taking part in the assault on his forward defences, but to get through his defences into his rear, and then to turn round and gnaw away at his vitals while their own main forces assail him from the front.

But we must now leave this fascinating subject and return to our main theme, which is the Soviet use of air and sea *desants*; and since airborne *desants* were not technically possible until shortly before the Second World War, we will begin with those that are seaborne.

The Russians began to put soldiers on ships at least as early as the seventeenth century, and probably a great deal earlier; but these were not used in a fashion which, according to Soviet reckoning, would qualify as a *desant*.[6] According to Soviet reckoning, the first proper Russian *desants* were those made by General Lyakhov on the southern shores of the Black Sea in February 1916.[7] These were comparatively small affairs, each consisting of about two battalions of infantry, together with some artillery and some machine-guns. Their aim was to co-operate with the Tsarist ground forces, which were advancing along the coast near Rize, by landing in the rear of the Turks and attacking them from behind. The three *desants* were reasonably successful; and their success was due, according to Soviet sources, to the very careful reconnaissance of the intended landing-places and to the gaining of complete surprise. The latter was achieved, say Soviet writers, by not permitting a preliminary artillery bombardment of the intended landing-places by the ships' guns, and by arriving at dawn off the target area, halting a couple of miles offshore, and ferrying the troops to their place of disembarkation in specially designed assault boats.[8]

The first *desants* of the Soviet period occurred during the Civil War of 1918–20, but none appear to have been of any significance. The first Soviet *desant* of importance, as Soviet historians themselves agree, was therefore the Kerch-Feodosiisk operation of December 1941, which was designed to relieve the Nazi pressure on the besieged garrison of Sevastopol.[9]

The Kerch-Feodosiisk *desant* was a very big one, totalling approximately 42,000 men. The troops were to be landed at a number of points on the eastern end of the Crimea (chiefly around the towns of Kerch and Feodosia); and they were to be transported thither by the Black Sea Fleet and the Azov Naval Flotilla from the western end of the Taman' Peninsula and from the Georgian ports of Tuapse and Novorossiisk (see Figure 9.2).

Opposing them was a mixed force of Germans and Romanians which, even according to Soviet sources, never exceeded 25,000 men.[10] The Nazis, however, did have the advantage in the air. The whole operation lasted a week and failed to achieve its main objective, that of significantly relieving the pressure on besieged Sevastopol. It did, however, manage to capture the Kerch Peninsula, and to hold on to it until the summer of 1942, when German pressure in the Caucasus and on the Don compelled its evacuation. It might have achieved much greater successes if the *desant* had been better organised; but, in addition to the really terrible weather, which did not make things easier for the Soviet forces, there were no proper landing craft available, so that the troops had to be got ashore in whatever sorts of boats there were to hand; furthermore, totally inadequate time had been allotted for teaching the men how to get in and out of boats with all their equipment in very inclement weather; and, above all, command and control was far from what it should have been.[11]

Soviet writers usually claim that the Kerch-Feodosiisk *desant* was on such a large scale that it cannot be called a tactical *desant*, and must be reckoned to be strategic. In terms of size, there is something to be said for this argument; but, in terms of that classification according to the western notions of seaborne and airborne landings that has been set forth at the beginning of this paper, the Kerch-Feodosiisk *desant* must surely be considered as belonging unquestionably to the third category. It was not aimed at imperial expansion; nor was it able, even had it been successful, to 'open up a new theatre of war', since the Crimea, on which it landed its troops, was already the scene of heavy fighting, which had begun a long time before the *desant* got started, and which continued after its collapse. It therefore seems unquestionable that, at least for the purposes of this present paper, the Kerch-Feodosiisk *desant* must be classified as belonging to that third category of seaborne and airborne landings, which is devoted to those undertaken for the purpose of co-operating with one's own troops (usually one's own *advancing* troops) by operations in the enemy's rear in comparatively close proximity to one's main forces.

The Kerch-Feodosiisk *desant* was followed by a number of others, of which some were more, while others were less, successful. The

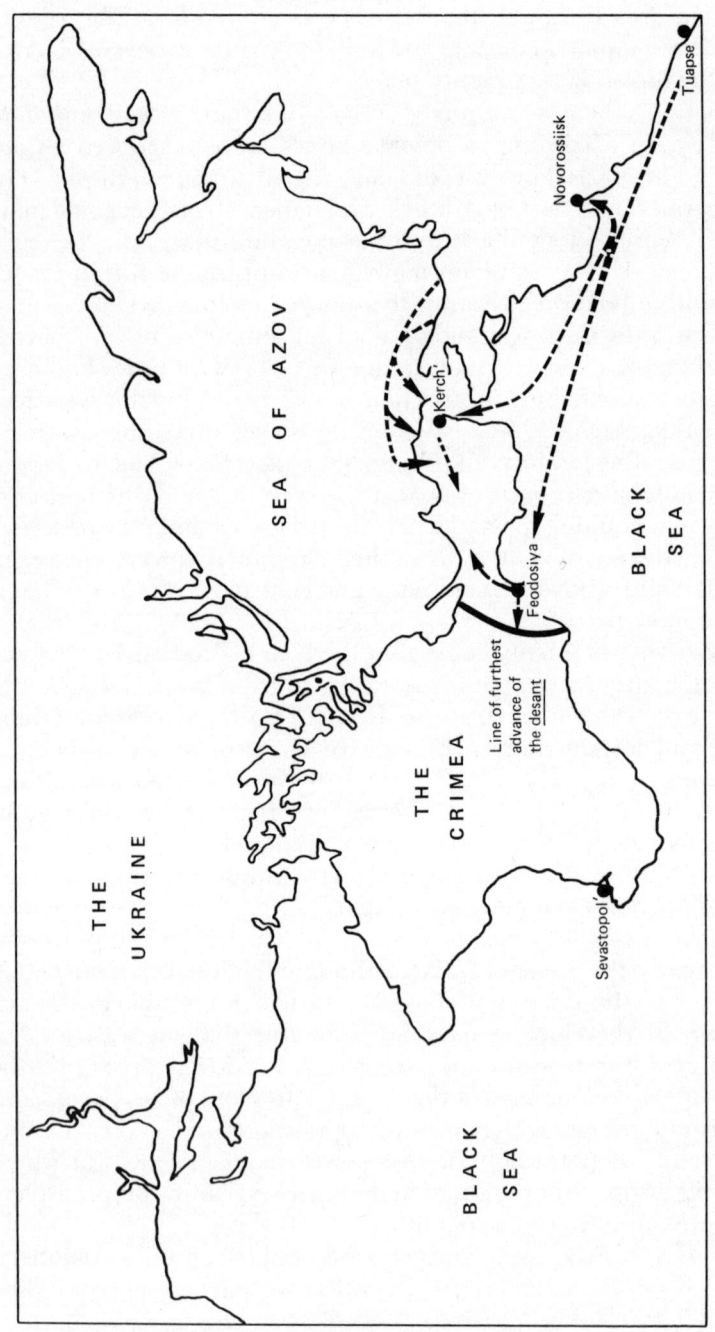

FIGURE 9.2 The Kerch-Feodosiisk *Desant*

The Soviet 'Forward Reach'

Novorossiisk *desant* of September 1943, is an example of one that was totally successful, in the sense that it aimed at the capture of Novorossiisk, and the city was duly captured as a result of it.

It was, moreover, a true example of a tactical *desant*; because it formed part of a much larger operation, the purpose of which was to pierce the German 'Blue Line' defending the eastern approaches to the Taman' Peninsula (see Figure 9.3), to smash the Nazi forces in the area, to advance through the Taman' Peninsula to the Kerch Straits, and there to make ready for a subsequent operation to aim at the liberation of the Crimea (the latter was actually accomplished in the summer of 1944).

But, although what the Russians call the 'Novorossiisk-Taman' Operation of 1943'[12] aimed at much larger goals than the mere capture of the city of Novorossiisk, the latter was the sole aim of the Novorossiisk *desant*; and it is this *desant's* effectiveness which must therefore be our criterion for judging the Soviet Union's ability to mount a seaborne landing.[13] The plan was to capture Novorossiisk by using elements of 18th Army to converge on the city from the east and the west by land, while at the same time putting ashore in the neighbourhood of the harbour a number of units whose combined total was approximately 6,500. A large proportion of the seaborne forces was composed of naval infantry; a naval officer was in charge of the whole *desant*; while another naval officer was in charge of the business of actually getting the troops ashore at the places where they were wanted.

There was thus a unity of command and unity of plan which were noticeably absent from the Kerch-Feodosiisk *desant*, and also a willingness on the part of the Soviet generals to admit the value of naval expertise in matters concerning the sea and passage across it. This, too, had been missing from the Kerch-Feodosiisk *desant*. Finally, the troops who were selected to take part in the Novorossiisk *desant* were given thorough and prolonged training in embarking and disembarking; and the lessons of the Kerch-Feodosiisk *desant*, in this and other particulars, were carefully studied.

As a result, the *desant* was a success, which in turn contributed greatly to the success of the Novorossiisk Operation, the aim of which, it will be remembered, was to effect the capture of that city. The fall of Novorossiisk, in turn, played a big part in ensuring the success of the overall Novorossiisko-Taman' Operation and the consequent eviction from the Taman' Peninsula of German and Romanian troops.[14] Judging by these criteria, therefore, one is

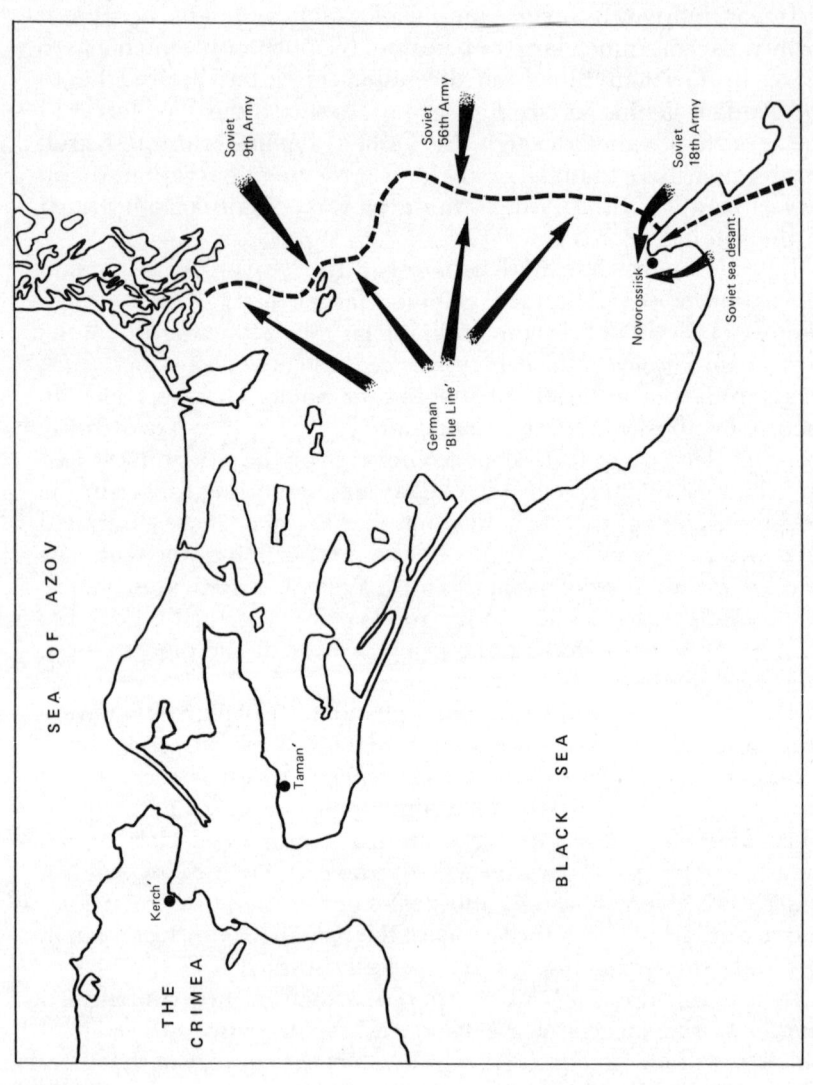

FIGURE 9.3 The Novorossiisk *Desant*

bound to agree with Soviet historians, who point to the Novorossiisk *desant* as proof that the USSR was capable of mounting successful seaborne landings, at least by the early autumn of 1943; though it remains true that the size of the *desant* was not particularly great.

The Soviet armed forces mounted a total of over a hundred seaborne *desants* in the course of the Great Patriotic War: it would be tedious, and not very profitable, to examine them all. The last example, therefore, to be examined in this paper will be the string of seaborne landings which were mounted by the Russians in the Far East in the course of their war against Japan in August 1945. A number of these seaborne landings were also combined with airborne. These landings, both airborne and seaborne, were all on a small scale, and some were mounted against very minor targets. We shall concentrate, therefore, on those landings which helped to capture South Sakhalin and those which captured the Kurile Islands.

Before going on to describe the operations, it might be helpful to say a few words on the historical and geographical background. As will be seen from Figure 9.4, both Sakhalin Island and the Kurile Islands lie very close to both Russian and Japanese territory. The question of who owns them is therefore a matter of great importance to both the Soviet and the Japanese Governments. The Treaty of Portsmouth, which put an end to the Russo-Japanese War of 1904–5, awarded South Sakhalin to the Japanese and gave North Sakhalin to the Russians. Prior to that war, the latter had, to all intents and purposes, ruled the whole of Sakhalin Island; in Russian eyes, therefore, the Japanese, by means of the terms imposed by the Treaty of Portsmouth, had robbed Mother Russia of sacred Russian territory; and this had to be recovered. With regard to the Kuriles, these were for long a bone of contention between Russia and Japan; but in 1875 they were formally proclaimed to be part of the Japanese Empire, though the Russians seem never to have accepted their new status, and always continued to covet them. Whatever hopes the Tsars might have had of gaining possession of them, however, were blighted by the Russian defeat in the Russo-Japanese War. It was to be left to the Soviet Union to succeed where the Tsars had failed.

The military operations designed to capture these territories in 1945 were not, however, identical in character. This was because in North Sakhalin there was a powerful Soviet garrison which, in order to get at South Sakhalin, had merely to march southwards.

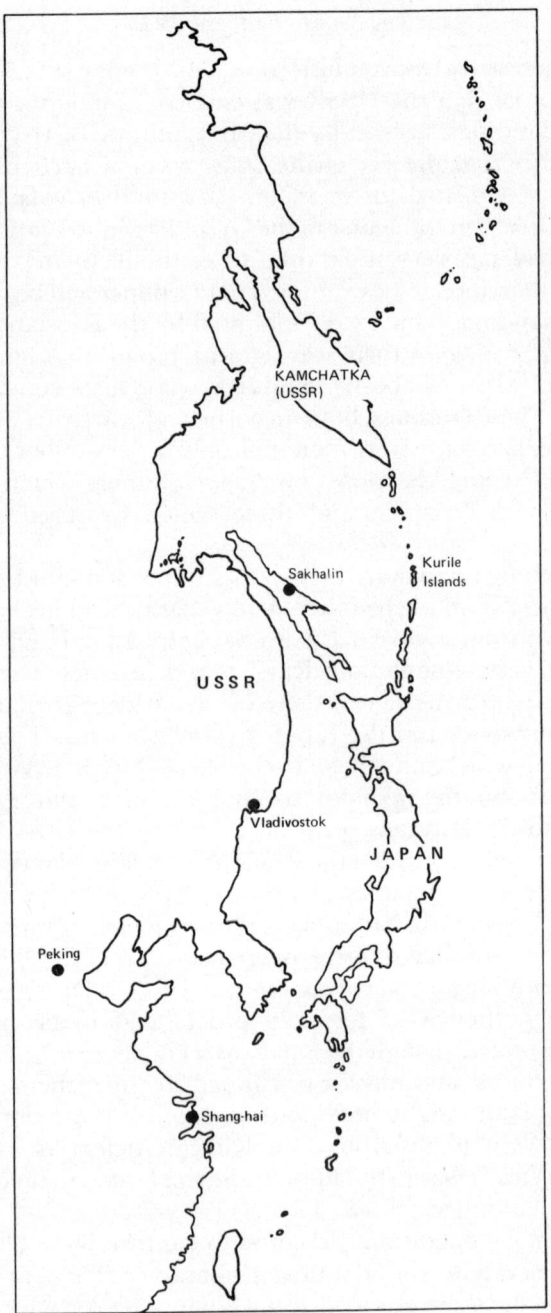

FIGURE 9.4 *Sakhalin and the Kuriles*

Airborne and seaborne landings could doubtless render assistance; but it was perfectly possible to do the job without any landings at all.

This was not the case in respect of the Kuriles, however. The USSR had no garrisons on any of these islands, which were all wholly and completely in Japanese possession. Landings of some kind, therefore, whether by sea or air, were absolutely essential, if these islands were to pass into Soviet hands. However, none of the Kuriles was more than a dot in the ocean; and the Japanese garrisons in all of them were correspondingly small. Their combined total, according to Soviet sources, was about 80,000 men;[15] and the bulk of these were in the two islands of Shumshu and Paramushir. If these two islands could be captured, the rest would fall without trouble.

Luckily, the two islands in question happened to be the nearest of all the Kuriles to Soviet territory. Indeed, Soviet coastal guns mounted on the Kamchatka Peninsula were near enough to Shumshu to be able to shell it.[16] The Soviet forces involved in the landing on Shumshu amounted to roughly two rifle regiments, with artillery and other support; but during the first day's fighting it proved impossible to get any guns ashore at all, and the landing parties had to rely for their artillery on the guns of the Soviet warships. Despite this the Russian forces continued to advance; and by the afternoon of the second day they had done so well that the Japanese garrison on Shumshu agreed to capitulate. The rest of the Kuriles were taken with even less difficulty, in most cases surrendering without any fighting at all. No airborne landings were made by the Russians in the Kuriles; and the whole operation is of little interest, except to observe that what had to be done, was done by the Russians efficiently.

The capture of South Sakhalin was a little more difficult, and was not finally accomplished till a fortnight after the original attack began. The bulk of the fighting, naturally, was borne by the land forces; and units of 16th Army, on the morning of 11 August 1945, began a frontal attack on Japanese defensive positions which was to prove extremely costly. As the Soviet division involved, the 79th Rifle Division, slowly forced its way down into Japanese territory, seaborne *desants* were launched from Sovietskaya Gavan' and landed at points on the west coast of South Sakhalin. In particular, the little part of Toro and surrounding villages were made the object of a seaborne landing that had a total strength of about 1,700 men. On 19 August, five days after the Japanese Emperor had agreed to unconditional surrender, larger *desants* were put ashore on the south-west tip of South Sakhalin; but the job of these was not so much to assist the advance of 79th Division as to prevent the defeated Japanese from removing to their homeland various stocks of machinery and stores of raw materials which the Soviet Government wanted for Russian use.[17]

Soviet airborne *desants* in the Far East in the 1945 campaign did almost nothing to affect the course of the fighting. There were quite a lot of them; but, as General Ivanov explicitly tells us, they were very *ad hoc* affairs, called forth by the speed of the Russian advance, which made it necessary to take unexpected measures to deal with the mass surrender of the Japanese forces, to prevent the destruction of important stores, and to stop the enemy engaging in a 'scorched earth' policy in China and Manchuria. The size of the airborne *desants*, he says, was invariably small, generally ranging between 120 and 500 men.[18] As well as senior staff officers and a few soldiers to guard them, the bulk of the troops transported in this fashion were engineers and airfield technicians: infantry battalions were not sent because they simply were not needed. To all intents and purposes, the fighting was over by the time that the decision was taken by Marshal Vasilievsky to mount his airborne *desant*; and they therefore tell us virtually nothing about the Soviet capacity to mount them.[19]

Overall, it cannot be denied that airborne drops featured very little in Soviet military activities during the Great Patriotic War. This, at first sight, might seem rather strange; since we all know that the USSR had pioneered the large-scale use of airborne forces between the two world wars. For instance, the 1935 manoeuvres at Kiev and the 1936 manoeuvres in the neighbourhood of Moscow had demonstrated successfully how airborne forces could be dropped behind the enemy lines in relatively large numbers. The technology of peacetime, however, is more forgiving than the technology of war; and when war came, the USSR was simply unable to manufacture transport aircraft of a reliable enough design and in sufficient quantities to realise on the field of battle the hopes of the peacetime experimenters.

The Red Army seems to have had five airborne corps on its strength in 1941, with an approximate total of 50,000 men;[20] but these did very little in the way of airborne *desants*, if the official Soviet histories are any guide. There was indeed one near Vyazma in early 1942, in which a total of roughly 10,000 men were dropped.²¹ For lack of aircraft, however, these had to be dropped in three stages, of which the first lasted from 18–22 January, the second, from 27 January to 1 February, and the third from 18–24 February. In the first stage 1,643 men were dropped; 2,100 men in the second; and 7,373 in the third; and these were supported by a few mortars, anti-tank rifles and machine-guns, but (so far as can be discerned from Soviet sources) no proper artillery. Committed piecemeal to battle as they were, deprived of proper air support, unable to link up quickly with their ground forces, the Soviet airborne soldiers at Vyazma were clearly not going to be able to win great victories.

Nor, in the event, did they do so. They contributed, no doubt, something towards the pushing back of the Nazi forces from the proximity of Moscow; and of their personal courage and self-sacrifice there can be no question. They did not, however, produce upon the enemy that kind of effect that those must have expected who had watched the peacetime manoeuvres of the Red Army only a few short years before. Admittedly, the Vyazma drop was done in particularly adverse conditions: the weather was cruel, and mastery of the air unquestionably belonged to the Germans in that area. On the other hand, 8th Airborne Brigade, even when joined by 11th Cavalry Corps, proved quite unable to take Vyazma; while those units dropped in the area of Zhelanie were forced to spend the next six months operating clandestinely in the rear of the Germans as some sort of super partisans.

Since it goes without saying that the First World War had seen no airborne *desants* of any kind because the aeroplane at that time was far too primitive an instrument to permit of it being used for the transporting of men and their equipment and the putting of them down successfully in the enemy's rear, we are bound to say that, by December 1945, the total wartime experience of air *desants* possessed by both Tsarist and Soviet forces was the few bits and pieces that have been outlined in the preceding paragraph. The great promise of the 1936 manoeuvres had not been fulfilled in battle.

On the other hand, we are equally bound to notice that the Soviet ability to mount seaborne landings improved considerably during the Second World War. Those they mounted at the beginning were badly handled; those at the end were in every way more successful. We thus have here a significant example of the USSR's innate capacity to improve on existing capabilities, or to acquire new ones, whenever she thinks it important that she should do so. The marked improvement since the Second World War of the capabilities of the Soviet navy is yet another, and disturbing, instance of this.

Having now completed our study of the Soviet Union's use of air and sea *desants* in the period up to the end of the Great Patriotic War, we must next proceed to examine the affairs of the present; and we may start by asking to what extent the USSR's capability to mount such landings compares with what she possessed in 1945.

So far as numbers are concerned, her airborne forces are roughly what they were at the start of the war. In 1941 the Red army had something approaching 50,000 men in this category; the USSR today has about the same number. Put as a percentage, these figures are not very different. The Soviet armed forces in January 1941, were 4,207,000 strong;[22] the 50,000 men of the airborne forces therefore represented 1.2% of this figure. The Soviet armed forces today, however, are only 3,575,000 strong; so the 60,000 men of the modern airborne forces are a giddy 1.4% of today's total. 0.2% is no tremendous figure; so it seems that, whether we are talking about percentages or total numbers, the USSR's *numerical* capability in the matter of airborne forces has not increased dramatically.

If we turn from air to sea *desants*, we find that in the Second World War the maximum strength of the Soviet naval infantry was 150,000.[23] Their present strength, so far as can be determined, is of the order of 10–12,000 men. The maximum total strength of the Soviet forces during the Great Patriotic War was 11,365,000;[24] so the naval infantry then comprised about 1.3% of them. In modern times, their 10–12,000 men constitute roughly 0.3% of the overall total of the Soviet armed forces.

On the other hand, it is beyond question that the Soviet capability for both air and sea *desants* has improved enormously since 1945 in terms of military hardware. Indeed, it would be astonishing if it had not! Military hardware of every kind has improved enormously since 1945 in every country of the globe. It would be quite astounding if one of the world's most militarily advanced nations had failed to follow suit. Indeed, one may fairly comment that, if the improvement in Soviet *desant* equipment seems to us in 1977 to be particularly striking when compared with that available to them in 1945, the reason may be not that their kit today is so exceptionally good, but that at that time it was so appallingly primitive.

In general, then, it cannot be said that the USSR today possesses any horrendous capacity for making air or sea *desants*. With regard to the former, western experts believe that, at the present moment, only one division can be para-dropped; though obviously, if an airfield could be seized, the innumerable aircraft of Aeroflot could ferry in substantial additional numbers very quickly. As for heliborne troops, the present estimate is that about six to seven battalions could be transported in this fashion. This constitutes a significant tactical, but hardly a strategic, threat.

As for sea *desants*, western opinion very much doubts whether the USSR is at present capable of transporting more than its current number of naval infantry units. These are widely dispersed around the four fleet areas, the Northern, Black, Baltic and Pacific fleets, so that a considerable redeployment of these units would obviously become necessary if any major seaborne landing was to be envisaged by the USSR.

However, studying numbers and military hardware will provide no more than some of the military answers. Such a study, with a bit of luck, will make you aware of what *cannot* be done and (somewhat less certainly) of what *can* be done; it cannot tell you what *will* be done, because it cannot detect the thinking behind the hardware. In order to obtain the answer to the third question, we are therefore obliged to study military thinking; and accordingly it is Soviet military thinking on the subject of the *desant* which is going to form the subject of our next section.

Soviet thinking classifies airborne *desant* into two categories: (i) the tactical; (ii) the operational and strategic. Tactical airborne *desants*, according to Soviet sources, are usually carried out by ordinary motor-rifle units or sub-units. The Russian words employed, *chast'* and *podrazdelenie*, imply that no more than a battalion will be used in any one tactical *desant*. The means of transport for these *desants* is the helicopter. The troops employed are to be landed in the enemy's rear in order to co-operate with their own advancing ground forces; or to destroy the enemy's tactical nuclear weapons and also his command posts and communication centres; or to seize bridges, etc.[25]

On the other hand, airborne *desants* at the operational or strategic level are carried out by the airborne forces proper, though it is accepted that these will sometimes have to be supplemented by ordinary motor-rifle units. Obviously, since the latter have had no special parachute training, they can only be used when, somehow or other, an enemy airfield has been captured; so that they can be flown on to the airfield in ordinary aircraft. When these conditions do not prevail, the airborne forces proper have got to be used, as has already been said above. In either case, the landings will be *deep* in the enemy's rear; and their object will be to seize and hold militarily and economically important areas, to disrupt the enemy's civil and military administrative centres, and to destroy his strategic nuclear, and other really important, installations.[26] Soviet sources emphasise that no major air *desant* is possible today without possession of at least the local mastery of the air.[27]

In general, it is fair to say that airborne landings, in the Soviet view, are useful supplementaries to existing military operations, but cannot be regarded as an independent form of warfare. This is true, whether we are speaking of tactical, operational or strategic air *desants*. Their aim is to get their troops into the enemy's rear, there to commit the maximum damage possible. As has been said already, the USSR made little use of air *desants* during the Great Patriotic War; but recent Soviet comment insists that the importance of this type of operation has much increased since 1945.[28] This, one supposes, is largely because the Soviet technology of the 1940s was not sufficiently good to encourage their use; while now, of course, it can mount them without any trouble.

As for sea *desants*, Soviet thinking classifies these into three categories. First, there are the small landing-parties which are put ashore for reconnaissance or demolition; secondly, there are tactical seaborne landings; and thirdly there are seaborne landings at the operational or strategic level.[29] The first category is usually implemented by the naval infantry, acting alone, though at other times the crews of warships or ordinary army units may be employed. The second category is also usually implemented by the naval infantry, acting alone; though, once again, these may be supplemented by ordinary army units. It is also regarded as possible that *desants* of this category may have to be carried out by ordinary army units acting alone (that is to say, without any help whatever from the naval infantry). As for the third category (the seaborne landings at operational or strategic level) these, by definition, are far too big to be capable of being carried out by the naval infantry alone. The latter, however, whenever possible, form part of the *desant*; but then they act as the forward detachment or first echelon of the main forces, their job being to see to it that these get safely ashore.[30]

The tasks allotted to the three categories in Soviet writing are as follows: those of the first category are reconnaissance and demolition, as has already been mentioned above. Those of the second category, the tactical *desants*, are the seizure of islands or of important sectors of coasts, or the capture of ports or naval bases or of airfields near a coast. As for operational or strategic sea *desants*, their chief tasks are said to be the attacking in flank or rear of groups of enemy armed forces located near the coast, or the seizure of islands or ports or naval bases, or the capture of airfields or other important military installations located near the coast.[31] In the Soviet view, no major seaborne landing is possible without possession of at least the local mastery of the air.[32]

As has been said above, an important role in any Soviet sea *desant* is likely to be played by the naval infantry. Soviet writers ascribe to them the following characteristics: (i) they are chiefly armed with small calibre weapons; (ii) when acting alone, their task is to seize islands, or ports and naval bases, or airfields near the coast; (iii) when acting in co-operation with the ground forces, their task may be as at (ii), though on a larger scale. Usually, however, in such cases they will be involved in a big *desant*; and their task then will be to act as the forward detachment or first echelon of the main wave of the ground forces, and see that these get successfully ashore; (iv) they may also be used for defensive purposes, such as holding a stretch of the Soviet Union's own coastline or one of the any islands that belong to the USSR.[33] It is therefore possible that one of the reasons for the Pacific Fleet having that second regiment of naval infantry is that in that area there are more Soviet islands to defend than there are in other areas; and that these particular Soviet islands are somewhat less inaccessible to foreign attack than are those in, say, the Baltic or the Arctic.

It has already been mentioned that modern Soviet doctrine regards mastery of the air as an essential pre-requisite for both air and sea *desants*, except perhaps for the very smallest. For all others, at least local command of the air is mandatory. Furthermore, if the *desant* is to be of any consequence, the command of the air must pertain not merely to the moment of making the landing, but must continue throughout its operation (i.e., until its link-up with the main forces), in order to ensure supply. Soviet criticism of Arnhem focusses upon this very point. The British, they say, provided only nugatory air support after the *desant* had landed; and his, they claim, was one of the major reasons for its failure. It therefore follows that, in the Soviet view no *desant*, whether by sea or air, is possible at either the operational or the strategic level without an assured command of a considerable air space over a relatively long period. Readers of this paper must form their own conclusions as to the extent to which the USSR is, or is not, able to achieve this in today's circumstances.

Having thus set out the basic principles of the Soviet approach to air and sea *desants*, and having also summarised the history of the Tsarist and Soviet experience in actually mounting them, we may now turn to consider the ways in which the USSR might possibly use them today. It will be convenient to group such uses under two principal headings: their use in wartime and their use in what, in the somewhat whimsical jargon of the twentieth century, passes for peace.

We will start with their wartime uses. But this in turn immediately raises the question as to what war we are talking about. Thousands of different 'scenarios' (i.e. sketches for possible wars) are floated around the community of western defence experts every day of the week. We cannot possibly consider them all, even if it were profitable to do so, which is extremely doubtful. It is therefore necessary to group these wars into a small number of manageable categories; and in this paper these will be reduced to (i) major and (ii) minor wars.

Major Wars will be defined here as those between the Warsaw Pact and NATO or those between Russia and China. They are themselves reducible to three sub-categories, according to the type of weapons with which they are fought: (*a*) *all-out nuclear*, (*b*) *conventional wars in which tactical nuclear weapons are employed*, and (*c*) *purely conventional wars with no nuclear weapons*.

It is difficult to see how, in a modern all-out nuclear war, an air or sea *desant*, whether at tactical, operational, or strategic level, could be of any value. In the old days, when the number of missiles and their efficacy was less, it was possible to think of an area in the theatre of war (in which expression is included the civilian economic installations, such as cities and factories in the flat areas) which was of considerable tactical, operational, or strategic importance, but for which no nuclear missile was available. In such a case, the appropriate *desant* might just possibly have proved to be the most effective means of dealing with it. Sokolvsky's *Military Strategy* went further, however, and asserted positively in all three of its editions, the last of which was published in 1968, that air *desants* of every kind would be a large and important feature of nuclear war, not only for the purpose we have been just discussing, but also for ferrying ground forces across large areas of nuclear devastation and there engaging them with what remained of the stricken enemy forces. Such *desants* would have to be able to be mounted sufficiently rapidly, said Sokolovsky, to prevent the enemy from having time to reorganise, or to bring in troops from areas unaffected by the nuclear bombardment.[35]

Sokolovsky, in his *Military Strategy*, whether wittingly or unwittingly, added a third requirement for a *desant* in nuclear war; by declaring that total victory can only come after the complete defeat of the enemy's armed forces and the seizure of his territories. He also said that it required not merely the seizure of his territories, but also their occupation; so that a 'proper order' could be established in the enemy country, and 'peaceful control over all problems after the war' could be attained.[36] Since in a major war between NATO and the Warsaw Pact the principal enemy of the USSR would be the United States of America, it therefore follows that Sokolovsky's *dicta* require the invasion and occupation of the USA. The Soviet Union and her Pact allies are simply incapable of mounting such an operation, from which we must conclude that, in the Soviet view, meaningful victory in an all-out war between Capitalism and Communism is totally impossible, whatever the Russians may sometimes say to the contrary; or that Sokolovsky was wrong; or that Sokolovsky was right enough, but that his words are no longer heeded by Soviet decision-makers.

We turn now to the use of *desants* in *conventional wars in which tactical nuclear weapons are employed*. If *desants* are envisaged by Soviet thinking as having a place in all-out nuclear warfare, there is no doubt that the same thinking ascribes a much bigger role to them in the sort of war we are now engaged in discussing. Soviet sources are fond of declaring that proper value cannot be extracted from the use of tactical nuclear weapons, unless airborne troops are landed near the burst only a few short minutes after the nuclear explosion has occurred. Only thus, say Soviet writers, can due advantage be taken of the demoralisation which the nuclear bursts will cause to the enemy forces.[37] It goes without saying, in view of what has been set forth above, that such airborne forces are likely to be heli-borne; and therefore they will not be 'airborne forces', properly so called, but ordinary motor-rifle units which happen to have been transported by helicopter. In addition to *desants* of this sort, it is reasonable to envisage a widespread use of the proper airborne forces to operate deep in the enemy's rear for the purpose of capturing his nuclear weapon sites, his main military and civilian administrative centres, and his principal communications centres.

If we now turn to a *war that is purely conventional*, with no nuclear weapons of any kind being employed by either combatant, we must expect the use of air *desants* of the kind described in the preceding paragraphs to be correspondingly augmented. It is hard to believe that their character will differ from what has been suggested above, but it is highly likely that their frequency and importance will increase fairly dramatically under these circumstances.

The above has been directed almost exclusively to an examination of air *desants*; because air *desants* figure larger than sea *desants* in Soviet writing concerned with modern strategy. In the context of a war against NATO, the possible Soviet targets for sea *desants* appear to be somewhat limited; and this is true whether we are talking about nuclear war or some kind or other of conventional war. In every case, we are forced to conclude, the Warsaw Pact would like to seize the northern ports of Norway and also Denmark, and has made what it hopes to be sufficient preparation to allow it to achieve this. The Warsaw Pact (or, to be more accurate, Russia) would also dearly like to seize Japan; and the seizure of Japan would also involve a sea *desant*, though in this case one of very considerable proportions. It is, one imagines, precisely because it would involve a *desant* of such significant proportions that no correspondingly valid preparations for its accomplishment have yet been made by the Soviet Far Eastern Forces.

We have so far been speaking about major wars that we assume to have erupted between the Warsaw Pact and NATO; but there remains a second category of major war, a war between China and the USSR, which so far we have not analysed. Once we proceed to do so, it is surely clear that the same Soviet principles will be applied to this war as would be applied to a major war against the western alliance. Nuclear war against China will demand just as much back-up to the nuclear strikes by the various arms of the ground forces as we have come to conclude would be necessary in a nuclear war against NATO.

The same is true in the event of one kind or the other of conventional war against China; though it is hard to imagine the Russians deciding to attack China by conventional means only, since here for once they enjoy no clear advantage. (A defensive war against Chinese attack is obviously another matter; and if the People's Republic were to invade the Soviet Union, using purely conventional weapons, it is hard to think of any reason that could induce the Russians to escalate. Certainly they did not do so in the case of the skirmishes across the Ussuri; but admittedly in this case it is pertinent to urge that the scale of the fighting was far too small to make escalation even theoretically justifiable.)

The only thing that may be expected to differ is the scale and frequency of seaborne landings. These can be much more easily mounted against China (assuming, of course, no western intervention on behalf of the Chinese People's Republic) than would be possible against the NATO Alliance; and Peking itself is obviously aware of the fact, as is shown by the kind of navy that Communist China has built. It bears an uncanny resemblance to that sort of navy which was built by the USSR between the wars, when the latter feared a western maritime invasion, and, though herself possessed of only a limited and somewhat primitive technology, built the best kind of fleet to repel the invasion that the technology in question could produce for her. In this matter, if in no other, the Chinese have copied Russia.

We now come to the category of minor wars; and these too can be divided into two sub-categories. There are minor wars of the Soviet Union against one or more of the capitalist countries; and these, one would imagine, would have to be fought somewhere outside Europe, if they were not to come within the categories we have just been discussing above. They would therefore have to be fought on the high seas or somewhere in the Third World; and in 1973, at the height of the Yom Kippur War, it was by no means beyond the bounds of possibility that such a war would break out. Had there been, in 1973, a direct clash between American and Russian troops in the Middle East, it could only have happened as a result of the latter being transported to the battlefield in aircraft. It was, in fact, precisely an air *desant* with which the USSR threatened the USA; and it would still have been a tactical *desant* in the sense of the third of the western categories that was outlined at the beginning of this paper. In other words, it would *not* have been designed to open a new theatre of war, but to co-operate with existing forces (in this case, with Egyptian forces) in an existing theatre of operations.

One finds it very difficult to envisage any *minor* war against any of the western countries in which the sort of conditions outlined above are not almost bound to prevail; and this means that one finds it very difficult to envisage the USSR allowing a war of this kind to erupt, if she can help it. For, how could the war be fought, how could the troops be supplied and reinforced, without a far greater lifting capacity than the USSR possesses at the present moment, or seems to want to possess? If the ferrying of men and supplies to the scene of battle were to be totally unopposed, that, of course, would be different; but then we would be talking about a peacetime operation, whereas what we are discussing is war.

The same sorts of considerations must surely apply to the second of the two sub-categories of minor wars, that in which the USSR is fighting a war against one of the Third World countries; for, with the exception of Finland, Austria, Yugoslavia, Iran, Afghanistan, India, and Pakistan, Third World countries are not directly accessible to the USSR. In other words, if she wants to wage a war against any one of them, then, barring these seven exceptions, she has got to cross the seas or indulge in airlifts in order to be able to do it. If the Third World country is small enough, so that the war can be made to be so short that it resembles more a military *putsch* than a war, then all the difficulties which the USSR at present experiences regarding the projection of armed force could easily be surmounted. A war against Mauritius, for instance, if properly prepared in peacetime, could be brought within these parameters, and therefore won. On the other hand, a war against Sri Lanka would be a very different proposition. The chances of a quick 'kill' could not be rated high; while the likelihood of international complications arising as a result of the delay would obviously be considerable.

It is clear from the above that the key question is that of opposition. If there is to be no opposition, or opposition so slight as to be virtually non-existent, then armed force can be projected by anyone wheresoever in the world he chooses. The doughty inhabitants of the Isle of Wight could cross the Atlantic, invade Brazil, and occupy Rio de Janeiro without the slightest difficulty, so long as the Brazilians were not prepared to resist them; on the other hand, the slightest Brazilian resistance would make such a thing impossible. So, too, in the case of the Soviet Union. The USSR does not possess, and shows no signs at present of trying to acquire, the means of projecting armed force across any significant distance in any situation where strong resistance is at all to be expected. She has not the means to seize and hold a bridgehead in the teeth of determined opposition in any place where such a bridgehead is more than a couple of stone-throws from the borders of the Soviet empire. Nor, even if we suppose that by some chance she has managed to grab such a bridgehead, does she possess the means to supply the troops who must hold it. We are therefore reduced to the proposition that the USSR, at present at least, is only capable of projecting force across more than trifling distances when there is no opposition to be expected from either the intended victim or from another, protecting power. This means that she can only do it in peacetime. It is therefore the Soviet Union's capacity to project armed force in peacetime that should be the main concern of the western world today.

The Soviet willingness actually to use whatever capacity of this nature the USSR possesses is strongly influenced by two basic propositions. The first is that an enterprise of this kind must necessarily be directed against a Third World country; because if it were directed against a NATO country, it would lead to a major war. But military effort against Third World countries comes under the heading of 'wars of national liberation'; and Soviet doctrine insists that wars of this kind may only be directly supported by communist military units (as distinct from military advisers or supplies of arms) when there already exists a pro-Soviet political party in the victim country of sufficient size and influence to make it seem probable that, with only the smallest application of force, it will be able to seize power. Better still, it should actually have successfully accomplished the seizure of power; and communist troops can then be sent in to prevent the new government being forced from office by those who disagree with it, and the 'will of the people' being thwarted as a result. This is what happened in Angola. Once the MPLA had got itself into a position where it could proclaim itself to be the government, the question of how many Angolans actually wanted that government could conveniently be ignored, and the Cubans could be brought in to prevent the numerous opponents of that government from giving effective expression to their views by staging a successful counter-coup. Communist media proclaimed that the MPLA represented the 'will of the Angolan people'; and that the Cuban troops were there to ensure that the people's 'will' was respected.

The second basic proposition underlying the Soviet Union's willingness to use force in this particular fashion is that, if the enterprise in question is not certain to be successful, but that if the advantages inherent in it are perceived to be of such a degree of magnitude as to justify the taking of an amount of risk that the Soviet leaders would normally not permit themselves, then *Soviet* troops must not be sent, but those of one of the 'satellites'. This is because the defeat of the latter, though tiresome, brings none of the loss of 'face' and collapse of prestige that would be seen to follow the rout of a Soviet battalion. The USSR is very chary of committing her own troops to battle; and hitherto she has only done so in defence of vital Soviet *domestic* interests. The victory of the MPLA in Angola is certainly welcome in Moscow; but it cannot be said that, as viewed from the Kremlin, it was absolutely *vital* that it should occur.

The use of the Cubans, therefore, slew a brace of most desirable, but not essential, birds with a single stone. The MPLA were maintained in power in Angola, and the Soviet Union's own prestige was never put at risk. In the eyes of the Kremlin, the Cubans were expendable; and if the West had decided to fire on them, and sink their ships and shoot down their planes, it is highly unlikely that their ensuing deaths would have been regarded by the Russians as anything more than regrettable, and as something furnishing good material for an anti-western propaganda campaign and for spirited diplomatic protests. The Cubans being expendable, they would duly have been expended; and it would have been time for the Kremlin to cut its losses and think of something else. As things were, however, there were no Russian losses; and all that remained for the Russians to do was to capitalise on Cuban gains. It is clear, therefore, that, just as the West today is faced on the domestic scene with a new threat, the threat of urban terrorism, against which she has got to devise, and is indeed devising, acceptable and effective counter-measures, so now, on the international scene, it is the sort of projection of force on the Angolan model that is the threat that is most likely to concern it, at any rate in peacetime. Traditional commando-type operations, carried on Soviet aircraft-carriers and mounted by Soviet naval infantry, should not be regarded as our prime concern so much as activities of the kind now being undertaken by Cuban troops in Africa.

If there has been no mention of the air *desant* on Prague in 1968 in this paper, it is because, although it was technically a highly successful tactical *desant*, it was unopposed and it was not a projection of force across a great distance. On the contrary, Czechoslovakia is territorially contiguous to the military bases of those Pact countries which took part in the invasion. Furthermore, the air *desant* was merely one small part of an operation which overall was bound to succeed and which was, in any case, conducted within the confines of the Soviet empire. The *desant* is therefore interesting, technically even instructive, but not really relevant to the purpose of this paper.

SUMMARY OF DISCUSSION

In the discussion of his paper Mr Vigor stressed that the Russians were unlikely to initiate a major operation in the form of an airborne or seaborne *desant*, unless they could be sure of incurring very small risks or meeting very little opposition. They were likely to be very cautious about getting themselves into the situation of having to maintain substantial forces at a distance against opposition. When asked about possible operations in the European theatre, such as the seizure of Hamburg, or a descent on Belgrade, attacks in the sensitive thinly-held areas of Northern Norway, or in Berlin, Mr Vigor again thought the Russians were unlikely to take great risks for small gain. He considered the intervention in Angola the type of operation the West would be more frequently faced with in the future. The Soviet Union would support what it considered legitimate governments against attempts to overthrow them and it would respond to invitations to intervene from such governments. It might use satellite forces, such as the Cubans, in operations of this type and in case of failure the forces would be expendable from the Soviet point of view. There was general agreement that the idea of legitimacy was of great importance to the present Soviet leadership, as evidenced by their desire to conclude such agreements as the quadrupartite treaty on Berlin, the treaty on the non-use of force in international relations, and by the Brezhnev doctrine. In conclusion Mr Vigor felt that all this held good while detente remained an important goal of Soviet policy, but it was impossible to predict what would happen if there was a revival of the Cold War.

NOTES

1. The first proper treatment in English of the Soviet concept of the *desant* was contained in C. N. Donnelly's article on the subject in the RUSI *Journal*, September 1971, to which interested readers are referred.
2. *Bol'shaya Sovetskaya Entsiklopediya* (henceforth shown as *BSE*), 3rd edn., vol. 8, p. 131. See also *Slovar' Osnovnykh Voennykh Terminov* (Moscow: Voenizdat, 1965), p. 71. On the other hand, the 1975 edition of Ozhegov's dictionary continues to give both meanings. In nineteenth-century Russian, *desant* meant exclusively the troops engaged in the operation, not the operation itself.

3. *BSE*, 2nd edn., vol. 14, p. 99.
4. See, for instance, *BSE*, 1st edn., vol. 21, p. 541 for examples of this.
5. Ibid.
6. *BSE*, 1st edn., vol. 21, pp. 539 *et seq.*
7. Ibid.
8. *Istoriya Voenno-Morskogo Iskusstva* (Moscow: Voenizdat 1969), pp. 125-7.
9. *Istoriya Velikoi Otechestvennoi Voiny Sovietskogo Soyuza 1941-1945* (henceforth shown as *IVOVVS*), vol. 2, p. 669.
10. Ibid.
11. There is a useful account of the Kerch-Feodosiisk *desant* in *Istoriya Vtoroi Mirovoi Voiny 1939-45* (Moscow: Voenizdat, 1975) vol. 4, pp. 295-9, including some fairly objective criticism.
12. *BSE*, 3rd edn., vol. 18, p. 76.
13. There is a good account of the Novorossiisk *desant* in *Istoriya Vtoroi Mirovoi Voiny 1939-1945* vol. 7. pp. 219-31.
14. Ibid. It is perhaps worth spelling out that, in Soviet eyes, there were three bits of military activity going on in connection with Novorossiisk in September 1943. There was the Novorossiisk *desant* 10-16 (Sept. 1943) which was merely designed to assist, by means of a seaborne landing, the efforts of 18th Army to take Novorossiisk by land; there was the Novorossiisk Operation 9-16 (Sept. 1943), which is the name given by Soviet historians to the combined efforts of the *desant* and of 18th Army to capture Novorossiisk, a task in which they succeeded on 16 Sept. 1943; and there was the Novorossiisko-Tamanskaya Operatsiya of September-October 1943, which had the much wider task of capturing not merely Novorossiisk, but the whole of the Taman' Peninsula in addition.
15. R. Ya. Malinovskii (ed.), *Final* (Moscow: Nauka, 1966), p. 229.
16. Ibid., p. 237.
17. Ibid., p. 227.
18. General S.P. Ivanov, *Nachal'nyi period voiny* (Moscow: Voenizdat, 1974), p. 297.
19. Ibid.
20. *BSE*, 3rd edn., vol. 5, p. 258 and *IVOVVS*, vol. 2, p. 669.
21. For an account of the Vyazma drop, see *IVOVVS*, vol. 2, pp. 325-9.
22. *KPSS i Stroitel'stvo Sovietskikh vooruzhennyk Sil* (Moscow: Voenizdat, 1971), p. 244.
23. *BSE*, 3rd edn., vol. 16, p. 586.
24. Khrushchev's speech of January 1960.
25. *BSE*, 3rd edn., vol. 5, p. 264
26. Ibid.
27. See, for instance, General Ivanov's comments in his above quoted work.
28. *BSE*, 3rd edn., p. 258.
29. *BSE*, 1st edn., vol. 21, pp. 539 *et seq.*
30. *BSE*, 3rd edn., vol. 16, p. 586.
31. Ibid.
32. Ivanov, op. cit.
33. *BSE*, 3rd edn., vol. 16, p. 586.
34. *Voennaya Entsiklopediya* (Moscow: Voenizdat, 1976), vol, p. 262.

35. Harriet Fast Scott (ed.)*Soviet Military Strategy: V. D. Sokolovsky* (New York, Crane-Russak, 1975), p. 249.
36. Ibid., p. 291.
37. V.E. Savkin, *The Basic principles of Operational Art and Tactics* (Moscow: Voenizdat, 1972), pp. 253–5. Translated and published by USAF, pp. 193–5.

Conclusion

The conference ended with a general discussion, the first part of which had as its theme the strategic power of the USSR and its implications for the West. Many of the contributors to the debate were concerned with the motivation behind the build-up of Soviet Power. The function of military power was defined within the framework of Soviet ideology: Marxism-Leninism regarded military capability as one of the means by which a correlation of forces more favourable to the Soviet Union and the progressive camp could gradually be brought about. Stalin had still envisaged that this process would ultimately entail war, but under the impact of nuclear weapons his successors had revised this view. The international class struggle and support for national liberation movements would continue; meanwhile the policy of detente and arms control negotiations would keep the risk of general war low. The growth of Soviet strength would produce an accumulation of quantitative change leading ultimately to qualitative change.

The general view however was that the actual use of military force would still be treated by the Soviets with the utmost caution. In this connection the question was raised as to what extent the Russian build-up was the result of military influence, bureaucratic politics, or inertia within the Soviet system. It was felt, notwithstanding the traditional fears of Bonapartism in the Communist leadership, that there was in fact no divergence between the interests of the political and of the military leaders. If it was the Soviet Union's policy to use military strength to produce a gradual shift in the correlation of forces in its favour, then the chief effects of this policy might be felt in western Europe. Without any change in present trends a scenario might be envisaged in which Soviet power would help to frustrate western European dynamism and produce a sense of stagnation. In particular the EEC might not move beyond the present stage of a customs union and all attempts to create a more powerful western European political identity might fail. This could well have repercussions on the allegiance of the more peripheral members of NATO to the Alliance. All this would constitute a major western defeat and a Soviet gain. At present the Soviet Union respects spheres of influence as a practical necessity, as was shown by the cases of Czechoslovakia and Portugal. In the future military strength might make them more confident and they might be guided by the slogan 'what is mine is mine, what is yours is up for grabs'.

Some speakers were concerned with the economic aspects of detente.Could the Soviet need for western technology or American grain be exploited by the West? It was felt that the West did not have much leverage, not even in the specific case of the exploitation of Siberian energy resources. On the other hand, Soviet attempts to use opportunities in the Third World for the acquisition of overseas bases could be seen in the light of an increasingly fierce global struggle for resources.

The second discussion session, on the nature of Soviet expansion and the problem of negotiating with the USSR, was opened by Professor Peter Nailor. Actions such as the creation of a *cordon sanitaire* in eastern Europe were not necessarily seen by the Soviet Union as expansion. Since 1945 the USSR had acted very much in the traditional mode as an expanding power and had behaved like any other unit of the international system. The west had only begun to oppose Soviet expansion when it saw it as military adventurism. Future expansion might be in the traditional military powerpolitical mode; it might take the form of economic warfare or it might be in the area of the mind and of ideology. In the latter field both super-powers had attempted to capitalise on their claim to be post-revolutionary powers in the period since 1945 but the USSR had had the best of the argument in an era of decolonisation.

Soviet society was changing but the theory that western and Soviet society were converging had only limited credibility. The most important change in the Soviet Union would come when a new generation of leaders who did not know the pre-nuclear world took over. It might produce greater caution or the willingness to take greater risks. Even in the US there was too much faith in mechanistic solutions to the problems of a nuclear world, for example, with the multilateral force in the past or the cruise missile at present. It was part of the convergence theory that ideology was declining, but ideology absorbed into the political culture does not go away. The usefulness of ideology is that it provides a framework within which a programme of action is easier to determine. The West with the dissolution of great empires had found itself in a period of confusion and retreat which had put it on the defensive. Nevertheless the West had dealt with the situation not too badly. NATO had been created not only out of fear but also out of repentance and determination to do better than in the thirties.

As for negotiating with the Soviet Union, the West laboured under the disadvantage that negotiations were public property. The Carter Administration was trying to make a virtue out of this necessity. The USSR with its ideology did not really negotiate. Nevertheless Professor Nailor felt that agreements that gave the Soviet Union less than its total objectives were possible. They were concerned for legitimacy, they were legalistic, they shared some international objectives, they liked to be seen as reasonable, they did not believe that historic determinism would do it all for them, and one could do business with them. They had a special relationship with the United States and it was this which really enabled them to claim world-wide super-power status.

In the wide-ranging discussion that followed Professor Nailor's introduction several speakers further explored the nature of Soviet expansion. Seen from Moscow it might well seem that the USSR was to some extent encircled and that it was necessary to push back the potentially hostile circle through the creation of *cordons sanitaires*. This policy could be pursued with caution, yet also with a sense of mission about the virtues of the Soviet systems. Fears were expressed that the Soviet Union might in the future find opportunities to put pressure on the West through the denial of vital resources: the instability of the Middle East, for example, might create situations which the USSR could exploit without too much risk.

The problem of negotiating with the Soviet Union received attention from several participants. Strategic arms talks could, it was felt, only deal in simple comparabilities and crude numerical categories. The cruise missile and other technological advances might be too complex to be the subject of Soviet-American arms control agreements. There was some debate about the degree to which the Soviet command was alarmed by the cruise missile. The MBFR negotiations in Vienna were also discussed and the opinion was expressed that a failure to produce results from these talks would cause great strains in the western alliances. There would be renewed pressure both in USA and western Europe for unilateral troop reductions, but some disputed this view, pointing to the high of unemployment in many western industrial countries. There was a general plea for strengthening the western alliance, by 'not merely serving but transcending national interests'. Another problem the West faced in negotiating with the Soviet Union was the pressure of public opinion in the countries of the western alliance. This could, however, be turned to advantage, particularly now that the Russians displayed much greater sophistication about the domestic politics of the US and her allies. The way in which the Brandt Government used its narrow majority to extract concessions from the Soviet Union in the Berlin negotiations was given as an example. Finally there was a plea that extremes should be avoided in interpreting Soviet expansion: the truth lay neither in theories of conspiracy for world domination nor in a simple denial of any danger from Soviet Russia.

Index

Aeroflot, 94, 199
Airborne troops, 52, 64–5, 94, 110–11, 188–9, 195–201, 203–4
Aircraft: 60, 88–97 *passim*, 196
  An-12 (Cub-C), 93–4
  An-22, 94
  AWAC, 31, 169
  B-1, 172
  B-52, 169
  Badger, 77
  F-14, 31
  FB-111, 169
  Il-14, 94
  Il-76 (Candid), 94
  Il-86, 95
  Li-2, 94
  Mi-24 (Hind), 95
  MiG-17 (Fresco), 90
  MiG-21R (Fishbed-H), 93
  MiG-21 SMT (Fishbed-K), 89
  MiG-23 (Flogger-B), 31, 89, 91
  MiG-25 (Foxbat), 31, 88–9, 91
  MiG-25R (Foxbat-B), 93
  MiG-27 (Flogger-D), 89, 91
  SU-15, 31, 88
  SU-17 (Fitter-C), 89, 91
  SU-19 (Fencer), 89, 92
  TU-(26?) (Backfire), 93, 176
  TU-28p (Fiddler), 88
  TU-126, 31
  V/STOL 80, 87
  YaK-28 (Brewer-D & E), 93
  YaK-28p (Firebar), 88
Air defence, 26, 29, 31, 53, 65, 90, 110–11, 158–9
Alexander II, 186
Alexander III, 186
Anfilov, Colonel, 20
Angola, 82, 207–9

Anti-submarine warfare, 77, 79–82, 87, 168, 170–1, 174
Armour, *see* tanks
Artillery, 3, 6–7, 9–13, 15, 33, 53, 56, 58, 64, 195, 197

Baranovsky, V. S., 6
Batitsky, Marshal, 88
Bethmann Hollweg, 3
Blitzkrieg, 20–1
Bloch, 9
Borovykh, Colonel-General, 88
Braun, J. K. L., (Prussian Artillery Officer), 7
Brezhnev, Leonid, 36–7, 129, 136, 160, 209
Budenny, Marshal, 144
Büchner, 7

Carter, President, 172, 175
Catherine the Great, 186
Cavalry, 7, 11, 15, 197
Chemical Warfare, 47, 61, 63, 114
China, 80, 104, 126, 169, 196, 202, 204–5
Civil Defence, 26, 170, 171
Civil War (1918–20), 14, 24, 39, 131, 188
Communist Party of the Soviet Union: 102, 106, 108, 113, 122–3, 131, 136, 139–40, 144
  Komsomol, 103, 105–6, 122
  Young Communist League, 137, 139, 141
Czechoslavakia (invasion of, 1968), 69, 135, 208

DNIEPER (exercise), 23
DOSAAF (Voluntary Organisation for

Index

Co-operation with the Army, Air Force and Navy), 39, 105–6, 110
DVINA (exercise), 23

Efimov, Marshal, 96
Electronic warfare, 29, 38, 53, 54, 56, 60, 84, 91
Engineers, 15, 54, 56, 59

Falaleev, Marshal, 96
Fedorov, N. P., 6
Fortresses, 12–13, 15
Frunze Academy, 22, 117
Frunze, Mikhail, 132–3

General Staff, 7, 15, 18–21, 25–6, 36–7, 41, 86
Gorshkov, Admiral, 18, 35, 77–9, 80–3, 85, 87–8
Grechko, Marshal, 23, 139, 142
Grinkevich, Colonel-General D., 37–8
Group Soviet Forces Germany (GSFG), 37, 49, 71–2, 89–90, 95, 107–8

Hitler, 4

Infantry, 3, 11–13, 15, 111, 188; infantry combat vehicle (BMP), 19, 33, 52, 56, 58; (BTR), 52; motor rifle troops, 38, 51–2, 58, 63, 71, 108, 110–11, 117, 199, 203; naval infantry, 191, 198, 200–1.
Isserson, G. S., 21
Istomin, Col. V. P., 32
Ivan the Terrible, 5, 6, 186
Ivanov, General, 196

Japan, 90, 94, 193, 195–6, 204

KGB, 83, 104, 107, 123
Khrushchev, 26–7, 77, 159
Khudyakov, Marshal, 96
Kiev (aircraft carrier), 80, 84, 86–7, 168
Korean War, 76
Kulikov, Marshal, 20, 38
Kurochkin, General, 32
Kutakhov, Air Chief Marshal P. S., 88–9, 94, 96

Lagovskii, Major-General, 22
Lebanon (operation, 1958), 77
Lemnitzer, General, 71
Lenin, 22, 131–2, 139–41
Lomov, Colonel-General, 94
Luftwaffe, 90–1
Lyakhov, General, 188

Malenkov, 25
Mendeleyev, 6
Ministry of Defence, 32, 88, 108, 121, 137, 140, 144
Missiles:
   Anti-Ballistic (ABM), 29–32, 157–8, 168, 177
   Intercontinental (ICBM), 19, 27–32 *passim*, 47, 158, 166–7, 170–80 *passim*
   Intermediate Range (IRBM), 167, 175
   Multiple Independently-Targeted Re-entry Vehicles (MIRV), 30–1, 166–7, 175, 177
   Naval, 76, 79, 171
   Poseidon, 81
   Submarine-Launched (SLBM), 28–9, 158, 164, 166–8, 171–3, 179
   Surface-to-Air (SAM), 19, 29, 31, 53, 66, 169
   Trident, 79, 81, 171
Mochavsky, 6
Motor rifle troops, *see* infantry

NATO, 18, 35, 41, 49, 70–1, 79, 81–3, 90, 93, 126, 176, 179, 202–4
Navy, 29, 35, 74–87 *passim*, 199–200, 205
Nicholas I, 39, 186
Non-Commissioned Officers, 7, 69, 104, 112–13, 142, 145
Non-Proliferation Treaty, 179
Novikov, Chief Air Marshal, 93, 96

October Revolution, 75, 103, 131
Odom, Colonel, 39
Okean (exercise), 83

Pakilev, Lieutenant-General, 94
Penkovskii, 26

Index

Peter the Great, 5, 7, 186
Podgorny, President, 82
Political officers, 37, 122–5, 139
Pyot, Captain (French Liaison Officer), 11

Radzievskii, General, 22
Roshetnikov, Colonel-General, 92
Royal Navy, 76, 78
Russo-Japanese War, 11, 75, 193

SALT, 30–1, 157–80 *passim*
Savkin, Colonel, 94
Schlesinger (Secretary for Defence), 179
Shtemenko, General, 93
Sidorenko, Colonel, 93–4
Silant'ev, Marshal, 96
Skrypnik, Mykola, 132
Smirnov, General, 13
Sokolovskii, Marshal, 26, 202–3
Sredin, Colonel-General, 37
Stalin, 4, 36, 75–7, 96, 134, 186
Strategic Rocket Corps, 29, 110, 111, 129
Suez (operation, 1956), 77
Sukhomlinov, 15
Suvorov academies, 113

Tactics, 7, 14, 19, 32–4, 55–66
Tanks: 49, 58–9, 63, 71, 110, 187
    T-55, 50, 71–2
    T-62, 50,
    T-72, 50, 71–2

Tannenberg (battle of, 1914), 3
Timokhovich, Colonel, 91, 95
Tokarev, 6
Tolubko, General, 93
Trotskii, 24, 40
Tsushima (battle of, 1904), 75
Tukhachevskii, Marshal, 21

United States of America:
    Air Force, 96;
    Navy, 76–7, 82;
    Polaris force, 77–9, 81
    Strategic Air Command, 161

Vasilievsky, Marshal, 196
Vershinin, Chief Air Marshal, 89, 96
Vladivostok Summit, 175–8
Voroshilov, Marshal, 144
Vorozheikin, Marshal, 96

Warnke, Paul, 163
Warsaw Pact, 59, 70, 84, 90, 131, 135–6, 141, 202–4, 208
World War, First, 4, 7, 8, 12, 15
World War, Second (*also* Great Patriotic War), 20–1, 25, 36, 76, 88, 90–2, 94, 96, 103, 134, 139, 143, 188–9, 191, 193, 195–8, 200

Yom Kippur War, 205

Zhigarev, Chief Air Marshal, 89
Zhukov, Marshal, 25